A GEOGRAPHY OF SCOTLAND

A GEOGRAPHY OF SCOTLAND

K. J. LEA
Lecturer in Geography, University of Strathclyde

with contributions from

G. GORDON
Lecturer in Geography, University of Strathclyde

and

I. R. BOWLER
Lecturer in Geography, University of Leicester

DAVID & CHARLES
Newton Abbot   London   North Pomfret (Vt)   Vancouver

For Christina, Jane and Val.

0715 374 222 1225

ISBN 0 7153 7422 2
Library of Congress Catalog Card Number 77–076096

Printed in Great Britain
by Redwood Burn Limited Trowbridge
for David & Charles (Publishers) Limited
Brunel House   Newton Abbot   Devon

Published in the United States of America
by David & Charles Inc
North Pomfret   Vermont 05053   USA

Published in Canada
by Douglas David & Charles Limited
1875 Welch Street   North Vancouver   BC

914.1 L46

HN 4656

CONTENTS

INTRODUCTION:
SCOTLAND AND THE SCOTS

Scotland presents in a territorial sense no problems
of definition.   Between latitudes 54° 37' N (Mull of
Galloway) and 60° 52' N (Muckle Flugga, Shetland) and
between longitudes 0° 45' W (Out Skerries, Shetland) and
7° 40' W (Mingulay), 79,000 sq km of land are clearly
identified as Scotland on the world map.   Since the
name of Scotland was first used, very little change has
occurred in the area to which it has referred.   This land
area is greatly fragmented by the sea, and parts of it
consist of small islands and island groups.   The sea bites
deeply even into the mainland of Scotland, the northern
part of the largest of the British islands.   Only the
short land boundary with England prevents the complete
encirclement of Scotland by the sea.

The persistence of the identity of this territorial
unit owes a great deal to its clear definition;   almost
complete isolation from other land areas by the surrounding
seas.   It also owes a great deal to the fact that this
territorial unit has been, and is, the homeland of the
Scottish people.   Indeed, their presence gives the term
Scotland additional connotations much less easy to define
than its areal extent.

Historically, Scotland achieved the status of a
nation state in the late middle ages as a result of the
culmination of centuries of struggle to extend the
authority of the Scottish crown over the various groups
of Picts, Britons, Scots, Norsemen, Angles and other
peoples of diverse origin who provided the first settlers
in various parts of the Scottish territory.   This
centralising power however was at no time either strong
or secure.   History also records, by the same process,
the steady extension of the authority of the English
crown over the whole of the British Isles.   By the
Union of the Crowns in 1603 and the voluntary Act of
Union in 1707, the Scottish nation state was absorbed

into the larger British unit.   The extent to which the
Scottish people have retained a separate identity rather
than been assimilated into the general British population
is extremely difficult to measure.

Scotland is no more linguistically distinct than any
other part of the British Isles.   Gaelic has never been
the everyday tongue of more than a small proportion of
the total population even in the north and west, and today
is spoken by less than two per cent of the Scottish people.
Accents and dialects abound in the spoken language and
spill over into the literary heritage, especially the
poetry of Burns, but they are all essentially variations
of English.   The promotion of Lallans, the supposed pre-
seventeenth century language of the Scottish lowlands, by
a group of recent Scottish literary figures is an
interesting attempt to create, or recreate, a distinctly
Scottish linguistic form, but it has made little headway
and bears little relation to the everyday language of
modern Scotland.   The literary heritage in general is
much more a part of the British and European tradition
than of a peculiarly Scottish one.   In some other
artistic fields, Scotland has been influenced more by
continental European than English styles.   Scottish
architecture for example owes more to the influence of
France and the Low Countries than to the influence of
England.   Even so, purely Scottish styles are weakly
developed, and together with distant memories of statehood
and artificially promoted linguistic forms are hardly
sufficient to explain the degree of cohesion which the
population of Scotland displays today.

Much more significant has been the influence of the
religious, educational and legal systems, evolved in
Scotland from a combination of native, English and
continental ideas and protected under the 1707 Act of
Union.   They have given a distinctive character to many
aspects of Scottish culture and social life.   In addition
they have necessitated special arrangements and
institutions for the management of Scottish affairs as
distinct from the affairs of other parts of Britain.
They have, as a result, helped to keep alive the identity
of Scotland in an administrative and political sense.

After the Reformation, the official religious
system evolved from a combination of hostility to the
essentially English power of the episcopal establishment

8

and the appeal of the single-minded doctrines of Calvinism.
Whether or not the intolerance and grim utilitarianism of
the Presbyterian Church reflected the Scottish character,
there is no doubt that from the seventeenth century onwards
it was a powerful institution exerting considerable
influence in that direction.   In the absence of a strong
local aristocracy or a local political assembly, both of
which were based in distant London after 1707, the Church
provided the only real leadership to the social development
of Scotland.   This leadership continued through the
nineteenth century, in spite of schisms, the acceptance
of other religious communities like the Roman Catholic
and the loss of some of the Church's social and educational
functions to the state.   In the late twentieth century,
the Established Presbyterian Church of Scotland is still
supported by a large proportion of the Scottish population,
significantly larger than the proportion of the English
population actively supporting the Established Episcopal
Church of England.   Indeed the strength of the animosity,
especially in the west of Scotland, between the Catholic
and Presbyterian communities is indicative of the continued
importance of religion in the everyday social life of
Scotland.   Some of the bleaker influences of the church,
the strict observance of the sabbath and the strong
disapproval of frivolous artistic pursuits, are much less
all pervading than they were earlier in the century.
Nevertheless the views of the church elders and ministers
as expressed from the pulpit and in the debates of the
General Assembly still mould as well as reflect a great
deal of Scottish thought.

Before the great Disruption of the Established Church
in 1843 and the establishment of the Free Church, the
Established Church almost totally controlled the educational
system of Scotland.   While benefitting from the Church's
belief in the value of learning, possibly deriving from a
much older pre-reformation Scottish belief, the schools
also provided the Church with additional institutions for
the dissemination of its own general philosophy in a sense
wider than the purely religious.   Protected by the Act
of Union, the education system of Scotland survived as
distinctive in spite of the decline of church and the rise
of state influence after the mid-nineteenth century.   Some
of this distinctiveness derived from a not wholly admirable
inbreeding.   Scottish teachers were largely drawn from

9

the Scottish population, while Scottish school pupils
generally advanced to Scottish universities. This
parochialism was greatly encouraged by rigid entry
qualifications which made movement between the Scottish
and other, notably the English, educational systems
difficult at all stages for both pupils and teachers. It
had the effect of strengthening the Scottish character of
education by maintaining distinctively Scottish courses,
especially in the field of history, and distinctively
Scottish ideals, such as utilitarian rather than artistic
learning. The second half of the twentieth century has
seen much drawing together of the Scottish and English
educational systems, to the benefit of both. This has
led in turn to a considerable decline in the role of
education in the maintenance of a distinctive Scottish
society. However, the process of assimilation is far
from complete and in any case the legacy remains.

The Scottish legal system, also protected by the
1707 Act of Union, differs fundamentally from the English
system in its strong codified Roman and Feudal basis as
opposed to a dependence on precedent. The detailed
differences, now mainly confined to the fields of personal
and property law, are complex and often purely technical.
They have though, two important ramifications; the need
for a separate set of Scottish legal institutions and the
trained professional staff to man them, and the need for
separate Scottish legislation in the Westminster parliament.
The Scottish legal profession is, even in the late twentieth
century, more of a closed shop than the educational
profession. Undiluted by much infiltration of new blood,
trained in Scotland for unique Scottish institutions, the
Scottish legal profession constitutes a powerful high-
status group with a vested interest in the separateness of
Scotland. The Scottish legal system is perhaps less
responsible than either the religious or educational
systems for the persistence and cohesion of the social
character of Scotland. It is far more responsible for
the persistence of Scotland's administrative and political
identity. The removal of the Scottish Office from London
to Edinburgh in 1939 gave that city a real capital status,
but this was only a formal recognition of the administrative
role which Edinburgh had long performed, arising from the
separate legal and local government organisation of Scotland.

Economic considerations provided the strongest motives

for the original Act of Union in 1707, and in the period since that time there has rarely been any strong pressure in Scotland for the separation of the Scottish from the general British economic system. Even during periods of economic depression, agitation has been muted, partly because little advantage would accrue to Scotland as a result of breaking away, and partly because a great deal of aid has been made available to Scotland as a result of British economic legislation. Towards the end of the nineteen sixties however, a major new element entered into the economic equation, North Sea oil.

The addition of a prospect of economic self-sufficiency to the various feelings of cultural and social distinctiveness, and feelings of second-class status within Britain, has produced a powerful surge towards the devolution of greater political power to Scotland. In the general elections of 1974, the Scottish National Party, campaigning on the single platform of Scottish independence, returned an unprecedented seven MPs to the Westminster parliament in February, and raised the number to eleven in October. Under this growing pressure, all the major British political parties committed themselves to providing Scotland with greater political freedom, based on the establishment of some kind of assembly sitting in Edinburgh. The limits which this trend will eventually reach are by no means clear, but the various strands of Scottish cultural, social and political identity are more closely and strongly interwoven as the twentieth century approaches its last quarter than at any other time in the last two and a half centuries.

The Scottish community is nevertheless not completely united and is certainly not uniform in character. The strength of the Roman Catholic church and the workers' movement in Scotland are but two illustrations of powerful opposition to the religious and social establishment. Not all Scots are dour, thrifty and uncultured as the stereotyped image would suggest. Long association with the rest of Britain has blurred the differences between some sections of the Scottish community and the British community as a whole. It has also loosened some of the feelings of kinship between different sections of the Scottish community. Nevertheless, the bulk of the Scottish population has retained a degree of cohesion and common feeling which amounts to the retention of a

11

national consciousness.   In that sense, Scotland is a
nation.

1 THE NATURAL ENVIRONMENT

THE LAND

The summit of Ben Nevis, 1343 m, is the highest point in the British Isles (Plate 1A) and the plateau of the Cairngorms is the largest continuous area at an elevation of more than 1220 m. Scotland, by British standards contains a considerable area of high ground, but by world standards the heights attained are only modest, and the altitudinal range of the Scottish landscape is comparatively small. Nevertheless, as a result of the location of Scotland, the range is sufficient to assume great significance climatically. Scotland lies sufficiently far north for the rather modest altitudinal range to introduce climatic variations from temperate at sea level to sub-arctic on the summits; indeed in most years snow lies on some sheltered parts of the highest hills throughout the year. In addition the significance of the altitudinal range is greatly enhanced by the ruggedness of the terrain, the juxtaposition of high and low ground. The summit of Ben Nevis is only about 8 km from the coast, indeed no part of Scotland is more than 70 km from the sea. The landscape is extremely accidented, especially in the west, with low lying valleys winding and inter-connecting between steeply sloping often precipitous upland terrain. In few parts of Scotland, even in the Central Lowlands or the coastlands of the east, are extensive stretches of level ground to be found (Fig 1). This ruggedness, a dominating feature of the landscape of Scotland and one which exerts a powerful influence on the activities of man, reflects a long and complex history of rock formation, earth movements, erosion and deposition. Much of this history, and many of the influences responsible for the present landscape, are only imperfectly understood, perhaps not surprising since few of the rocks which now form the basis of the Scottish landscape are younger than 300 million years, and the oldest are approaching 2000

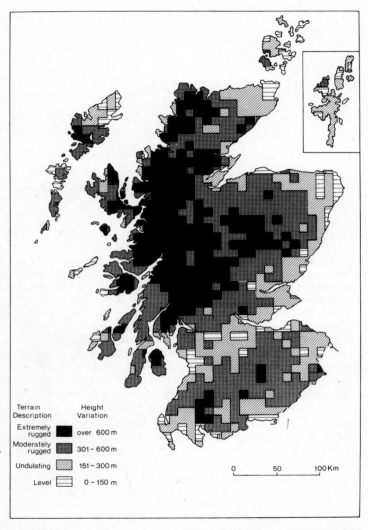

Terrain Description		Height Variation
Extremely rugged	▓	over 600 m
Moderately rugged	▓	301 – 600 m
Undulating	▨	151 – 300 m
Level	▤	0 – 150 m

0   50   100 Km

Figure 1.   The nature of the terrain, based on the height variation between the lowest and highest points in each 10 km grid square

million years in age.

The contribution to the present scenery of different types of rock

Rocks vary from one another in many important characteristics, and even minor variations occur within one broad rock type. Differences of jointing, chemical composition, grain size, porosity, colour and resistance to the various agents of erosion all contribute to variety of scenery. The complex juxtaposition of different types of rock in Scotland, generalised in Fig 2 therefore suggests considerable scope for landscape variation. The age of the rock is not in itself of any great significance, while the significance of the contribution to the landscape made by any one rock type may depend just as much on the characteristics of neighbouring rocks as on the characteristics of the rock itself. These two points are well illustrated by the contribution to the Scottish landscape made by igneous rocks.

Intrusive igneous rocks of the granite or gabbro type are now revealed at the surface widely in Scotland, especially in the Highlands and Southern Uplands. They vary considerably in age. North of the Great Glen most of the granitic intrusions occurred in Lower Palaeozoic times or even earlier – that is at least 440 million years ago. Further south, in the Grampians and Southern Uplands, most of the intrusions are of Devonian age, up to 50 million years younger. Most of the granites of the Inner Isles, Skye, Mull and Arran are younger still, dating from Tertiary times which began less than 70 million years ago. Irrespective of age, these granitic outcrops are extremely resistant to erosion and therefore stand out as high ground unless surrounded by even more resistant rocks. The Cairngorm plateau, the Red Hills of Skye, Goat Fell on Arran, Ben Nevis, Ben Cruachan and many of the highest hills of Galloway are all largely formed of granite. On the other hand relatively low ground on Rannoch Moor, around Loch Doon and on the Sutherland-Caithness border, is also formed mainly of granite. Granite has a massive crystalline structure which tends to create a broadly smooth landscape when viewed from a distance, but one which is rugged and

15

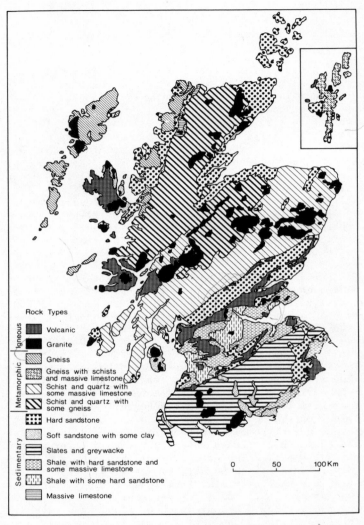

Rock Types

Igneous
- Volcanic
- Granite

Metamorphic
- Gneiss
- Gneiss with schists and massive limestone
- Schist and quartz with some massive limestone
- Schist and quartz with some gneiss

Sedimentary
- Hard sandstone
- Soft sandstone with some clay
- Slates and greywacke
- Shale with hard sandstone and some massive limestone
- Shale with some hard sandstone
- Massive limestone

0   50   100 Km

Figure 2.   The geology of Scotland: rock types

16

irregular in detail, reflecting small and irregular variations in the character of the rock. This is noticeable especially where granite rocks reach the coast, as for example in the rugged granite cliffs north of Aberdeen.

Extrusive igneous rocks of the basalt or andesite type are more limited in distribution, occurring mainly in the Central Lowlands and the Inner Isles. Most of these extrusive igneous rocks date from Devonian and Carboniferous times, 350 to 440 million years ago, although in the strip of country from Skye through Mull, Ardnamurchan, Kintyre and Arran to the central Southern Uplands they are much younger, being of Tertiary age. These rocks tend to give rise to less massive blocks of distinctive landscape as they were in general poured out at or near the surface in a series of sheets. They make a considerable contribution to the scenery however, largely because of their resistance to erosion. Most of the high ground in the Central Lowlands, like the Sidlaw, Pentland and Ochil Hills is chiefly constructed of nearly horizontal layers of basaltic rocks. Often the different layers of basalt can be seen in the series of steep rises and intervening levels which give a stepped appearance to the hill slopes. Sometimes the steep edges of these sills give rise to marked inland cliffs, as in Salisbury Crags in Edinburgh. In Skye and parts of the Inner Isles high ground resulting from basalt layers meets the coast to produce some of the highest and steepest cliffs in Scotland. Inland and on the coast, basalt scenery is much more angular than granite scenery, due largely to the more regular structure of the rock, which reaches perhaps its most spectacularly geometric form in the columnar formation of Fingal's cave on the Isle of Staffa. The much darker, often almost black colour of the basalt also makes a distinctive contribution to the scenery, especially in the coastal cliffs of the west.

More vertical intrusions of basalt also give rise to important elements of the Scottish landscape. The dyke swarms of the Inner Isles and the western peninsulas of the mainland from Ardnamurchan southwards generally produce sharp narrow ridges, while the old volcanic vents of the Central Lowlands and Southern Uplands produce sharp hills or steep islands offshore, such as the Eildon Hills, Bass Rock and Ailsa Craig.

17

The complex variety of very ancient, largely metamorphic rocks which form most of the northern half of
Scotland is still not fully surveyed, although differences
of rock type clearly lead to marked contrasts in the
landscape.   The Precambrian Lewisian Gneiss rocks,
widespread in the Outer Isles, Skye and the extreme north
west of the mainland, are thought to be the oldest rocks
in Scotland, approaching 2000 million years in age.
Although they are extremely resistant to erosion, they now
give rise to a lowlying landscape, albeit an extremely
rugged and rocky one with occasional rough hills rising
over three hundred metres.

Over most of the rest of the Highlands and in Shetland,
the varied metamorphic rocks of the Moine and Dalradian
series, probably only a little younger than the Lewisian
Gneiss, produce a landscape in which broad rock types are
less important than other factors in producing variations
of scenery.   The mountainous terrain is predominantly
developed on schists, which in general produce fairly
smooth slopes.   However more resistant quartzites
especially in the more southerly Dalradian series tend to
form noticeable ridges and peaks, as in the strip of
country from Jura to Buchan, which includes Schiehallion
and Glas Moal, while more resistant grits often produce
more rugged hills like Ben Ledi and Ben Vorlich close to
the southern edge of the Highlands.   Narrow outcrops of
less resistant limestone, frequent in Shetland and the
Dalradian series tend to form lower ground and inlets on
the coast.   However the most dramatic example of the
variation which limestone introduces into the Highland
scenery is found around Inchnadamph and Durness in the
north west.   Small outcrops of massive Cambrian Limestone
occur in this region, producing a landscape whose verdant
grassland contrasts sharply with the acid moorland of
neighbouring formations, and in which caves and swallow-
holes resulting from the rock's solubility abound.

In the gneiss country of the extreme north western
part of the mainland, two other rocks make a vivid
contribution to a spectacular landscape.   In places the
sedimentary Precambrian Torridonian Sandstone overlies
the gneiss.   Occasionally the more regular structure of
the sandstone produces low lying country less rugged in
character than that developed on the gneiss.   Generally
however the sandstone beds form steep sided mountain

18

masses, as in the Torridon and Applecross areas, or isolated hills like Suilven, Quinag and An Stac (Plate 1B). The generally reddish colour of the mountains contrasts with the grey of the gneiss, and the contrast is heightened by the capping of whitish Cambrian Quartzite which forms the resistant summits of many of the sandstone mountains. On mountains like Liathach and Beinn Eighe, the quartzite weathers to produce dramatic white screes against the reddish mountain slopes (Plate 2A). The bedding and jointing of the sandstone also produces weathered formations very different from the gneiss, most clearly illustrated perhaps in the towers, buttresses, cliffs and chasms of the summit of An Stac.

Another hard sandstone, the much younger Devonian or Old Red Sandstone, formed about 400 million years ago, influences the landscapes of Orkney, the fringes of the north eastern mainland, the eastern Southern Uplands and the northern and southern stretches of the Central Lowlands. Although a resistant formation, the Old Red Sandstone for the most part gives rise to gently undulating low or intermediate level plateaux fringing higher ground formed from even more resistant rocks. Rarely does the land rise much above about two hundred and fifty metres. In the north east and Orkney more resistant grit beds give rise to occasional higher hills, and on the coast the bedding, jointing and reddish colour of the rocks gives rise to a distinctive coastline of cliffs, arches and stacks. The Old Man of Hoy is perhaps the best known example of these Old Red Sandstone coastal features.

The only other rocks forming major relief features in Scotland are the broadly uniform thin bedded slates and greywackes of the Southern Uplands. These are Ordovician and Silurian in age, some 450 to 500 million years old, and they form smooth rounded upland terrain, hills rather than mountains.

The mixed Carboniferous rocks which floor most of the Central Lowlands are all of generally low resistance to erosion. Rarely does a more resistant band of limestone or sandstone produce significant landscape features. The inclusion of coal seams in the series has however exerted a considerable influence on the present day appearance of

the region.   Purely in terms of the physical landscape
though, these rocks and the even newer friable sandstones,
shales and clays which occur in small patches in the
valleys of the Southern Uplands, in the islands and on the
coastal margins of the mainland, exert little influence,
apart from being largely responsible for the general lowlying character of these localities.

The contribution to the present scenery of pre-Quaternary geological events

In their long life, the rocks of Scotland have been
subjected to many changes.   Although later events tend
to obscure the scenic effects of earlier ones, so that
most of the features of the present landscape result from
geologically recent influences, there are nevertheless
some very significant traces of much earlier events.
The igneous and metamorphic rocks themselves are
evidence of considerable instability in the earth's
crust in the area which is now Scotland.   The uplift,
folding and faulting of all the rocks, another facet of
this instability, has also left its mark on today's
landscape.   Although several periods of marked instability certainly occurred in very early geological
time, the earliest such period to which the present day
scenery bears clear witness was the Caledonian orogeny
of about 400 million years ago.   The mountains produced
by the Caledonian folding and uplift have long since been
eroded away, though the folds themselves can still be
widely seen in rock outcrops, especially on the coast.
The general NE-SW trending alignment of the main fold axes
is often still evident in the present grain of the landscape, as a result of NE-SW alignment of different rock
beds revealed by erosion of the folds and emphasised by
differential erosion.   More graphic and obvious however
is the influence of the faults (Fig 3).
From southern Mull to the Black Isle, a series of
deep sea inlets, lochs and low ground follows the zone
of weakness along the Great Glen Fault.   Lateral movement along this fault seems to have resulted in the area
to the northwest now being out of line with the area to
the south east to the extent of about 105 km.   Further
south, the Central Lowland belt of later rocks and

generally less elevated ground is basically a rift valley block let, or forced, down between the Highland Boundary Fault, running from Helensburgh to Stonehaven and the Southern Uplands Fault, running from Girvan to Dunbar. The former line still broadly coincides with the marked break between the landscapes of the Highlands and those of the Central Lowlands. It has been suggested that a similar though rather more recent rift valley feature may account for the broad trench between the Outer Isles and the Scottish mainland. The major Caledonian fault in the north west however is the Moine Thrust. A line from Skye to Loch Erribol marks the north western edge of a block of land which was thrust over and buried much of the former land to its north west, leaving only a narrow strip of territory in north west Scotland not dominated by the schistose rocks typical of most of the northern Highlands.

Many other major and minor fault lines, originating or greatly emphasised in Caledonian times, are still evident in the present landscape. For the most part they form low ground or control valley lines due to their weakness and hence low resistance to erosion. Most produce linear features with the characteristic NE-SW alignment, though some, such as the Loch Maree fault run at right angles to this trend, and others on a more local scale diverge completely from this clear pattern.

Later orogenies, such as the Hercynian about 300 million years ago and the Alpine about 50 million years ago introduced few new features, although both were accompanied by considerable volcanic activity, some uplift and further movement along the Caledonian faults. Rocks newer than the Devonian, especially in the Central Lowlands, were gently folded in Hercynian times, with the main fold axes trending N-S or E-W. Although not of great significance as far as present day landforms are concerned, subsequent erosion of the anticlines is in part responsible for the limited occurrence of coal bearing rocks today, almost entirely confined to the synclinal basin areas.

Although culminating in these major mountain building periods, the instability of the earth's crust in the region of present day Scotland seems to have been a persistent characteristic. Even in the last hundred years, quite severe earthquakes have been recorded in

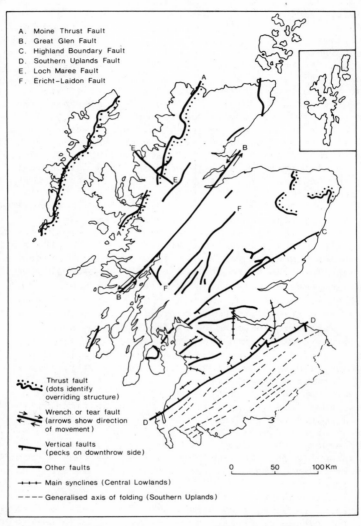

A. Moine Thrust Fault
B. Great Glen Fault
C. Highland Boundary Fault
D. Southern Uplands Fault
E. Loch Maree Fault
F. Ericht–Laidon Fault

Thrust fault
(dots identify
overriding structure)

Wrench or tear fault
(arrows show direction
of movement)

Vertical faults
(pecks on downthrow side)

Other faults

Main synclines (Central Lowlands)

Generalised axis of folding (Southern Uplands)

0   50   100 Km

Figure 3.   The geology of Scotland: structure

22

Scotland, notably at Inverness and Comrie, clearly associated with the ancient Caledonian fault lines. Minor tremors are by no means rare.

Apart from uplift, folding and faulting, the rocks of Scotland have also been subject to erosion over immense lengths of time, often under climatic and other conditions markedly different from those obtaining today. There is some evidence to suggest that in some parts of Scotland, for example the gneiss country of the north west, a landscape produced by erosion in very early geological time may have been subsequently buried under and preserved by later rock formations. The removal of these later rocks by erosion in more recent geological time might then exhume these ancient landscapes, but sufficient time may not have yet elapsed to have allowed erosion to remove all traces of the very ancient scenery. Indeed it is possible that the small patches of secondary rocks now found in Scotland are the last remnants of rock strata which perhaps as little as 50 million years ago buried almost the whole of Scotland. Such a possibility would imply that the broad outline of present day Scotland and its broad landscape features might have been recognisable more than 200 million years ago. The embryo Scotland would then have been preserved for some 150 million years, and only in the last 50 million years have been once more exposed to further erosion and modification.

Two aspects of this theory have given rise to considerable controversy, the development of erosion surfaces and of the drainage pattern. Even a casual observer, looking over any part of Scotland from a vantage point, could scarcely fail to notice the general accordance of summit heights or the occurrence at various elevations of broadly level land surfaces. Map evidence and field research has in fact shown that these levels are widespread and may be present at almost any height. Very rarely do they bear any relationship either to geological structure or to any contemporary erosion processes. Some geomorphologists have argued that they were formed by marine erosion, and are therefore related to different levels of the sea since mid-Tertiary times (about 40 million years ago). They are broadly similar in origin to the much more recent and more limited raised beach features common around much of Scotland's coastline. Others also postulate

Tertiary changes of sea level, but suggest that the levels in the present landscape were produced by sub-aerial erosion working to the base level of the sea. They are more the remnants of coastal plains than wave cut platforms. In the absence of any clear evidence for the necessary sea-level changes there has recently been re-advanced a theory involving uplift, sub-aerial erosion and parallel slope retreat in relation to local river base levels rather than general sea levels. This theory could also explain the origin of the puzzling inland basins like Rannoch Moor and the region around Loch Shin. Of con-troversial origin, these erosion surfaces are an important feature of the present landscape of Scotland.

As far as the drainage pattern is concerned, certain features clearly relate to the structure and present day relief of Scotland. The main watershed between the Atlantic Ocean and the North Sea runs much closer to the former, corresponding to the main axis of high ground. Many valleys, like those containing the river Spey, Loch Ericht and Loch Ness, clearly follow major lines of structural weakness. Minor anomalies are explainable in terms of river capture and normal processes of valley development. Other elements, such as the W to E or NW to SE trending valleys like the Tweed, Dee and Tummel are not so readily explained. Attempts have been made to explain these and similar anomalies by postulating an original drainage pattern developed on a different land surface. The sub-sequent removal of this land surface allowed this original drainage pattern to readjust to the character of the exhumed land surface, but parts of the system did not so readjust, and were superimposed to produce those elements of the pattern which now appear discordant. Controversy still rages over the detail of this original pattern - whether the main watershed was further west than it is today and whether the main rivers flowed eastwards, south eastwards or varied locally in direction. There is little doubt however that these studies reveal yet another contribution made to the present landscape patterns of Scotland by the shadowy events of the 70 millions years of the Tertiary era, almost unrepresented in the record of the sedimentary rocks of Scotland.

The contribution to the present scenery of recent post-Tertiary events

Although not substantially changed since the end of Tertiary times, the present day landscape of Scotland owes much of its detail and hence visual character to the processes of erosion and deposition operating over the last one or two million years. Climatic conditions play a considerable role in determining these processes, and during the period in question, the climate has varied considerably. The normal processes of landscape evolution associated with the present temperate climate have varied in degree and sometimes in kind as higher or lower temperatures have prevailed and more or less water has been at work. None of these fluctuations have been of more significance than those which led to the advance and retreat of ice-sheets and glaciers over Scotland. Superimposed on these recent climatic fluctuations, there persisted much the same kind of regional variation of climate that obtains today. This led to considerable differences in the lengths of time during which various parts of Scotland were affected by particular processes, and also differences in the intensity at which these processes operated. Thus glaciers and sub-arctic conditions developed first and persisted longest in the higher mountain areas, while the western mountains, with their persistently higher precipitation, tended to suffer the most intensive erosion at all periods.

Although the detailed chronology of these climatic changes is by no means clear, the landscape most clearly bears the marks of the most recent changes, and the effects of earlier conditions tend to be obscured or have been removed. Thus although there have been probably at least four major ice-ages and intervening periods of warmer climate in the last two million years or so, the sequence over the last 50,000 years since the height of the last glaciation is of greatest significance. At that time, probably the whole of Scotland was covered by ice and affected by glacial processes. Although the last glaciers finally disappeared about 8000 years ago, there is considerable evidence to suggest that before the final retreat several partial retreats and readvances occurred, each readvance extending less far from the main mountain areas. As a result, it is the mountain areas, and especially the western mountain areas, which display the results of glacial processes least modified by subsequent normal processes. However, even in those areas of the east, probably not glaciated at all in the last 40,000 years, normal processes have not had a sufficient length of time to entirely eradicate glacial features.

Most of the effective erosive power of ice is undertaken by ice moving under the influence of gravity in confined channels, aided by meltwater and debris frozen into its mass. Features resulting from glacial erosion in Scotland are therefore particularly strongly displayed in the upland valleys and neighbouring hill slopes in regions already considerably dissected prior to the appearance of ice. In regions of less dissected pre-glacial relief, such as the plateau uplands of the east and the lower ground of the north west, where the ice was for the most part less confined, features of glacial erosion are less dramatically displayed in the present landscape. Indeed there is still some doubt as to whether slow moving unconfined ice sheets undertake any erosion apart from removing already loose material. It seems likely however that some differential scouring, scratching and gouging of the land surface occurs, producing a generally level, but in detail ruggedly hummocky and hollowed scenery. This kind of landscape, with the hollows now filled with water, is very common in the Outer Isles and the north-west mainland. The summits of the higher mountains, above about 1000 metres, also display few features of glacial erosion, either because at such elevations ice had little erosive power, or because they were for most of the time above the ice. The vast accumulation of angular debris, mountain top detritus, which characterises most of Scotland's higher summits today, probably results from an accelerated freeze-thaw weathering process in glacial times, a process still operative in the sub-arctic conditions obtaining in such areas to the present day.

An area subjected to glacial erosion looks very different from one affected only by normal processes, and the landscape of Scotland displays numerous examples of features resulting from these distinctive processes. Glaciers tend to move in fairly straight lines, gouging in time an almost straight, steep sided valley trough, well illustrated for example in the valleys radiating from Rannoch Moor. Variations in ice thickness and pressure also enable ice to gouge hollows in the valley floor and to move uphill, producing rock basins now mostly occupied by the hundreds of ribbon lochs and fiords. Similar variations in a glacier's erosive power, often in association with variations of rock type, can also produce steep steps in a valley or between tributary valleys and a main valley. Such steps are often marked today by waterfalls such as the dramatic Falls of Glomach in Wester Ross or the more modest rapids of the Falls of Killin above Loch Tay. At the heads of valleys or on the flanks of surrounding mountains, small centres of ice accumulation produce deep hollows. Hundreds of these corries as they are called are found in the higher parts of Scotland, often supporting small lochs in their centre. Sometimes neighbouring corries eat into the mountain mass to such an extent that they reduce it to a series of sharp ridges or aretes. The ridge to the north of Glen Coe is a fine example. Most glacier movements in Scotland were controlled by existing river valleys, often themselves related to lines of structural weakness, but in some circumstances glaciers seem to have created new valleys. Generally such new valleys were carved either because ice was unable to negotiate sharp changes of direction in the original valley or because tongues of excess ice spilled over the watershed to produce new cols. Glen Falloch, above Loch Lomond, is thought to be an example of the former, and the short col between Loch Lomond and Arrochar of the latter, but similar glacial breaches abound in the heavily glaciated regions of the Western Highlands, producing numerous interconnections between different valley systems. (Plate 2B).

The Scottish glaciers also undertook herculean tasks of transport and deposition, removing vast quantities of rock waste and dumping it elsewhere, mainly outside the areas of heavy glacial erosion (Fig 4). Identifiable rock fragments with limited possible sources of origin found amongst this boulder clay or till provide much useful information about the movements of the ice. Even at high levels, above eight hundred metres, ice-carried erratic boulders, often weighing many tons, occur quite frequently, but more widespread and significant are the unsorted till deposits, chiefly found on lower ground. For the most part this till forms an uneven veneer to the

underlying landscape, producing a rounded and smoothed
appearance, but some more distinctive ice-moulded depositional landscape features do occur.   In many areas,
for example in the Glasgow district, the till is formed
into a series of low mounds, up to twenty or so metres
high;   features known as drumlins.   Often behind
resistant rock outcrops, like for example Edinburgh Castle
rock, a long tail of till accumulated to produce a feature
known as a crag and tail (though in some examples, boring
has revealed that much of the tail is also solid rock, and
the deposition tail only very thin).   Broadly linear
mounds of till known as moraines also occur widely, representing the concentrations of deposition at the edges
and snouts of former glaciers.   If unmelted blocks of ice
were included in the till deposits, their eventual melting
produced marked collapse hollows which are often today
water filled.   The Lake of Mentieth is in part such a
kettle-hole lake.

During warmer seasons, and associated with the retreat
of the ice sheets, vast quantities of melt water must have
been available, and this too has had its influence on the
landscape today.   Ice itself, or glacial deposits,
frequently blocked the natural valley escape routes for
much of this water.   In such circumstances, temporary
lakes must have developed before the water level reached
an overspill and began to carve a new valley.   Successive
levels of one of the larger such temporary lakes are still
clearly marked by the well known parallel roads of Glen
Roy.   Thousands of small valley features formed by meltwater streams have been identified in all parts of Scotland.

Many of the deposits of such streams are also present
in the landscape today, forming features often very
similar in appearance to glacial landforms, but differing
in composition.   Fluvio-glacial deposits tend to be of
sorted materials, sands and gravels especially, rather
than the undifferentiated mixture of glacial boulder clay.
Material originally deposited by meltwater in hollows or
tunnels in the ice now forms irregular mounds known as
kames, or sinuous ridges known as eskers.   Such a landscape, well illustrated in the area around Carstairs in
Lanarkshire, looks very like a landscape composed of
glacial moraine.   In the lower reaches of most glaciated
valleys, and in many parts of the lowlands, broad spreads

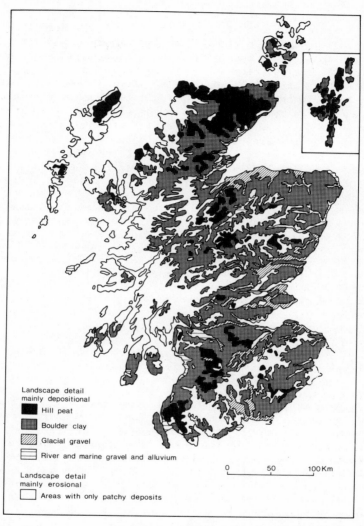

Landscape detail
mainly depositional

▓ Hill peat

▓ Boulder clay

▨ Glacial gravel

▤ River and marine gravel and alluvium

Landscape detail
mainly erosional

☐ Areas with only patchy deposits

0   50   100 Km

Figure 4.   Erosional and depositional landscapes

29

of meltwater outwash sands and gravels testify to the work of water in sorting deposits left behind by retreating glaciers.

Since the disappearance of the ice, more normal processes have been steadily adding their own stamp to the landscape. To a considerable extent these processes have been working to remove many of the irregular features introduced into the scene by glaciation. The steep valley walls and other steep slopes of glaciated areas are being eroded by gullying, softened by the steady accumulation of scree at their base and rounded at their crests by weathering. Streams are busily reimposing more regular profiles to their valleys by eroding away such irregularities as hanging-valley and valley-step waterfalls, and by filling in with alluvium the numerous rock-basin hollows. Some lochs have disappeared already, and all others are much reduced in length and depth by the accumulation of river-borne debris. At the same time streams are busy sorting the materials left behind by the glaciers and adding their own gravel and alluvium deposits to the landscape. Because they are geologically so recent, features of glacial origin abound in Scotland, but year by year they become more modified by the processes now at work in the present, latest, stage of the landscape's evolution.

The Scottish Coast

The broad pattern of the coastline of Scotland results mainly from the regional variations of rock type, structure and erosional history of the land already discussed, since the present sea-level represents a partial drowning of a once more extensive land mass. Major lines of weakness, such as the line of the Great Glen Fault and the Central Lowlands thus correspond with the greatest inland penetration of the sea. The general pattern of the west coast clearly reflects the drowning of a highly accidented, glacially modified landscape: the islands are the higher parts of former mountains, while the sea inlets and channels are the flooded, often fault-guided valley lines. [The much smoother outline of the east coast results from the drowning of a much less accidented and glaciated landscape.]

The familiar map outline of Scotland tends to create

30

an entirely erroneous impression of the permanent nature of the Scottish coastline. In fact both the land and the sea are constantly varying in level relative to one another. Over short periods of time the tidal movements of the sea lead to continual minor changes in the shape of the coast, though between the definable limits of the lowest and highest tides. On the more rugged and cliffed coasts, this oscillation merely exposes or submerges a few metres of rocky foreshore, but in shallow estuarine or bay inlets several hundred metres of mudflats, sand and marsh may be alternately covered and exposed. In parts of the Outer Hebrides and the inner parts of the Solway, Moray, Clyde, Tay and Forth Firths these daily tidal variations are responsible for dramatic variations in the shoreline and coastal scenery.

Over longer periods of time, much greater variations of land and sea levels occur. Indeed during and since the ice-age, complicated isostatic and eustatic movements have led to changes of sea level relative to the land such that at times the relative level of the sea has been perhaps fifty metres above and at times perhaps fifty metres below its present level. Over even longer periods of time much greater variations than this have occurred. The implication of the relatively short time during which the sea has stood at its present level in relation to the land, is that the sea has not had time to create major coastal landforms related to its present level, apart from some minor differential erosion on rocky coasts, some slight cliff erosion and the development of localised bay head, beach and estuarine deposits. For example, many of the major cliffs are believed to have been largely formed in pre-glacial times, and some may even have been formed directly by faulting in tertiary times and owe very little to erosion by the sea at all. Considerable stretches of the coast, especially in the west and on the islands display virtually no coastal landforms at all, the tides rising and falling over a rugged, rocky landscape, in which elements of land, sea and fresh water are often difficult to distinguish. As a result a widespread and perhaps the most dominant characteristic of the Scottish coasts is the remains of former coastal landforms often well above and well inland from the present tidal zone. These are the

remains of features formed by the sea when it stood
relatively higher than at present, especially in late, and
post, glacial times.

Bands of level or nearly level ground, often backed
with low cliffs, caves, stacks, etc. and covered with the
remains of beach deposits, occur at heights up to about
thirty metres above present sea level. Although very
common, especially on the central part of both east and
west coasts and on the western islands, where a series of
such raised beaches may occur one above the other, they
are neither continuous nor constant in level. Clearly
differential movements of the land as well as overall
movements of the sea must have occurred in a sequence far
from fully understood. On the more rugged coastlines
of Scotland, these former coastal features generally have
only a narrow horizontal dimension, but on lowlying coasts,
and especially on parts of the eastern estuaries, their
horizontal extent is much greater. The carselands of the
Tay, Forth, Moray and Solway estuaries extend several kilometres inland from the present coast, yet together with
similar level areas related to innumerable smaller coastal
inlets, they are coastal features - former mudflats,
shingle accumulations etc. now well above present sea level.
In many cases, especially on the open coast, such raised
levels provide a base for the accumulation of blown sand
from present areas of coastal deposition. The Culbin Sands
on the Moray Firth for example and many of the famous
coastal golf courses occupy such sites. Somewhat similar,
although less clearly associated with raised beach features,
are the machair lands of the Outer Hebrides.

THE CLIMATE

Reference has already been made to the dramatic
effect of the ice-age on the scenery of Scotland. Variations
in the prevailing climatic conditions clearly occur over
periods of time, and even minor changes may have significant
effects on landscape, soils, vegetation and the activities
of man. Scotland undoubtedly bears many traces of the
influence of past climatic conditions. However, as an
aspect of the total environment of present day Scotland,

Plate 1 Mountain Landscapes
A. Ben Nevis, Scotland's highest mountain, still carrying snow in late June. The pipeline serves the Lochaber aluminium works in Fort William.

B. Canisp and Suilven. Isolated hills of Torridonian Sandstone rise from the irregular platform of Lewisian Gneiss near Lochinver in Sutherland.

Plate 2 Mountain Weathering and Erosion

A. Liathach and Loch Torridon. The weathering of the white quartzite summit of Liathach in the Torridonian mountains produces screes which clearly trace the downslope movement of weathered material.

B. The Torridon Mountains. The effects of glacial erosion on a mountain mass: the view east from Sgurr Mhor.

it is the present day climatic conditions which are of
prime interest.   In describing this climate, moderation
and variability best summarise its characteristics.
Moderation because Scotland does not suffer from large
daily or seasonal extremes, yet variability because within
these limits the climatic conditions tend to vary over
short periods of time in a haphazard and largely unpredictable manner.   This latter characteristic, an
apparent lack of pattern, gives rise to the common
assertion that Scotland has no climate only weather.
However, always bearing in mind this variability, broad
generalisations about the climate of Scotland and regional climatic differences can be made.

    Two factors in particular exert a powerful influence
on the Scottish climate; the position of the country on
the globe and in relation to areas of land and sea, and
the shape of the terrain.   The country is situated in
high northern latitudes, a zone of generally low pressure
and westerly air flows.   Since the Atlantic Ocean, and
specifically the warm waters of the North Atlantic Drift
lie to the west, maritime influences prevail.   This
results in a moderation of temperature extremes, frequent
precipitation and considerable exposure to wind.   However,
the generally high relief of the western part of the
country modifies these prevailing influences quite rapidly,
and more continental conditions obtain in the eastern parts
of the country.   The westerly air flow though is by no
means regular in the latitude of Scotland.   Seasonal and
short term variations of pressure distribution can and
frequently do introduce air flows from other directions,
or the build up of pressure may introduce spells of stable
anticyclonic weather with little discernible air flow.
These variations introduce considerable climatic changes,
which influence different parts of Scotland to differing
degrees and with differing frequency depending on location
and the relief of the land.   For example, northern coasts
are clearly more directly and frequently affected by cold
northerly air flows than is the south, while the western
mountains protect the west coast from the effects of
easterly air flows.   Because the cold polar latitudes lie
to the north, warm subtropical latitudes lie to the south,
the open ocean lies to the west and a major land mass
(broken only slightly by the North Sea) lies to the east,

very different weather conditions are brought to Scotland
by the different flows.   The names given to the broad air
mass types which are brought to Scotland by these flows
themselves graphically illustrate these variations;   Arctic
Maritime, Arctic Continental, Polar Maritime, Polar
Continental, Tropical Maritime and Tropical Continental.
Marked weather changes occur especially when one air mass
is replaced by one of very different character, as for
example when the cold showery Polar Maritime gives way to
the warm wet Tropical Maritime and this in turn gives way
once more to the Polar Maritime, the usual sequence when
a depression crosses the country from the west.   The change
in temperature and the character of the rainfall as one air
mass gives way to the other at the warm and cold fronts is
often clearly identifiable without meteorological instruments.
        Scotland is not large enough for latitudinal and
longitudinal extent to cause major regional climatic
differences.   It is large enough however for a number of
significant minor differences to occur.   The eastward
increase in continentality, albeit more due to relief
patterns than distance, is one.   Seasonal variations
in daylight hours and insolation is another.   In mid-
summer, daylight in Shetland lasts about nineteen hours
compared with only seventeen hours in Galloway.   In mid-
winter on the other hand, daylight in Shetland lasts only
about six hours compared with about seven hours in Galloway.
Although the average day length is about twelve hours in
each case, the average daily insolation lessens markedly
northwards.   Because of the lower angle of the sun and
the consequently greater absorption of sunlight by cloud
and haze, the Shetlands only receive an average of 2.5
hours of bright sunlight a day, compared with 4 hours in
Galloway.   With low sun elevations, especially in the
north and in winter, relief also introduces dramatic
regional variations of insolation.   This is especially
so in areas of rugged terrain, where not only steep north
facing slopes may be completely sunless, but where many
other slopes may be shadowed for long periods by high
ground to the east, south and west.   This is but one
illustration of the way in which the' ruggedness of
Scotland helps to introduce marked climatic variations
over very short distances.   It is not simply a question

34

of the influence of altitude on temperature and rainfall, but a complex interplay of aspect, slope, elevation and degree of exposure affecting all the elements of the climate.

The broad regional variations which all these controlling influences produce in relation to various elements of the Scottish climate are illustrated in Fig 5. Even at this level of considerable generalisation, any attempt to combine these separate elements and produce a pattern of climatic regions requires substantial over-simplification. In considering the climatic regions depicted on Fig 6 therefore, it is imperative to bear this in mind and to remember that quite substantial local microclimatic variations may occur from place to place, especially in areas of accidented terrain.

Although the climate is generally characterised by moderation, short term extremes of particular weather phenoma do occur from place to place and from time to time, and may have a considerable disruptive effect on both the physical and human environment. High winds are perhaps the most frequent and most serious of such phenomena. Storms like those which demolished the Tay Bridge in December 1879, sank the Princess Victoria in January 1954 and ravaged Central Scotland in January 1968, cause considerable loss of life and substantial damage to buildings and forests. Intensive rain causing flooding is also a recurrent hazard. The natural drainage system is unable to cope with falls like the record 200mm in 24 hours near Loch Hourn in September 1916. Two days of prolonged heavy rain in Southern Scotland caused £1 million damage in August 1948 (Plate 4). Other disruptive exceptional weather phenomena by no means rare in Scotland are periods of drought, severe blizzards, fog, early and late frosts and electrical storms. No part of the country is immune from sporadic occurrences of these conditions.

SOILS AND VEGETATION

The intimately associated evolving soil and vegetation cover of Scotland was so disrupted by the events of the ice-age that to all intents and purposes

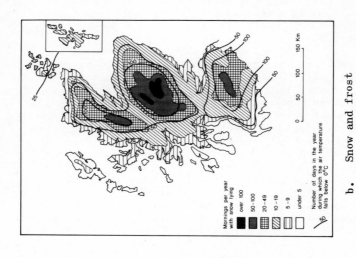

Mornings per year
with snow lying

■ over 100
▓ 50-100
▦ 20 - 49
▨ 10 - 19
▢ 5 - 9
□ under 5

Number of days in the year
during which the air temperature
falls below 0°C

b.   Snow and frost

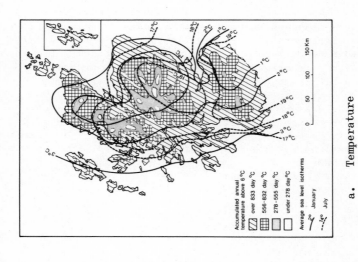

Accumulated annual
temperature above 6°C

▨ over 833 day °C
▦ 556-832 day °C
▨ 278 - 555 day °C
□ under 278 day °C

Average sea level isotherms

January
July

a.   Temperature

36

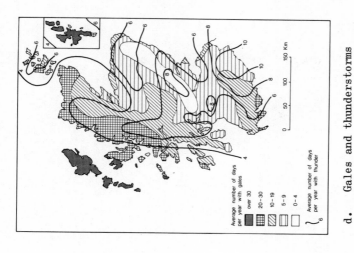

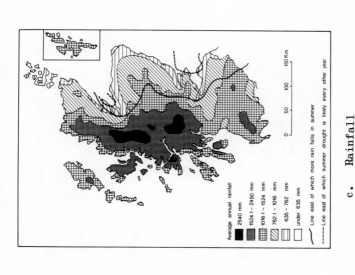

c. Rainfall

d. Gales and thunderstorms

Figure 5. Climatic features of Scotland

37

1. Lowland climates with generally high annual accumulated temperatures between 853 and 1400 day °C.

A. Atlantic Coast Type. Moderate rainfall, generally between 1000 and 1500 mm p.a., more falling in winter than in summer. Very mild winters with less than fifty days p.a. with air frost and less than ten mornings with snow lying. Cool summers. Exposed, with a high incidence of strong winds.

B. North Coast Type. Similar to A, but much cooler in summer with annual accumulated temperatures everywhere falling below 853 day °C. Also drier.

C. Western Lowland Type. Slightly drier than A, with rainfall falling below 1000 mm p.a. in places. Also less mild with generally more than fifty days p.a. with air frost and more than ten mornings with snow lying. Sheltered, with a low incidence of strong winds.

D. Southern Lowland Type. Similar to C, but cooler in winter and warmer in summer. Over one hundred days p.a. with air frost in places, and a high incidence of thunderstorms.

E. North Sea Coast Type. Low rainfall, generally below 750 mm p.a., more falling in summer than winter. Cool winters but less than fifty days p.a. with air frost and less than fifteen mornings with snow lying. Rather exposed, with a moderate incidence of strong winds. High incidence of sea mist.

F. Eastern Lowland Type. Similar to E, but wetter with colder winters. More than fifty days p.a. with air frost and warmer summers. Sheltered, with a low incidence of strong winds. Moderate incidence of thunderstorms, decreasing northwards.

2. Upland climates, with generally low annual accumulated temperatures between 0 and 852 day °C.

G. Western Mountain Type. High rainfall, generally above 1500 mm p.a. Cool winters with generally not more than one hundred days p.a. with air frost and generally less than fifty mornings with snow lying. Cool summers. Exposed with a high incidence of strong winds.

H. Northern Mountain Type. Rather drier than G, with rainfall generally less than 1500 mm p.a. Slightly less exposed and cooler with more frosty days and longer snow lie.

I. Central Mountain Type. Moderate rainfall, generally between 1000 and 1500 mm p.a. Very cold winters with more than one hundred days p.a. with air frost and well over fifty mornings with snow lying. Warm summers. Sheltered with a low incidence of strong winds.

J. Eastern Upland Type. Similar to I but generally drier and warmer at all seasons. Fewer frosty days and shorter snow lie.

K. Southern Upland Type. Similar to J, but warmer in summer with a higher incidence of thunder storms.

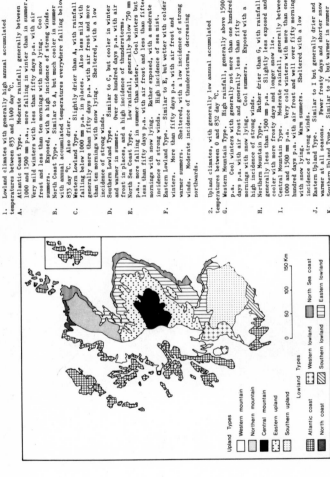

Upland Types

Western mountain
Northern mountain
Central mountain
Eastern upland
Southern upland

Lowland Types

Atlantic coast
North coast
Western lowland
Southern lowland
North Sea coast
Eastern lowland

0   50   100   150 Km

Figure 6. Climatic regions of Scotland, based on Figure 5

the present day soils and vegetation can be regarded as post glacial. Pre-existing soils were either swept away or inextricably mixed with other debris and deposited en masse elsewhere, while the vegetation was virtually wiped out by the extreme conditions. Since the end of the ice-age soils have been evolving in and vegetation recolonising the landscape, influenced by a range of variable factors. Climatic conditions, the shape of the land, the underlying geology and the influence of man have all contributed to the present extremely complex pattern of soils and vegetation.

Climatic conditions have been particularly influential, but they are known to have varied over the last 10,000 years, with important effects on the evolution of the vegetation. Drier phases encouraged more widespread tree growth, wetter phases encouraged greater development of peat moors, while variations in the altitudinal limits of different plant communities must also have occurred. Less is known about the corresponding fluctuations in the evolutionary story of the soil mantle. However, important as this detailed past history is, broad climatic characteristics over this whole period suffice to explain the influence of climatic conditions on the present soil and vegetation pattern of Scotland.

In association with the shape of the land, generally high rainfall has played a particularly important part in the evolution of the soils, leading to excessive leaching in better drained and excessive waterlogging in poorly drained areas. Nearly all the soils of Scotland therefore, depending on regional rainfall and drainage characteristics, are either podsols or gleys of one kind or another. Often these two broad types are not easily distinguishable. For example, the frequent development of an iron pan in the B horizon of the podsols (caused by the accumulation of leached minerals) impedes soil drainage to such an extent that gley characteristics develop in the A horizon. Over considerable areas of Scotland, a combination of high rainfall and poor drainage leads to the accumulation of partly rotted vegetation remains on the surface. If such a layer exceeds a depth of 40 cms it is classified as peat. True peats, occurring in small basins or other limited areas of poor drainage (topogenic or basin peat) or more continuously on all but the steeper slopes in areas of high rainfall (blanket peat), are themselves widespread, but the tendency towards peat development is almost universal in Scotland. Only very rarely on base rich parent material in the drier east, or in small flushes fed periodically by mineral rich ground water, are small areas of more fertile natural soils of the brown earth type found.

These variations of soil character due largely to rainfall and drainage conditions are reflected to a certain extent in broad vegetation patterns. Waterlogging and peat development in particular inhibits woodland, while different species characterise the grassland and heath communities developed on the various types of podsols and gleys. However other climatic characteristics also influence the vegetation (and hence soils), especially the climatic characteristics resulting from differences of altitude and of aspect. Trees (which tend to slow down the podsolisation of the soil) are confined to lower altitudes, but the tree line tends to be higher on south facing and sheltered slopes than on north facing and exposed slopes. Thus the general tree line today lowers from about six hundred metres in the eastern to less than three hundred metres in the western mountains, and virtually to sea level on the exposed west coast and islands. Different species also tend to dominate in different zones. To the east pine and to the west oak tend to give way upwards and northwards to birch. Above the tree line, different grass, herb and shrub communities also display altitudinal zoning, giving way at the highest levels and most exposed sites to communities largely composed of mosses and lichens.

These broad natural patterns of soil and vegetation, largely a result of climatic factors, are disrupted however by the influence of other factors. Apart from the resistance to erosion of most of the solid rocks of Scotland, resulting in considerable areas of only thin soil development, the main influence of the underlying geology on the present soils and vegetation of Scotland is through the general absence of base rich or calcareous parent materials. Soils in consequence are generally rather acid and the vegetation generally devoid of lime-loving species. Where soils have developed on such parent materials, the very different plant species which occur reflect the very different character of the soils. This influence is especially evident in the rendzina type soils of limestone areas such as Durness and a few locations in the Highlands such as Ben Lawers, and in the base rich brown earth type soils of some of the igneous areas.

Variations of slope are another disruptive factor since the degree of slope controls the stability of the soil and vegetation mantle. On steep slopes, no soil mantle is able to develop because of gravity movements of material; vegetation is thus confined to mosses, lichens and liverworts. Even on moderate slopes, the mantle may be subject to frequent erosion, preventing the development of a true soil profile and a stable vegetation community. Since steep and moderate slopes are common in Scotland, true soils and stable vegetation associations are far from universal. In some areas of level terrain, notably in river valleys and on the coast, true profile soils may also be prevented from developing because the accumulation of soil forming material is too rapid. Incipient soils of this type, with very specialised plant communities occur for example in the alluvial haugh lands, coastal marshes and areas of blown sand.

However, far and away the biggest disruptive influence on the broad natural patterns of soil and vegetation has been man. Since man began to cultivate the land on any scale in Scotland about three thousand years ago he has increasingly interfered with the natural evolution of the soils and vegetation. For the most part man's activities tend to maintain temporarily a set of environmental conditions different from those which would otherwise obtain, rather than to permanently alter the environment. Thus the repeated interference with the natural evolution of the soils and vegetation which results from cultivation in general, drainage, peat stripping, fertilising, burning, animal grazing, land management for sporting and re-creational purposes, forest clearing and planting, building and construction, air pollution, etc. only continues as long as these particular practices of man continue. Their cessation would lead over a period of time to a reappearance of more natural soil and vegetation development. However, at the present time all these aspects of man's activity are factors of the real environment to which the soils and vegetation of Scotland must respond. Obviously this man-affected environment is most complete in the densely settled and farmed lands of the lowlands,

but in fact very few parts of the uplands are free from
some influence, whether it be through animal grazing,
grouse moor management, burning or land drainage. Some
of man's activities do perhaps change the soil and
vegetation patterns more permanently. Especially is this
the case in relation to woodland clearance and planting.
Clearance, long characteristic of the lower lands, but
extending into the uplands from the fifteenth century onwards with the demands for charcoal and the needs of the
sheep farmer, can lead to increased waterlogging or other
permanent changes to the environment which prevent the
natural reappearance of woodland. It is known for example
that older thickets above about three hundred metres are
relics of past conditions, and are no longer regenerating
themselves. If they were to be removed, the tree cover
would be permanently lost. It is undoubtedly true that
clearance of woodland from areas where conditions were
marginal for tree growth has, in many parts of Scotland,
led to sufficient environmental changes as to prevent a
natural redevelopment of woodland vegetation. On the
other hand, man has also introduced many alien plant
species, especially trees, to Scotland. Many of these
introductions would remain and spread under natural conditions, so that species such as the larch, Douglas fir
and Sitka spruce have been permanently added by man to the
Scottish vegetation complex.

    As a result of the complex interplay of all these
influences, it is impossible in a short space to elaborate
all the detailed regional variations of soil and vegetation
in Scotland. Fig 7 attempts to illustrate some of the more
significant broader regional patterns.

    The alpine zone on the higher slopes and summits of
the mountains possesses prevailing climatic conditions
which allow very limited soil development. Most of the
more level surfaces are strewn with angular rock fragments,
sometimes arranged into polygons or stripes by frost action
under tundra conditions. Such soil as does occur displays
almost no horizon development and vegetation is under-
standably patchy. Lichens and mosses predominate, with
occasional dwarf alpine shrub and herb species especially
on ledges and soil pockets in areas of calcareous rock.
This zone is almost completely free from the influence of
man.

    The lowland zone on the other hand is almost entirely

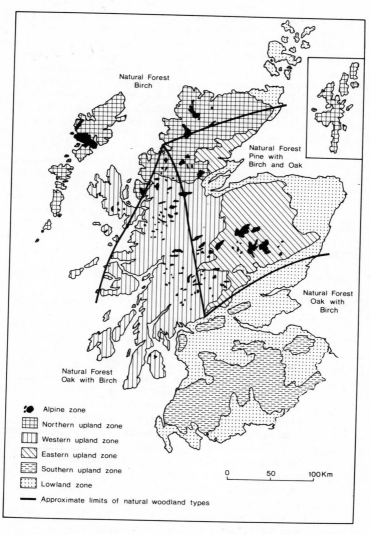

Natural Forest
Birch

Natural Forest
Pine with
Birch and Oak

Natural Forest
Oak with
Birch

Natural Forest
Oak with Birch

Alpine zone
Northern upland zone
Western upland zone
Eastern upland zone
Southern upland zone
Lowland zone
Approximate limits of natural woodland types

0   50   100 Km

Figure 7.   Soil and vegetation zones in Scotland
(For explanation see text)

43

controlled by man, and natural soils and vegetation communities have been much altered. Small patches of marsh, woodland and hedgerow areas are the least often disturbed elements of this zone, and in these environments soil processes and plant communities are often allowed to evolve naturally over long periods of time. For the most part however, disturbance occurs frequently, ranging from the effects of grazing animals and periodic reseeding in meadowlands, to the annual ploughing, planting and heavy fertilisation of arable fields and the intensive control exercised in private gardens. Apart from land completely built over however, soil and vegetation still occurs, not all of it completely controlled by man. For example, arable fields support not only the planted crop, but also a natural community of annual grasses and herbs able to thrive in the specialised annually disturbed environment. Similarly species other than those planted or encouraged for grazing, haymaking or enjoyment in meadows, parks and gardens are able to thrive in the specialised conditions, appearing to man as weeds of various kinds. The variety of man influenced environments, and the irregular intensity of his control produces in fact a kaleidoscopic pattern of soil and vegetation communities in the lowland zone. Man's influence is less complete, but nevertheless significant in the upland zones.

In the eastern upland zone, fairly well drained pod-solic soils predominate, with only limited areas of basin peat development. Between about 150 and 950 metres, shrubby moorland, dominated by heather (Calluna) is the characteristic vegetation. Heather shares the dominant status with cotton grass (Eriophorum) in the wettest areas and deer grass (Trichophorum) above about 450 metres. Above 900 metres cowberry (Vaccinium) and crowberry (Empetrum) replace the dominant heather as the shrubby moor land vegetation begins to merge with the hair moss (Rhacomitrium) moors of the tops. Only occasionally do very damp areas and flushes occur, giving rise to sphagnum moss and heath (Erica) bog or sedge (Carex) fen communities. Grassland is rare except on calcareous soils such as those of the Clova-Glen Shee region where extensive mat grass (Nardus) and poor bent-fescue grass (Agrostis-Festuca) communities occur. Tree felling and controlled moor burn-ing are clearly major factors in the creation and retention of these heather dominated communities, hindering the development of the natural open pine (Pinus) and birch (Betula) forest and juniper (Juniperus) shrub communities still found up to altitudes of about 800 metres where burning is infrequent. The now limited areas of native forest are being supplemented by reafforestation schemes, chiefly using larch (Larix) and native pine (Plate 3A).

The soils of the northern upland zone are much less well drained, with gleys and extensive areas of blanket peat rather than podsols predominating. Cotton grass and deer grass moorland with much sphagnum moss is the dominant vegetation, with moor grass (Molinia) frequent in areas where the ground water is not stagnant. Heather is common but not dominant, except on a few well drained sunny slopes, and seems to be kept down rather than encouraged by the less systematic moor burning practised in this region. Other shrub and grassland communities are rare, though hair grass (Deschampsia) and fescue grass does occur with the moss moors of higher levels, and mat grass is locally common at lower levels. The one exception to this lack of grassland is found in the Durness region, where a rich bent-fescue grassland has developed in association with the calcareous soils and heavy grazing. In this area, and around other formerly farmed and grazed land, bracken (Pteridium) is rampant and spreading widely. (Plate 3B). Pine trees are rare and the remaining patches of native forest, probably never widespread, are mainly of birch. Afforestation, mainly with Sitka spruce (Picea) and North American pines is becoming widespread, but only after considerable drainage and soil improvement.

The western upland zone also possesses mainly poorly drained acid soils, but blanket peat is less widespread. Although cotton grass, deer grass and heather are common, the greater part of the region is dominated by grassland communities. Grassland with moor, bent or fescue grass dominant is almost universal, with mat grass and rush (Juncus) species also locally dominant especially above 600 metres. In the highest parts of this zone, species-rich mountain grassland and dwarf herb communities are commoner than elsewhere in Scotland, due to the more frequent occurrence of calcareous soils. Heavy grazing in part maintains these patterns, but it also encourages the spread of bracken now dominant in parts of the region. Relics of native woodland mainly consist of oak

(Quercus), ash (Fraxinus) and hazel (Corylus) scrub, but the considerable reafforested areas contain a wide range of introduced coniferous species.

The southern upland zone possesses more areas of better drained podsolic soils and only limited areas of peat, chiefly in the west. Vegetation communities other than grassland are very rare, largely as a result of the long history of almost universal hill sheep farming. Only in a few wetter and higher areas do cotton and deer grass, sphagnum, cowberry and heather communities replace those dominated by mat, hair, bent, fescue and moor grasses. Only limited relics of the natural oak, birch, hazel and juniper scrub remain, usually on steeper slopes, but large areas have been reafforested mainly with alien coniferous species.

2 POPULATION AND PLANNING

Population trends since 1801

The first official census enumeration of the Scottish population in 1801 revealed about 1.6 million inhabitants, representing a population density of about twenty to the square kilometre.   At this time, the population density of the United Kingdom as a whole was just over forty to the square kilometre.   Throughout history, the higher proportion of rough terrain and other environmental limitations have undoubtedly limited Scotland's share of the total United Kingdom population to well below the proportion which might be expected on the basis of size alone.   In 1801 the Scottish population represented just over 15% of the total United Kingdom population, and without suggesting that this was in any sense a norm, it does provide a base against which to measure the population trends in Scotland over the last century and a half compared with those in the whole of the United Kingdom.

The decennial census returns for Scotland since 1801 show an almost uninterrupted population growth (Fig 8). By 1851 the number of inhabitants had reached nearly 3 million, by 1901 nearly 4.5 million, by 1951 just over 5 million, and by 1971 just over 5.25 million.   Throughout the nineteenth century, except in the periods 1851-61 and 1881-91, the rate of population increase remained at about ten per cent every ten years.   Since the beginning of the twentieth century however the pace of increase has slowed down, and has not exceeded five per cent in any decade since the first of the century.   Indeed in the decade 1921-31 the population of Scotland actually declined by almost one per cent and the increase in the period 1961-71 was less than one per cent.   Estimates suggest that this increase occurred in the first half of the

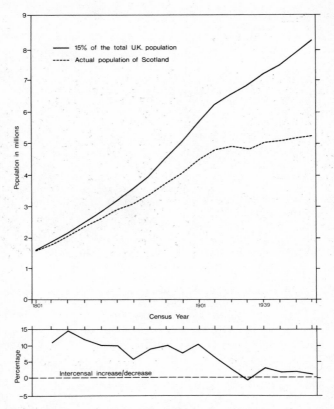

Figure 8.   Scottish population trends since 1801

decade and since 1965 the Scottish population has been
virtually static, if not slightly declining (Fig 8).
     In broad terms this population growth trend since
1801 parallels the growth trend in the rest of Britain,
and indeed the population trends in other nations which
underwent the great socio-economic changes of the period.
The slowing down of the rate of increase in the twentieth
century reflects the slowing down of the processes of
industrialisation and urbanisation, and the closing of
the gap between the birth and death rates, all factors

Plate 3 Vegetation Patterns

A. Sheriff Muir. Heather moor is characteristic of much of the upland areas of Scotland, especially in the east. The coniferous plantation in the background is also characteristic.

B. Glen Cannich. On rougher terrain, especially in the west, vegetation is very mixed. Bracken (foreground) is often a considerable problem for the farmer.

Plate 4 Variations of River Flow
A. The River Nevis in August 1961 after three days heavy rain.

B. The River Nevis in late September 1961 after a dry month. The white rock on the left provides a guide to the variations of flow in this short highland river as a result of variations in rainfall. Minor floods occur frequently on most Scottish streams.

involved in the very rapid rates of population growth in the nineteenth century (Fig 9).

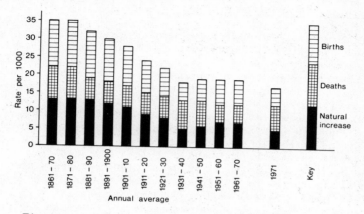

Figure 9.   Birth, death and natural increase rates in Scotland since 1861

Although the general growth trend of the Scottish population broadly parallels the United Kingdom growth trends since 1801, it does differ significantly in degree. Ever since 1801 the population of Scotland has been growing more slowly than the population of the United Kingdom as a whole.   If Scotland had maintained its 15% share of the total United Kingdom population throughout the period, then the 1901 census would have revealed a population of nearly 5.7 million instead of the actual 4.5 million;   the 1971 census would have revealed about 8.2 million instead of the actual 5.25 million.   This substantial shortfall of the Scottish population in the context of the United Kingdom pattern is clearly not a result of a consistently lower rate of natural increase (excess of births over deaths) in Scotland.   Indeed throughout this period, Scotland has generally possessed a higher rate of natural increase than the United Kingdom average, which would suggest that the rate of population growth since 1801 should have been higher not lower than the United Kingdom rate.   The recorded trend can only be explained by a persistent net loss of population by migration to other parts of the

49

United Kingdom and overseas.

Migration to and from Scotland

Migration is a perfectly natural characteristic of human populations, and emigration and immigration movements are normal features of Scottish population history as they are of the population histories of other countries. Much of the present population of Scotland is in fact composed of immigrants or the descendants of immigrants from all parts of the world. After a time most of these incomers are absorbed into the general population, but as in most other advanced countries, individuals or small groups of people from many nations and races can be identified in the Scottish population. However, for most years since 1801, the number of immigrants to Scotland from the rest of the United Kingdom and from Overseas, contributing new elements to the population, has been far outweighed by the number of emigrant Scots. The resulting long-continued net loss of population by migration represents the cumulative effect of the responses of individual people to a complex set of factors. Relative to other parts of Britain and the world, environmental, social and economic conditions in Scotland since 1801 have encouraged far fewer people to move to Scotland than the number who have been encouraged to leave.

Detailed information on migration to and from Scotland is extremely limited, especially during the nineteenth and early twentieth centuries. For the most part net migration figures are based on the difference between the population enumerated at a census, and the estimated figure based on rates of natural increase obtaining since the previous census. During the nineteenth century the shortfall, presumed to be the net loss by migration, varied between about 40 and 120 thousand people every ten years, rising to a peak of nearly 225 thousand in the decade 1881-91. In the twentieth century however the net migration loss has exceeded 225 thousand in each decade, reaching a peak of almost 400 thousand in the period 1921-31.

Fig 10 illustrates the recent fluctuations in the estimated annual Scottish net migration losses and the proportions lost to or gained from the rest of the United

50

Kingdom and overseas respectively.

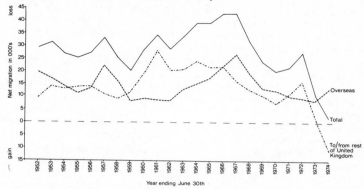

Figure 10.   Migration patterns 1951-74

During the period 1951-74 it can be clearly seen that
although about equal numbers were lost to the rest of the
United Kingdom and to overseas countries, there was a considerable variation from year to year both in the total
loss, and the proportion of that loss to the respective
areas.   Thus the high losses in 1957 clearly resulted
from an upsurge in net loss overseas, while the 1961
peak clearly resulted from an upsurge in the net loss to
the rest of the United Kingdom.   The peak loss of 1966
on the other hand resulted from high net loss rates to
both areas, and the trough in 1970 to a decline in net
losses to both areas.   These marked fluctuations indicate
the complexity of the relationships which exist between
the actual or perceived economic and social conditions
obtaining within Scotland and those obtaining elsewhere.
Superimposed on these fluctuating natural repelling and
attracting forces, changes in legislation also influence
the flows, as for example the introduction of limitations
on immigration into Canada since the late 1960s, for long
one of the main destinations of Scottish overseas emigrants.

Future population trends

Estimates of the future population trends of Scotland

51

are based on estimates of migration, birth and death rate
trends.   Except perhaps for the death rate trend, these
are extremely unpredictable, and therefore any estimates
of future population levels must be treated with considerable caution.   Table 1 illustrates the way in which
the estimates were altered in the light of new evidence,
in the early 1970's.

Some indication of the likely future population trends
of both the country as a whole and its regions, is of vital
importance because of the implications of these trends for
economic and social planning.   On the other hand economic
and social planning policies may be adopted with the express
aim of altering the predicted national and regional
population trends.   It is therefore possible, within limits,
to suggest what the future population might be if the present
trends continue.   It is not possible to estimate with any
degree of confidence what the population will be at a
specific date in the future.   So much depends on economic
and social policies adopted, not only in Scotland, but in
other parts of the world.

Internal Variations in population trends

The general pattern of population growth in Scotland
as a whole since 1801 hides a great deal of variation in
the population trends in different parts of the country.
In 1801, the population was far from evenly distributed,
but long continued divergent regional trends have led to
the development of extreme regional variations of
population density at the present time.   In 1801, the
East Central Lowland Counties of Angus, Perth, Clackmannan,
Fife, Kinross, the Lothians and Stirling, contained about
a third (35 per cent) of the total Scottish population.
The West Central Lowland counties of Ayr, Bute, Dunbarton,
Lanark and Renfrew contained about a fifth (21 per cent),
leaving 44 per cent shared between the remaining nineteen
counties to the north and south.   In 1861, the much
larger population was almost evenly divided between these
three regions.   However, by 1971, although the East Central
Lowlands still contained about a third (33 per cent) of the
enlarged population, the West Central Lowland's share had
risen to almost a half (48 per cent), leaving only 19 per
cent of the total population outside the Central Lowlands.
This changing regional population balance reveals the

* Regional variations

| | Date of Estimates (June) | | | | |
	1970	1971	1972	1973	1974
Live births					
Actual figure in previous year	87.9	87.5	83.0	76.3	71.0
Projection for following year	88.0	84.0	77.0	72.6	70.1
Projection for 1981	101.0	97.0	94.2	88.9	96.0
Projection for 2001	109.0	99.0	93.5	75.4	88.9
Projection for 2011	-	102.0	102.0	83.0	105.0
Migration (net loss)					
Actual figure in previous year	20.1	21.7	27.6	10.7	2.0
Projection for following year	28.0	25.0	24.0	15.0	Nil
Projection for 1981, 2001 and 2011	15.0	15.0	15.0	15.0	Nil
Population					
Actual figure in previous year	5225.0	5244.0	5235.0	5237.0	5252.0
Projection for following year	5223.0	5239.0	5225.0	5229.0	5256.0
Projection for 1981	5344.0	5315.0	5236.0	5180.0	5313.0
Projection for 2001	5891.0	5719.0	5589.0	5265.0	5910.0
Projection for 2011	-	5981.0	5828.0	5267.0	6217.0

Table 1. Estimates of live birth, migration and population trends to 2011 (figures in 000's)
Source. Annual Reports of the Registrar General for Scotland

results of a long-sustained internal movement of the
population, leading to a cumulative concentration of
population in a very small area of Scotland. A rather
more detailed understanding of the divergent regional
population histories which have led to the development of
this concentration emerges from a study of the population
histories of the individual counties. These histories can
be grouped into six main types as depicted on Fig 11. Three
of these groups display some growth in the nineteenth
century, but stagnation or decline in the twentieth, while
the other three display more general growth throughout the

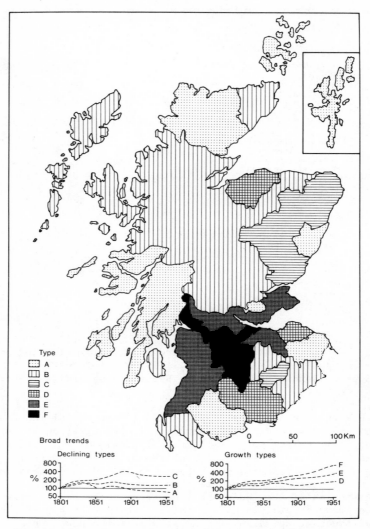

Figure 11. Regional population trends 1801-1971

present century. (For a key to the Scottish counties see Fig 15).

Eight counties (Argyll, Berwick, Kincardine, Kinross, Kircudbright, Orkney, Sutherland and Zetland), possess a history of almost unrelieved population decline (Type A). No census since 1801 has recorded a population more than twice that of the 1801 census, and in each case the population peak was attained at some time in the nineteenth century. The decline from the peak population has been so sustained that these eight counties had fewer inhabitants in 1971 than they had in 1801. A further nine counties (Banff, Bute, Caithness, Inverness, Peebles, Perth, Ross and Cromarty, Roxburgh and Wigtown), have a population history which is characterised by only slightly less twentieth century decline (Type B). Again no census has recorded a population more than twice that recorded in 1801, but the decline since the peak population was returned (in most cases during the nineteenth century) has been less severe. As a result these nine counties had slightly more inhabitants in 1971 than they had in 1801. Three counties (Aberdeen, Angus and Selkirk) resemble Type B in terms of stagnation during the present century, but display much more substantial growth in the nineteenth (Type C). In these three cases the peak population was between two and five times the figure recorded in 1801 and the three counties still possessed well over twice as many inhabitants in 1971 as they had in 1801.

Four counties (Dumfries, East Lothian, Moray and Nairn) have a history of modest growth in the nineteenth century, but this growth has been sustained through the twentieth century (Type D). Although the peak populations in these four counties were less than twice the 1801 population, they were recorded in 1971 (1961 in the case of Dumfries). Six counties (Ayr, Clackmannan, Fife, Midlothian, Renfrew and Stirling), display a history of much more sustained growth throughout (Type E). In all six counties the population recorded in 1971 was greater than that at any previous census, and was between two and five times the population enumerated in 1801. A history of rapid sustained growth has only been characteristic of three counties (Dunbarton, Lanark and West Lothian), (Type F). The peak population in these three cases was more than five times the population in 1801 and was recorded in 1971, (1961 in the case of Lanark with Glasgow).

The regional concentration of population resulting from these county trends is quite dramatic. Lanarkshire with Glasgow, an area which makes up about three per cent of the total land area of Scotland, was the most populous county in both 1801 and 1971. In 1801 this county already contained 9.2 per cent of the total population of Scotland, but the proportion had risen to no less than 29.1 per cent in 1971. The three counties classified as Type F, comprising just over four per cent of the total land area of Scotland, contained 11.6 per cent of the population in 1801, but this had increased to 35.8 per cent in 1971. If the six Type E counties are added, then these nine Central Lowland counties, accounting for about thirteen per cent of the total land area of Scotland, had increased their share of the population from 39 per cent in 1801 to over 72 per cent in 1971.

Urbanisation

The dramatic changes in the distribution of the Scottish population since 1801 have been particularly associated with the process of urbanisation. The population has progressively drained away from the rural areas and small rural settlements and has become more and more concentrated at high densities in a relatively small number of towns and cities. The 1971 census identifies about two hundred urban settlements in Scotland (the cities, large burghs and small burghs) which by that date contained just under 71 per cent of the total Scottish population. The rural areas (landward areas), which make up the bulk of the land area of the country contained only 29 per cent. Fig 12 illustrates the extremely localised character of the population concentrations which have resulted from urbanisation. In the mid nineteenth century (1861) less than 40 per cent of the population was located in the then designated urban areas, and more than 60 per cent in the rural areas.

The urbanisation of the Scottish population has, in general, displayed a snowball-like growth pattern. The smaller urban centres have grown as a result of population movements from their local hinterlands, but have in turn themselves lost population to larger centres. A few of

56

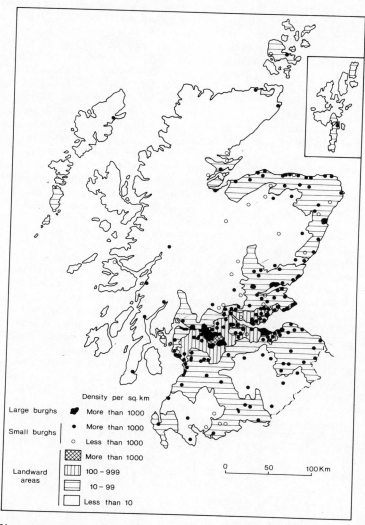

Figure 12. Population distribution and density 1971

57

the smaller and more isolated centres have as a result
suffered an overall population decline. The largest
urban centres and urbanised zones have, on the other hand,
enjoyed the most substantial population growth. Urbanisation in Scotland has therefore been spearheaded particularly by the growth of the four major cities of Glasgow,
Edinburgh, Aberdeen and Dundee. These four major urban
centres contained 11 per cent of the total population in
1801, 35 per cent in 1901, and 40 per cent in 1951. Since
1951 these four cities have suffered an apparent decline,
since they only accounted for 33 per cent of the total
population in 1971. This decline (and the resulting more
rapid growth of many smaller urban centres) is partly a
result of dispersal from these crowded centres through
planned overspill and the development of New Towns. It is
also partly explained by the fact that continued suburban
expansion outside the rigidly defined city boundaries is
not included in the city figures: the decline is therefore
more apparent than real.

Fig 12 also illustrates the extremely uneven distribution of the urban centres of population. Over half
of the small burghs, all but two of the large burghs
(Dumfries and Inverness), and all but one of the cities
(Aberdeen), are located in the central belt of Scotland
between the Firth of Clyde on the west and the Firths
of Forth and Tay on the east. Many of the urban centres,
especially in the Clyde valley have coalesced to form
large continuous tracts of densely populated urban territory.
Over much of this region, the landward areas also support
very high population densities. In a small region south
of Glasgow, the landward areas display a density in excess
of 1000 per sq km, a figure above that of many of the
smaller urban centres in other parts of Scotland. Suburban
developments in the countryside and around many small
villages, together with the close spacing of the smaller
settlements, largely explains these very high population
densities. This whole zone is of an urban character,
forming the nucleus of the concentrating tendencies of the
Scottish population. Lesser concentrations of urban
centres are found in a narrow strip along the east coast
between the Firth of Tay and the Moray Firth, along the
Solway coast and in the Border Lowlands. Over the rest
of the Scottish mainland and in the Islands urban centres

are few and far between, especially away from the coast.

Urbanisation of the population is however characteristic even of those parts of Scotland with very few and rather small urban centres. In 1861, twenty three of the thirty three Scottish counties had less than a quarter of their populations living in the then designated urban areas; only four counties had an urban population of more than half (Midlothian 78 per cent, Lanark 69 per cent, Angus 68 per cent and Renfrew 58 per cent). By 1971 the situation had dramatically changed. Only one county, Sutherland, still had less than a quarter of its population living in urban areas. Only 7 per cent of this county's population was recorded as urban compared with 26 per cent for the next most rural county, Ross and Cromarty. The anomaly of Sutherland results from its unique position amongst the counties of Scotland in possessing only one very small designated urban area, Dornoch. At the other end of the scale, twenty three counties had more than half, and four counties more than three quarters, of their populations in urban areas.

Although the process of urbanisation of the population is particularly associated with the larger towns, and the greatest concentrations are now in those parts of Scotland which are almost continuously built up, ever increasing proportions of the population in all parts of Scotland are found in urban settlements. Thus the two counties with the highest proportions of their total populations in urban areas are Angus and Selkirk. Although heavily built up counties like Midlothian, Dunbarton and Lanark are found in the list of the top ten, so too are counties with much less of an urban character such as Nairn, Dumfries and Roxburgh. The overall Scottish pattern of increasing population concentration into a small central urbanised region, with population decline throughout the rest of the country, is paralleled on a more local level by small urban growth centres set in a matrix of declining rural areas.

Urbanisation provides a measure rather than an explanation of the process of population concentration so characteristic of Scotland in the last century and a half. The explanations lie in a whole complex of fundamental economic and social changes. The term 'Industrial Revolution' is often used to broadly summarise these changes, and particular emphasis is rightly placed on the

59

part played by industrialisation in this context. However, the term industrialisation is itself used as a generalisation covering a whole range of significant factors which contributed, and still are contributing, to changes in the population geography of Scotland.

Industry, in the sense of manufacturing, was an important branch of human activity in Scotland long before the nineteenth century. Even the smallest communities possessed their craftsmen, producing everyday requirements such as tools, furniture, clothing and processed foodstuffs. To a limited extent local specialisms and local industrial concentrations were evident, as a result of particular local advantages such as raw materials, power resources, accumulated skills and enterprise and large local markets. In general though, industry was widely distributed and on a relatively small scale. As the eighteenth, and more particularly the nineteenth, century progressed, local advantages of power supply, raw materials and manpower skills became more and more significant as technical innovations and widening markets for industrial products encouraged an enlarged scale of industrial activity and the development of factories rather than workshops. Progressively therefore thriving industry became more and more concentrated in a few localities which were favourably endowed with these advantages. In particular, the harnessing of greater power resources, first water and later coal, caused localised growth concentrations of key industries such as textiles and the metal industries (especially iron making). Smaller scale, more widely scattered enterprises in these fields, dependant on wood or small scale water power resources decayed, either in relative or absolute terms. As home supplies of raw materials began to fail, access to overseas supplies became of increasing significance, stimulating industrial growth concentrations in and around coastal sites and major ports. The cotton and iron industries of the Clyde region, and the jute industry of Dundee represent this kind of import based industrial growth.

Over a similar period, great changes were also occurring in the character and scale of agriculture. Much of the pre-nineteenth century rural population depended on a very local subsistence pattern of agriculture, often in areas, especially in the Highlands, which today would be considered

impossible for arable farming.   The introduction of a more
commercialised outlook in agriculture, often stimulated by
outsiders, steadily eroded this long established basis of
life.   The improvements almost invariably meant a reorganisation of farming which lessened the demand for
agricultural labour and the carrying capacity of the land.
There were some improvements which led to new areas of rural
settlement, the reclamation of some of the carse lands in
the Central Lowlands for example, but overall the changes
forced migration from the countryside, often movement beyond
Scotland altogether.   Many however moved to the industrial
centres whose growth occasioned an almost insatiable demand
for labour.   The notorious and often harrowing story of the
clearances and the introduction of sheep farming into much
of the Highlands from the eighteenth century onwards has
become part of the folklore of the country, but this is
only one facet of the changes which contributed to the
transformation of rural Scotland.

Well before the nineteenth century, the accumulation
of commercial enterprise and wealth also played an important
part in the growth of towns, especially Edinburgh the
national capital associated with European trade, and Glasgow
associated with New World trade (sugar, tobacco, cotton).
Prior to the nineteenth century however, a large part of
the population was unaffected by the development and values
of a commercial society.   Many of the population trends
since 1801 can be related to the spread of these values,
associated with money, living standards and ideas of social
climbing, to the general population.   Education and improving
communications of all kinds played a key role in spreading
this philosophy in general, and publicising the greater
opportunities offerred by the growing towns in particular.
In spite of many drawbacks; disease, overcrowding, exploitation and drudgery, which in any case were often not
greatly different from the problems of rural areas, the
opportunities of the urban centres attracted a persistent
influx of people.

Today, if it ever were, the attraction is not entirely
economic, although the range of job opportunities is still
an important consideration.   The range of facilities which
the present population of Scotland, with its high living
standards, demands in terms of education, entertainment,
health, shopping and a whole host of other services, can

61

only be provided in the largest urban centres. Smaller centres and rural areas are consequently at a disadvantage in relation to the provision of services now almost universally regarded as necessities rather than luxuries. Over the last century and more, the evolving social aspirations of the population have played a vital part in encouraging net population movements to the large urban centres or their immediate surroundings.

Age-sex structure of the population

Fig 13 depicts the age-sex structure of the Scottish population as recorded at the 1971 census. The actual pyramid is plotted against an absolutely regular pyramid representing the mathematical ideal. As far as age is concerned, the most immediately noticeable feature is the break in the pattern between the 35-39 and the 40-44 age groups. Below 40, the actual pyramid is mostly inside the ideal, but above 40 the actual pyramid is mostly outside the ideal. A certain degree of top heaviness is almost inevitable in a real population sample, but the degree of top heaviness in this case is somewhat excessive.

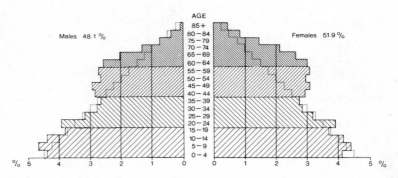

Figure 13.   Age-sex composition
of the Scottish population 1971

Leaving aside this feature, the pyramid is quite healthily broad based.   33.6 per cent of the total

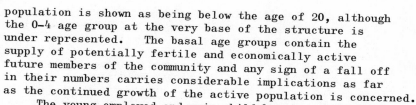

population is shown as being below the age of 20, although
the 0-4 age group at the very base of the structure is
under represented. The basal age groups contain the
supply of potentially fertile and economically active
future members of the community and any sign of a fall off
in their numbers carries considerable implications as far
as the continued growth of the active population is concerned.

The young employed and main child bearing section of
the population, aged from 20 to 39, accounts for 25.3 per
cent of the total, revealing a normally healthy reduction
in the breadth of the age pyramid. However the break at
40 reveals that the base is in fact inadequate to maintain
the level of population growth. There are already more
people in each five year age group between 40 and 64 than
in either the 30-34 or 35-40 age groups. Recent analyses
of migration movements suggest that a main part of the explanation for this feature of the age pyramid of the
Scottish population lies in long-continued age-selective
migration. Over a long period emigration from Scotland
has tended to show a slight predominance of the younger
age groups (below 40), sapping the base of the pyramid,
while immigration to Scotland has tended to show a slight
predominance of the older age groups (over 40), thus adding
to the top heaviness.

Within Scotland, regional variations in the age
structure pattern of the population, suggest the operation
of the same long-continued selective process. In general,
the more rural and remoter areas which have suffered long
from net emigration correspond to the regions with the most
top heavy population age structures, while those areas enjoying considerable net immigration, mainly the growing
outskirts of the major towns, generally possess a population
age structure much closer to the ideal pattern.

The crude breakdown of the Scottish population on the
basis of sex reveals a slight preponderance of females. In
1971, females accounted for nearly 52 per cent of the total
while males accounted for just over 48 per cent. However
males predominate in the younger age groups. 17.2 per
cent of the total population is seen to be composed of males
under the age of 20, while females below this age only make
up 16.4 per cent. The position is reversed at the upper
end of the age pyramid. 10.6 per cent of the population
consists of females over the age of 60, while males over

the age of 60 account for only 7.3 per cent.   Females also
slightly dominate the 20-39 age groups (12.8 per cent against
12.5 per cent) and more clearly the 40-59 age groups
(12.1 per cent against 11.1 per cent).

These differences in the sexual balance are explained
very largely in terms of the higher male birth rate but
greater female life expectancy, normal characteristics of
populations in advanced countries.   The higher mortality
rate amongst young males tends to cancel out the advantage
gained by greater initial numbers, and the sexes are
approximately in balance in the 20-24 age group.   There-
after the sexual balance tips increasingly in favour of
females, and in the over 85 age groups females outnumber
males by more than two to one.

There is little evidence to suggest that the balance
of the sexes in Scotland as a whole is greatly influenced
by sex-selective net migration movements, although research
has revealed a slightly greater net loss of males than
females in the over 20 age groups.   Within Scotland however,
there is some statistical support for the view that
population movements tend to intensify the preponderance
of females in the cities and towns, and lessen their preponderance in rural areas.   For example, the city of
Edinburgh has a preponderance of females above the national
average (53.2 per cent), especially marked in the 20-59 age
groups, whereas the county of Argyll has markedly less than
the national proportion of females in the 20-59 age groups
and males are in the majority in all age groups up to 50.
However the complexity of the factors underlying such
regional sexual variations is illustrated by the fact that
although the only three counties in Scotland which actually
have more males than females in their total populations
(Inverness, Kincardine and Moray), could be described as
predominantly rural, one large burgh (Dunfermline), also
displays this characteristic.

Occupational structure

Changes in the occupational structure of the Scottish
population over the last century and a half are clearly
associated with the redistribution of the population over
this period.   Especially is this obvious in the steady
decline of primary occupations and the rise in the significance of secondary, and more recently, tertiary

64

Plate 5 Changing Patterns of Transport
A. The Forth Railway Bridge and Queensferry in 1959. The car ferry is now replaced by a new road bridge, greatly improving road links between Edinburgh and Fife.

B. Port Dundas, Glasgow. The remains of the once busy canal basin of Port Dundas in the heart of Glasgow, with part of the new inner ring road beyond.

Plate 6 Landscapes of Power
A. Bedlay Colliery, Lanarkshire. A modern coal mine in a rural setting.

B. Longannet Power Station. Across the Forth lies the vast Grangemouth oil refinery complex.

employment.   Statistical comparisons between the balance
in recent years and various dates in the past are however
extremely hazardous as both the general character of employment conditions and systems of classification have
changed markedly over the last two centuries.

In 1971, 41 per cent of the total population of Scotland
was classified as in employment.   Under existing economic
and social conditions, with children, older people and a
large part of the married female population not normally
employed, it might be expected that less than half the
total population would be officially classified as working.
Indeed, a proportion of about 40 per cent is typical of
most industrialised countries today.   The 1971 figures
nevertheless reveal a decline of about five per cent in the
work force of Scotland since 1961.   Significantly the
trends in male and female employment in this period were
markedly divergent.   Male employment declined by over six
per cent while female employment increased by nearly seven
per cent.   As a result, women comprised nearly 39 per cent
of work force in 1971 compared with about 35 per cent in
1961.

Divergent trends in the main sectors of employment are
increasingly evident.   By 1971 employment in the primary
sector was at a very low level (below 5 per cent) and is
still tending to decline.   This trend is of long standing
in respect of the agricultural work force, but much more
recent in respect of the mining work force.   The sharp
decline in the manpower demands of the mining industries,
particularly coal mining, dates only from about 1950.
Employment in the secondary sector was clearly much more
significant (about 42 per cent), although it too had
declined since the early 1960's.   It was the expansion of
this sector in particular which led to the major redistribution of the Scottish population in the nineteenth
century.   The growth of employment in the tertiary
sector in the post-war period is however of greatest significance.   Service industries in general have an even
greater tendency than manufacturing industries to expand
in urban centres and in consequence this changing pattern
of employment is associated with an even greater tendency
towards an urbanisation of the population.   In the late
1960s, for the first time, the proportion of the Scottish
work force employed in the tertiary sector rose above
fifty per cent.   This is a characteristic shared with
only a very few economically advanced and highly urbanised

countries.

Within Scotland, the occupational structure of the population varies regionally quite markedly from the national pattern. Four regions, the South West, the Borders, the North East and the Highlands and Islands, have well above average proportions of their employed population in the primary sector. This is a reflection of the greater significance of agricultural and fishing activities in these less densely populated areas of the country. However only one region, the densely populated, highly urbanised West Central, has a very small proportion of its workers in the primary sector. This region, together with Falkirk/Stirling, has a correspondingly high percentage of its employees in the secondary sector. In the case of the East Central region on the other hand, it is the tertiary sector which is markedly more significant. This difference distinguishes between the main urbanised industrial regions and the chief metropolitan region of Scotland. The balance between secondary and tertiary employment in the other regions of Scotland generally tips strongly in favour of the tertiary sector, largely because of the lack of any significant development of manufacturing industry. This is well illustrated for example in the difference between the Highlands and Islands and the Borders. In the latter case the small urban centres do have an industrial significance, and the secondary sector is in consequence well represented in the employment figures.

At any one time, a small proportion of the working population of an area is likely to be temporarily out of employment, but if the proportion rises much above about two per cent, this is generally indicative of some short-fall in employment possibilities. If high rates of un-employment persist, then population emigration and economic stagnation are likely to become characteristic features of such an area. Since 1960 Scotland has been characterised by rather high unemployment rates. In spite of fluctuations from year to year in the average percentages, the figures have remained steady relative to those for the United Kingdom as a whole. The Scottish unemployment rate has run consistently at nearly twice the United Kingdom rate since 1960.

Within Scotland, regional variations in unemployment rates also tend to occur, indicating variations in economic and social conditions which also generate internal movements of population. Such movements however can

66

involve individual hardship, and create problems such as
urban overcrowding, the decay of rural communities,
abandonment of expensive capital facilities and loss of
regional manpower.   As a result the twentieth century
has witnessed a steady increase in the efforts of
interested parties, especially the government, to remove,
or at least reduce, regional differentials by means other
than large scale population movements.

ECONOMIC AND SOCIAL PLANNING

The redistribution of the Scottish population over the
last hundred and fifty years reflects the changing social
and economic balance of Scotland's constituent parts, and
of Scotland in relation to other parts of the world.   The
existence of these changing balances is an undeniable
geographical fact, but the pace of change and the scale of
its effects in the twentieth century has forced a change
in man's response to them.   Instead of the laissez-faire
attitude of the nineteenth century, which allowed the dramatic social and economic changes to occur unchecked,
Britain has adopted more and more positive measures not
just to check, but also to reverse the population movements
which result from regional differences.   Increasing concern with the quality of the environment has also played
its part in the evolution of planning attitudes and policies
which now form a vital part of the total British environment of which Scotland is part.

Town and Country Planning

Town and country planning, more concerned with social
and physical than economic and regional problems, gave rise
to the earliest examples of marked government intervention
in the natural evolution of Britain.   It grew essentially
out of public health concern, and was in its early years
particularly orientated towards the improvement of urban
housing conditions.   Legislation between the wars laid
the foundation for the development of council house estates,
comprehensive land use planning and the control of ribbon
development, all of which had an impact on the character
of present day Scotland.   However, the comprehensive

system of town and country planning in Britain is largely
a post-war development, owing much to three government
reports: the Barlow Report concerned with the problems
of industrial and population distribution changes; the
Uthwatt Report, concerned with the problem of land use
control in relation to land values and compensation; and
the Scott Report, concerned with the planning of rural
areas.

The resulting post-war town and country planning
legislation for Scotland differed markedly from that for
England and Wales. In Scotland, the wide powers over
the organisation and control of local planning introduced
by the Town and Country Planning Act of 1947 were invested
in the Department of Health for Scotland rather than in the
new Ministry of Town and Country Planning. The provisions
of the 1946 New Towns Act were extended to Scotland but
those of the National Parks and Access to the Countryside
Acts were not. Scotland therefore possesses New Towns but
no National Parks, (the Forest Parks of Scotland are not
quite the same). Scottish legislation is now more in line
with that for the rest of Britain following the establishment of the Countryside Commission and the Town and Country
Planning Act (Scotland) 1969.

The influence on the Scottish scene of the many facets
of town and country planning is not however dissimilar to
that in Britain as a whole. Slum clearance and comprehensive redevelopment of run down areas of the major cities,
especially Glasgow, and the control of urban expansion by
means of green belts, overspill and New Town developments,
have been perhaps the most obvious impact. Major achieve-
ments too in controlling pollution of rivers, air and land
and preserving natural and man made features of beauty in
the environment, reflect the growing concern over, and
interest in problems of the whole, rather than just the
urban parts of the country.

Economic Planning

Considerable influence on regional economic activity
can be, and has been exerted by government through the
provision of varying levels of subsidy to specific enterprises. Potentially subsidies provide a powerful weapon
for encouraging or at least controlling economic change,
but in practice they have more often been used to bolster

ailing enterprises in areas of economic difficulty.   In
the Scottish context, high levels of subsidy to hill
farming, fishing and shipbuilding amongst other activities
have undoubtedly done much to maintain a reasonable economic
basis to life in many regions.   Regions of economic
difficulty may also be aided as a result of central or local
government, or even private promotion, of other developments,
for example tourism and forestry.   However these influences
tend to operate on a haphazard basis rather than forming a
part of a coherent regional economic planning policy.

The first Scottish problem area to give rise to special
legislation as a result of social and economic distress, was
the Highlands and Islands.   The Crofters Holdings (Scotland)
Act of 1886 attempted to stem the severe population decline
and economic hardship then affecting this remote rural part
of the country by giving legal protection to the disinte-
grating crofting system of agriculture.   When the North
of Scotland Hydro-electric Board was established in 1943,
it was given responsibility not only for developing the
water power potential of the northern part of Scotland,
but also for encouraging the economic development of the
region.   Then in 1965, the Highlands and Islands Development Board was established and given the task not only of
planning the development of the region, but actually
carrying out this development.   In spite of a limited
budget, and controversies stemming largely from its lack
of direct electoral responsibility, the Board has achieved
considerable success in encouraging the expansion of existing, and the establishment of new, enterprises of all kinds
in all parts of the region.   While it remains the most
comprehensive and independant agency of regional planning
in Scotland, it is also unique.   No other region of Britain
has the benefit of a similar development body.   The Highlands
and Islands Development Board therefore is a model for,
rather than a part of, an integrated national system of
regional economic planning.   Part of the explanation for
this situation lies in the fact that the evolution of
economic planning philosophy in Britain has been dominated
by the growing twentieth century problems of the heavily
populated industrial districts.   This has led to the
development of legislation related to specific industrial
problems rather than to overall economic planning for all
kinds of regions.   Against this background, the very real
social and economic problems of the Highlands and Islands
appear distinct and seem to require unique measures.

As an indicator of the extent of the economic problems
of the industrial regions, no single index has been more
significant than the unemployment rate. Early in 1933
several British towns recorded unemployment rates of over
fifty per cent; among them were the west of Scotland
industrial centres of Wishaw and Clydebank. Unemployment
rates of this magnitude represented a culmination of trends
throughout the previous decade, when rising rates of unemployment were increasingly unevenly spread. Particular
problem areas emerged in formerly prosperous industrial
regions, especially those characterised by large elements
of coal mining, shipbuilding, iron and steel production and
textile manufacture. All four of these activities had
played a major part in the nineteenth century population
and industrial expansion of the West of Scotland: their
collapse as a result of overseas competition and the world
trade depression transformed this same region into a major
economic and social problem area. The Clydeside and North
Lanarkshire region (but excluding Glasgow) was thus one of
the four regions of Britain designated as Special Areas in
the Special Areas (Development and Improvement) Act of
1934 (Fig 14).
At the time, the provision of limited financial help
from central government funds and the appointment of
Commissioners to promote the rehabilitation of the Special
Areas were regarded as short term measures. Long term
planning for economic change was still mainly in the hands
of the Industrial Transference Board, set up in 1928 to
encourage the retraining of labour and the movement of
workers to areas of economic growth, both in Britain and
overseas. This policy, although strongly supported by the
government of the day, and tending to encourage rather than
counteract natural trends of population movement and
economic growth, ran into increasing difficulties not un-
associated with the world wide economic recession of the
mid thirties. In the event, the temporary emergency
legislation, designed to aid the unemployment blackspots
by encouraging industrial change and growth within the
problem areas, expanded to become a permanent and increasingly powerful facet of British social and economic policy.
The principle of moving workers to work has not played a
major role in economic policy, except in relation to specific
industries such as coal mining, since 1945. Indeed the
policy of providing work where the workers are, begun by

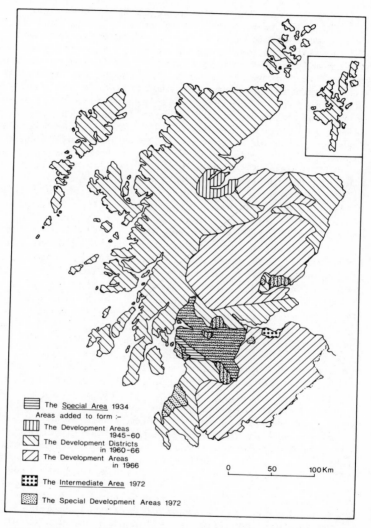

The Special Area 1934
Areas added to form :-
The Development Areas
1945-60
The Development Districts
in 1960-66
The Development Areas
in 1966

The Intermediate Area 1972

The Special Development Areas 1972

0   50   100 Km

Figure 14.   The evolution of the Development Areas

the 1934 act, has now extended to a policy of moving work and workers to the problem areas, e.g. the removal of the National Savings Department headquarters to Glasgow.

In 1937, two principles of great significance for the future were established by the Special Areas Amendment Act. The Special Area Commissioners were given wider powers to aid private industrial development, following the success of the first experiments with the trading or industrial estate principle whereby government finance was used to establish factory premises with full service facilities which could then be let to private firms. The Hillington estate in Glasgow, founded in 1937 proved, like similar estates in the other Special Areas of Britain, attractive to small, light industries both British and foreign. The industrial estate has come to play a major role in promoting greater industrial variety and hence economic flexibility in the problem regions. The Scottish Industrial Estates Corporation now administers nearly a hundred of these estates and individual factory sites, amounting to over 2.5 million square metres of factory space. Additional industrial estates have been promoted by private enterprise. Also under the 1937 act, the principle of the direct use of government money to aid private firms through grants, loans and tax relief was established.

By the end of the nineteen thirties it was clear that the problems of the Special Areas were the result of much more deep seated economic and social changes in Britain than short term difficulties arising from the depression. As a result the Government appointed a Royal Commission 'to inquire into the causes which have influenced the present distribution of the industrial population....and to report what remedial measures, if any, should be taken in the national interest'. The report of this Barlow Commission, published in 1940, firmly concluded that the trends evident at the time were highly undesirable, and made strong recommendations. These included the establishment of a central authority to monitor these trends and coordinate local measures to tackle regional economic and social problems. The Commission also recognised that the problem involved planned redevelopment of the congested areas of the country by means of decentralisation of population and industry, as well as the encouragement of growth in areas of decline. Garden cities, new and expanded towns and trading estates were seen as important instruments

of this policy.   This comprehensive approach was clearly
recommending a much greater liaison between regional
economic planning, and the rather more socially orientated
town and country planning.   However, the war time conditions obtaining when the Commission's report appeared
had temporarily alleviated the problems of the Special Areas.
The period of post-war redevelopment and the mild boom
conditions of the early nineteen fifties, with only limited
localised unemployment blackspots and other priorities,
prevented the full implementation of the Commission's
recommendations.

    The Distribution of Industry Act of 1945, which with
minor changes remained the basis of regional policy until
1960, did very little more than replace the old Special
Areas legislation.   The same part of Scotland, but with
the addition of Glasgow and the Dundee area reappeared as
one of the new Development Areas.   In 1948 the Dingwall
and Inverness region was added, as a potential industrial
focus of the problem region of the Highlands (Fig 14).
Responsibility for implementing the policy was removed
from the Commissioners to the Board of Trade and the
Treasury, but government expenditure remained modest.   In
the period 1945-60, Board of Trade financing of new factories and industrial estates in all the Development Areas
amounted to about £78 million, while loan and grant payments
by the Treasury in the same period totalled about £12
million.

    Two new developments immediately after the war, both
more associated with post-war town and country planning
than with economic planning policy, did make important
contributions to improving the economic and social conditions of the Development Areas.   The Town and Country
Planning Act of 1947 introduced the Industrial Development Certificate, an extension of a war-time measure which
in effect enabled the Board of Trade to exercise control
over the location of new large factory building.   This
new legislation was used, though with lessening vigour as
the nineteen fifties progressed, to curb industrial growth
in the well endowed regions and to direct a disproportionate
share of national industrial growth to the Development Areas.
The New Towns Act of 1946, primarily designed to alleviate
the problems of the over-crowded cities by encouraging the
establishment of new satellite towns, led also to the
establishment of significant growth points in the

Development Areas.   East Kilbride, Glenrothes and
Cumbernauld have already proved themselves important foci
for industrial growth and social improvement in Scotland,
while both Livingstone and Irvine, not designated as New
Towns until the nineteen sixties, are also rapidly
expanding.   A number of existing small Scottish towns
have also benefitted from industrial and population growth
as a result of planned overspill agreements with the major
cities, especially Glasgow.

     After 1957, the old regional disparities of the nineteen
thirties began to re-emerge as heavy industry, especially
coal mining and shipbuilding began to suffer recession.
Unemployment rates in the West of Scotland and the other
pre-war Special Areas began to rise to levels unacceptable
in relation to the government policy of full employment.
Once more the problem of the declining industrial areas
began to receive high priority as indicated by the passing
of the Distribution of Industry (Industrial Finance) Act
in 1958, which added a few more areas to the existing
Development Areas and increased the scale of Treasury aid
to them;   and the Local Employment Act in 1960.   This
latter act once more redefined the problem regions, on the
basis of a critical level of unemployment (4.5 per cent)
in individual local Employment Exchange Areas.   Because
districts could be scheduled and descheduled as the unemployment rate fluctuated, this gave considerable
flexibility to the application of regional aid, and to
the map of the new Development Districts.   At their
maximum extent the Development Districts of Scotland consisted of all the old Development Areas of the West of
Scotland, the Dundee region and the Inverness-Dingwall
region, together with considerable more rural areas;
most of Galloway, the whole of the northern and western
Highlands and a major part of the north east of Scotland
(Fig 14).   The growing scale of the regional economic
problem led to considerable strengthening of the financial
assistance to the Development Districts, especially after
the 1963 Local Employment Act.   Between 1960 and 1967 over
£230 million of government money was spent on factory
building, grants and loans in these areas of Britain.

     The Development District legislation had two great
drawbacks in practice, which did much to encourage
another major overhaul of the system in 1966.   The
possibility of descheduling areas as unemployment

74

fluctuated led to uncertainties in some regions, discouraging to new industrial enterprise, while the emphasis on the unemployment definition and the aim to remove unemployment, militated against a more comprehensive consideration of the planning required in the face of economic and social change.

In 1966 the Industrial Development Act abolished the Development Districts and replaced them with Development Areas. With the exception of a small area around Edinburgh and Leith, the whole of Scotland was included under this new designation (Fig 14). In 1967, small areas of special difficulty within the Development Areas were for the first time designated for additional development aid. Originally these Special Development Areas in Scotland were limited to small areas of the Ayrshire, Lanarkshire and Fife coalfields, suffering from the rapid rundown of the mining industry. Since 1967 however, a large part of the West of Scotland has been added. In addition, the Edinburgh region has been declared an Intermediate Area, making it eligible for limited aid. The whole of Scotland is therefore now covered by one of the three grades of development aid available.

Few, if any, of the industrial developments in Scotland since 1945 are unrelated to the various strands of the evolving development aid policy. Small enterprises on industrial estates alone now employ about 150,000 people. Several large scale private developments each employing over 3,000 people have also been encouraged, and have directly or indirectly helped to transform the quality and quantity of Scottish job opportunities. Especially associated with the motor car, business machine, electronics and petro-chemical industries, many of these key enterprises have involved foreign, especially American, companies.

Regional Planning

Regional planning, in the sense of a comprehensive and integrated approach to the question of balancing all developments between regions at all scales, is still very much in its infancy in Britain. There are examples of coordinated regional planning for specific purposes, e.g. electricity supply, hospital services and the police force. There are also many examples of regional agencies and promotional bodies designed to publicise regional assets and encourage regional development, e.g. Chambers of

Commerce, the Scottish Council for Development and Industry and Scotland West. Local authorities also have a statutory duty to prepare development plans for their areas, and this often involves consultation with neighbouring authorities and other bodies in an effort to coordinate planning over a wider region, e.g. the West Central Scotland Plan Steering Committee. None of these approaches however integrates the comprehensive planning of a region with that of all other regions and the country as a whole. Even classic regional studies, like the Clyde Valley Regional Plan of 1946 and Central Scotland: A Programme for Development and Growth of 1963, valuable as they are as surveys of existing conditions, suffered as detailed planning blueprints from the lack of an overall national planning strategy.

In 1965, the first real steps towards coordinated regional planning in Britain were taken. Britain was subdivided into eleven regions, each with a clearly defined centre, and advisory planning bodies were established. Scotland, with Edinburgh as its centre, was one of these new Economic Planning Regions. Two advisory bodies were established for each region, the Regional Economic Council and the Regional Economic Planning Board. The Council was composed of business and professional men, academics, trade unionists and others and its main function was to formulate regional planning strategies within the framework of an overall national plan. The Board was composed of civil servants and its main function was to coordinate the work of the central and local authorities involved in the region.

Various surveys and planning studies have resulted from this new structure, both for Scotland as a whole and for various subregions within Scotland. To some extent these have provided guidelines for new development. However they also illustrate some of the limitations which regional planning faces. To be fully effective, regional planning requires a sound national planning strategy, but this exists neither for the United Kingdom as a whole nor for Scotland. This situation results partly from the lack of sufficiently accurate forecasting techniques for economic and social trends and partly from a lack of clear identification of aims. In this latter respect, the balance to be struck between economic growth and environmental protection or between the material and aesthetic qualities of life, is a particular problem.

The definition of the planning regions themselves tends to lump together diverse areas and yet create an impression of an overall regional character. The problems of one subregion, e.g. the West of Scotland in the Scottish context, may then dominate the overall regional planning strategy. For a variety of reasons then, regional planning in Britain as a whole and in Scotland has by no means yet proved itself to be an effective tool for organising economic and social development.

Planning and the public

Planning of all kinds is undoubtedly increasingly influencing the pace and degree of change in Scotland. It is also producing increasing conflict between the planning bureaucracy and the public at large. At one extreme, planning controls on minor developments such as home extensions, tend to be irksome to the individual. At the other extreme major developments, such as the industrialisation of the Hunterston Peninsula, the routing of the Edinburgh ring road or the M9 motorway, or the siting of power stations or oil platform construction yards, may have wide repercussions on many people. However their complexity tends to preclude public discussion at the planning stage. Over the whole field of planning therefore, there is an increasing tendency towards confrontation between the planners and the public, or interested sections of the public. This confrontation is epitomised by the rising number of public inquiries and appeals designed to ventilate objections to planning decisions. Very often these objections challenge the very basis of the plan (e.g. stressing the environmental as opposed to the economic justification), and may succeed by argument or delay in preventing implimentation. Such interventions lessen whatever coordination the planning process might possess and may have serious regional repercussions. The abandonment in 1974 of major plans for the development of oil platform construction sites at Dunnet Bay in Caithness and Drumbuie in Wester Ross, are cases in point; the local environment was saved but many potential jobs were lost. Alternative sites subsequently developed (Loch Kishorn) have not necessarily possessed lower environmental quality.

The report of the Skeffington Committee in 1969 examined the gap between planners and the public without reaching any firm conclusions, although the 1968 Planning Act did attempt to provide a framework for more effective public involvement in the planning process. This unresolved conflict raises considerable doubts as to the complete effectiveness of the very considerable planning measures now in operation in controlling and shaping the future social, economic and regional development of Scotland.

3 ADMINISTRATIVE, TRANSPORT, ENERGY AND WATER SUPPLY INFRASTRUCTURES

THE ADMINISTRATIVE INFRASTRUCTURE

Administrative divisions are of considerable geographical significance since they create very real boundaries between areas in terms of many aspects of spatial organisation and management. If the administrative divisions are broadly in accordance with other spatial divisions, physical, economic and social, then they may become very strongly identified and accepted as entities with unique and highly prized characteristics, as well as functioning satisfactorily in their administrative role. If the administrative divisions are out of line with other spatial divisions, they may well still generate local feeling and pride, but are likely to present considerable difficulties to spatial organisation and management. The administrative framework of Scotland since 1966 has undergone a fundamental reappraisal, culminating in the introduction of a completely new system of local government areas in 1975. The administrative inefficiency of the old system, which originated under very different social and economic conditions clearly required change but the degree of attachment to that old system led to some substantial modification of the original revision recommended.

The Old Structure

For most of the present century, five types of local authority regions, with their elected councils, have formed the basis of the local government structure. The counties of cities, of which there were four in 1970 were the only areas to have full local government responsibility. The large burghs (twenty-one in 1970), had responsibility for all local government affairs except education and valuation; while the small burghs (176 in 1970), were responsible for

only a limited range of local government affairs - minor
roads, sewerage and cleansing, street lighting, entertainment establishments, parks etc.   The counties (33 in 1970)
were responsible for the remaining areas of local government in the large and small burghs, and the whole range of
affairs in the landward areas.   The districts (196 in 1970)
did however have some limited local responsibilities in
the landward areas of the counties.   There was clearly
some unevenness in terms of organisation.   In the small
burghs for example a local council had a wide range of
responsibilities, but the county council also had a considerable influence, whereas in the counties of cities
there was no second more local tier of control, and this
was only present to a limited extent too in the landward
areas of the counties.   Many large and some small burghs
had double administrative status, being the headquarters
of both burgh and county councils.   Apart from these
variations however, the administrative divisions themselves
were full of anomalies.

The county pattern of Scotland began to crystallise
some five hundred years ago, and changed little after the
early nineteenth century.   Apart from some differences
of name (Forfar for Angus: Elgin for Moray: and Linlithgow,
Edinburgh and Haddington for West, Mid and East Lothian),
the separate existence of Cromarty, and the presence,
especially in the north of some detached portions of counties,
the county map of early nineteenth century Scotland was much
the same as that of the mid twentieth century (Fig 15).

The pattern of the burghs has also been remarkably
static since their status was rationalised early in the
nineteenth century, although their earlier history shows
a less steady evolution than that of the counties.   Burgh
charters could and did lapse with changing circumstances.
However the massive urbanisation of the population since
the early nineteenth century was not matched by a dramatic
change in the pattern of burghs.

Given the recent history of population movements,
improvements in transport and communications and in the
location of economic activity, together with the increasing
scale and range of administrative activity, it is not
surprising that the administrative map, relatively un-
changing, should have become increasingly anomalous in the
twentieth century (Table 2).   Variations in the area and

80

Plate 7 Agricultural Land

A. Rural Scene near Kippen, Stirlingshire. Good quality arable and grass land on the flat ground of the reclaimed Flanders Moss. Sheep graze on the sown grass of the lower slopes, but the moorland edge is never far away.

B. The Edge of Urban Scotland. New building at Bishopbriggs on the edge of the Glasgow conurbation advances at the expense of good quality farm land.

Plate 8 Farm Contrasts

A. Croft at Rieff, Wester Ross. A small croft in a remote settlement just after electricity arrived in 1961. In spite of improvements, such small farms face severe problems and many are being allowed to go derelict or are being purchased for use as holiday cottages.

B. Farm near Dunblane, Stirlingshire. New buildings provide evidence of considerable expansion on this stock farm in Central Scotland.

Figure 15. The Scottish Counties and
Planning Regions to 1975

1. Aberdeen	8. Caithness	15. Kincardine	22. Orkney	28. Selkirk
2. Angus	9. Clackmannan	16. Kinross	23. Peebles	29. Stirling
3. Argyll	10. Dumfries	17. Kirkcudbright	24. Perth	30. Sutherland
4. Ayr	11. Dunbarton	18. Lanark	25. Renfrew	31. West Lothian
5. Banff	12. East Lothian	19. Midlothian	26. Ross and	32. Wigtown
6. Berwick	13. Fife	20. Moray	Cromarty	33. Zetland
7. Bute	14. Inverness	21. Nairn	27. Roxburgh	

shape of local government units with the same status are
geographically significant especially in respect of the
variable distances between the regional centre and parts
of its administrative territory.   The burghs, by
definition, were compact areas, but there was wide variation
in the size and shape of the counties and districts by the
mid-twentieth century.

Administrative Units	Area (km^2)		Population (000's)		Rateable Value (£000's)	
	Largest	Smallest	Largest	Smallest	Largest	Smallest
OLD						
Counties of cities	158	44	945.0	181.4	31,250.0	5,489.0
Counties	11,906	140	606.0	6.3	16,045.0	151.0
Large Burghs	28	5	95.1	21.2	2,900.0	434.0
Small Burghs	16	1	24.3	0.3	1,660.0	7.0
Districts	3,056	8	66.2	0.05	1,589.0	0.3
NEW						
Regions	36,500	2,590	2,536.0	145.0	72,900.0	3,300.0
Districts	9,500	104	1,186.0	17.0	38,035.0	151.0

Table 2. Variations in certain characteristics of the
          old and new administrative units, based on
          1968 values
Source : Appendices of the Royal Commission on Local
          Government in Scotland 1966-1969 (Wheatley)
          Report

To a considerable extent these differences reflected the
character of the terrain: thus Orkney and Shetland were
composed of groups of islands, Inverness contained a vast
area of rugged upland and numerous islands, while more
compact counties such as Renfrew or West Lothian were
largely made up of coastal lowlands.   In general, the
larger and more fragmented counties and districts were
less uniform in character, and larger areas of them were
remote from the decision-making centre.   This latter
characteristic was especially true in a large, irregularly-
shaped county such as Inverness, where the county seat was

82

far from centrally located, or as in the case of Dunbarton, where a part of the county was physically detached from the rest.

Also serious from the point of view of effective administration were the variations which had arisen in population and rateable value, since these significantly influenced the relative degree of local community involvement and the administrative power of the areas. By 1968, several of the districts of counties with very limited administrative functions, had greater populations and rateable values than most of the small burghs, several of the large burghs and even some of the counties. A handful of the small burghs were more populous and richer than some of the large burghs, while several of the counties, with a full range of administrative functions were less populous and poorer than any of the large burghs and even some of the small burghs.

The extent of these discrepancies by the 1960's was graphically illustrated by the way in which the parliamentary constituencies, areas in theory containing roughly equal populations, cut across the local authority pattern. The inadequate size of some of the areas was also illustrated by the growing number of voluntary or forced amalgamations of local authority areas for particular local government and planning purposes, notably for police and fire service organisation. In some instances, even this was not sufficient, and for a number of purposes, such as water and river purification, new statutory authorities were established by Parliament, with, in many instances, the area boundaries departing from even the long accepted county divisions. In view of these, and other problems, a Royal Commission was set up in 1966 to examine the whole question of local government in Scotland and to recommend changes in all aspects, including the basic areal units, of the local government structure.

The reappraisal

The reappraisal by the Wheatley commission had two main aims, to improve the efficiency of local government and to improve its relationship with local communities and the public. Therein lay the basic dilemma. Efficiency over a large range of functions was impaired

because many of the local government areas were too small.
Many non-government bodies, such as the electricity
authorities for example, had adopted a regional structure
on a much larger scale than the counties. On the other
hand, many of the existing local government areas were
considered too large for effective local public participation. The research sections of the commission, and
interested parties submitting evidence to it, naturally
therefore gave considerable attention to the identification
of communities within Scotland and to the question of
optimum size for local government areas.

Communities exist at various levels and with varying
degrees of intensity. Physical features, communication
networks, central foci, economic associations, and
historical associations all play their part in establishing and maintaining distinct areal units. Individuals,
in the course of their normal daily lives tend to associate
strongly with very limited areas, the immediate neighbourhood in a town, or a central village in a rural area. The
nearest thing to a defined system of communities on this
scale was found by researchers to be the 878 civil parishes
of Scotland, although these formed no part of the local
government structure, and did not exactly coincide with the
mid twentieth century patterns of local 'parish communities'.

A second, more intermittent, level of community was
found to exist in relation to the hinterland of a small town
or a suburban business, shopping and entertainment centre,
a pattern of units which tended to run counter to the
separation of burghs from their rural hinterlands in the
existing local government pattern. Research suggested
that there might be between 100 and 250 of these 'locality'
communities in Scotland, depending on the exact criteria
of hinterland definition adopted.

Rather less association was found to be felt by the
population with larger regions, although certain services
such as hospitals and administrative functions did operate
on such a scale. From a practical point of view, such
areas could be seen as the hinterlands of the larger urban
foci, and about 40 such 'shire' units could be defined in
Scotland, although they were by no means coincident with
the existing counties and counties of cities.

Even larger areas, often very vague in a community
sense but quite clear cut in terms of overall character
and sometimes identifiable in the administrative maps of
voluntary and commercial organisations, were also found

84

to exist, between 5 and 9 in all. Some of these regions
were clearly associated with the cities and their hinterlands, but others, such as the Borders, Galloway and the
Highlands were quite clearly not city regions. And
therein lay a major problem, because clearly these 'regions'
differed markedly in size, population, economic strength
and overall character one from another.

These four levels of 'communities' in Scotland
identified after considerable and varied research, were
by no means clearly apparent in all parts of the country,
nor were all the communities at the same level uniform in
respect of population, area or economic status. The
communities were also unlikely to remain constant over
time. However the commission argued strongly that this
hierarchical pattern, in spite of its limitations, provided
a realistic framework for a reorganisation of local government. The administrative and organisational requirements
of local government were also comprehensively reviewed,
and again a hierarchy of regions for different purposes
was found to be more realistic than one level of division
for all purposes. However, the adoption of too many
tiers was considered to give rise to grave dangers of
responsibility diffusion, and two tiers were concluded
to provide the most acceptable framework. Responsibilities
such as overall planning, housing, police and fire services,
health and education clearly required large areas and
substantial populations, while others such as environmental
and amenity matters could best be organised on a more local
basis. Some of the wider responsibilities seemed to
require areas on the regional scale, i.e. 5 - 9 regions
with populations of at least 200,000; but others seemed
more appropriately related to smaller units, perhaps
about 20 regions in all. Such a system however would have
produced a pattern which did not accord with any of the
community levels identifiable in Scotland. It was concluded therefore that an upper tier of 5 - 9 regions should
be recommended for these wider local government functions.

For some of the more local functions, compact
'locality' community areas with populations of between 10
and 50,000 were regarded as ideal, but such areas were
considered too small for the full range of activities.
On the other hand the 'shire' level of communities with
populations mostly between 50 and 200,000, ideal for some
local functions, were considered too large for the full

85

range, and especially too large for any real public and
community involvement in local government affairs. With
some dissent, the commission finally recommended the
adoption of the 'shire' scale, i.e. about 40 regions for
the second tier of administration, with some provision for
voluntary advisory community councils to be established
at the 'locality' or 'parish' scale, in order to satisfy
the demands for public participation in local government
affairs.

The New Structure

Even accepting the majority recommendation of two
tiers of local government, considerable difficulties
remained in defining the boundaries of the new regions
and districts thereby required. The map finally adopted
by the government, and accepted for implementation in 1975
by the Local Government (Scotland) Act of 1973 (Fig 16),
differed in several important respects from that produced
by the Wheatley commission. The strength of local feeling
and the different weighting given to the various factors
involved which resulted in the changes, testify to the
great difficulty involved in creating a rational pattern
of local government areas, especially in an area so
diverse in terms of landscape, population distribution,
economic character and historical heritage as Scotland.
The majority of the Wheatley commission recommended 7
regions and 37 districts, with considerable variations in
terms of area, population and rateable value as illustrated
in Table 2.

One region (West), although modest in terms of area,
contained nearly half the Scottish population, while another
(The Highlands and Islands) modest in population terms,
contained nearly half of the land area of Scotland. One
district (Glasgow) contained a population and possessed a
rateable value greater than all but one of the regions.
No less than ten of the districts had populations and
thirteen had rateable values greater than those of the
smallest region (South West). Clearly the recommendations
left considerable room for controversy, and even for some
doubts as to whether the anomalies in the new system
justified so radical a change from the old.

At the regional scale, controversy arose especially
on four counts; the population dominance of the West
region; the areal size and hence disparate nature of the

86

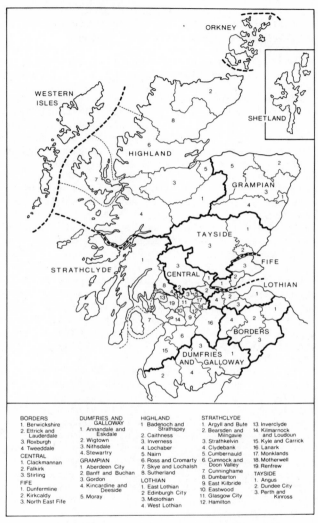

ORKNEY

SHETLAND

WESTERN
ISLES

HIGHLAND

GRAMPIAN

TAYSIDE

FIFE

STRATHCLYDE

CENTRAL

LOTHIAN

BORDERS

DUMFRIES
AND GALLOWAY

BORDERS
1. Berwickshire
2. Ettrick and
   Lauderdale
3. Roxburgh
4. Tweeddale

CENTRAL
1. Clackmannan
2. Falkirk
3. Stirling

FIFE
1. Dunfermline
2. Kirkcaldy
3. North East Fife

DUMFRIES AND
GALLOWAY
1. Annandale and
   Eskdale
2. Wigtown
3. Nithsdale
4. Stewartry

GRAMPIAN
1. Aberdeen City
2. Banff and Buchan
3. Gordon
4. Kincardine and
   Deeside
5. Moray

HIGHLAND
1 Badenoch and
  Strathspey
2. Caithness
3. Inverness
4. Lochaber
5. Nairn
6. Ross and Cromarty
7. Skye and Lochalsh
8. Sutherland

LOTHIAN
1. East Lothian
2 Edinburgh City
3. Midlothian
4. West Lothian

STRATHCLYDE
1. Argyll and Bute
2. Bearsden and
   Milngavie
3. Strathkelvin
4. Clydebank
5. Cumbernauld
6. Cumnock and
   Doon Valley
7. Cunninghame
8. Dumbarton
9. East Kilbride
10. Eastwood
11. Glasgow City
12. Hamilton

13 Inverclyde
14. Kilmarnock
    and Loudoun
15. Kyle and Carrick
16. Lanark
17. Monklands
18. Motherwell
19. Renfrew

TAYSIDE
1. Angus
2. Dundee City
3. Perth and
   Kinross

Figure 16.   The new Regions and Districts after 1975

Highlands and Islands region; the absence of a Borders region; and the division of the ancient kingdom of Fife between an East and a South East Region. The decisions not to split Fife, to create a Borders region and to give each of the three island groups of the Outer Hebrides, Orkney and Shetland the equivalent of regional status led to fundamental changes to the Wheatley map, especially in the east. The recommended East region centred on Edinburgh became three regions, Fife, Lothian and the Borders; the Highlands and Islands region became four regions, Highland, Western Isles, Orkney and Shetland. On the other hand, the recommended West Region was enlarged as Strathclyde to include Argyll. The Act also accepted some additional minor alterations to the recommended regional boundaries, especially where they departed from existing county boundaries, but the main results of the changes were to increase the number of regions from 7 to 12, and to greatly increase the population and rateable value discrepancies between them.

At the district scale, the overwhelming controversy arose over the recommended inclusion of most of the commuter settlements and small burghs around Glasgow in the Glasgow district. The small burghs, and the two large burghs of Rutherglen and Clydebank fought the proposal at all stages of the argument. In the end, the pressure succeeded in reducing the size of the Glasgow district by creating three new districts, Clydebank, Eastwood and Bearsden and Milngavie, and dividing the proposed Kirkintilloch-Cumbernauld district into two, Cumbernauld, and Strathkelvin. Rutherglen however was absorbed into the Glasgow district. Additional district subdivisions to those recommended were also created in most of the other regions, so that the Act of 1973 increased the number of districts from the recommended 37 to 56. This had the effect of slightly reducing the extreme variations of population, area and rateable value in the districts as recommended by the Wheatley commission, and retaining in only a slightly changed form some of the historic areal units of Scotland which would have disappeared under the recommended scheme (e.g. the large burgh of Clydebank, the small burghs of Bearsden and Milngavie, and counties such as Berwick, Roxburgh and Nairn).

The new structure replaced the old 430 local government areas with 12 regions and 56 districts, although since the three island regions (Western Isles,

Orkney and Shetland) consisted of only one district apiece, and were thus given all purpose status rather than a double tier, the actual number of new local government areas operative from 1975 was only 65. Obviously this represented a large increase in the average size of local government units, and although this arguably increased the efficiency of administration, it also reduced the local character of the units. Local community involvement was left to the voluntary organisation of community councils with no local government power. The fundamental change in the administrative regions is reflected in the names adopted for the new areal units, especially the districts. Some counties, large and small burghs and cities remain, but a number of the units take their names from physical features (e.g. Annandale and Eskdale, Inverclyde, Nithsdale), while others resurrect historic names which had no place on the old administrative map (e.g. Lochaber, Gordon, Monklands, Cunninghame). Perhaps the most radical change of all however was the departure from the principal of separating the burghs from their rural hinterlands. Some of the districts, such as the four city districts of Glasgow, Edinburgh, Aberdeen and Dundee, and Clydebank, Hamilton and Motherwell, are almost entirely urban, but the majority contain a mixture of the old burghs and landward areas.

THE TRANSPORT AND COMMUNICATIONS INFRASTRUCTURE

A modern society such as that of present day Scotland relies heavily on efficient transport and communication systems for the movement of people, physical objects, ideas and information. All these movements involve the development of networks such as roads, railways, canals, pipelines and transmission wires; nodal points such as air, sea and river ports, railway and transmitting stations, receiving machines and handling centres of all kinds; and vehicles and carriers. The construction, maintenance and operation of all these phenomena requires considerable finance and provides considerable employment. The fact that the incidence of these financial demands and employment opportunities varies regionally within Scotland is itself of considerable economic significance, so too is the regional variation in the availability of transport and communication facilities themselves.

From this latter viewpoint a number of the transport and communications systems of Scotland can be quickly dismissed. With minor exceptions, all parts of Scotland are equally accessible, at roughly equal cost, to postal and telephone services, broadcasting services, basic educational services and the distribution of certain basic commodities such as electricity and water. The main regional variations in terms of accessibility arise from the varying provision and standard of the road network and the varying distances from nodal points on the road, rail, sea and air routes. These are the variations which affect the flexibility and cost of movements of people and most goods. Fig 17 attempts to depict the accessibility of the various parts of Scotland in these respects.

Accessibility to the transport network can be assessed at a number of levels. At the international level, access to the main nodes on the international air and sea networks is of paramount importance. Since these nodes in Scotland, Prestwick airport and the ports of the Clyde and Forth, all lie in the narrow central isthmus of Scotland, accessibility in an international sense decreases rapidly away from this limited area. The main nodes in relation to the British transport network are located in the same general area, therefore at this second level a relatively small part of Scotland has a high degree of accessibility. Within Scotland, inter-regional accessibility depends mainly on rail and road transport, supplemented by internal air and ferry services in the fragmented territories of the west and north. However, because of the importance of the central belt of Scotland on a British and international level, it is accessibility to this particular part of Scotland which is of greatest significance at the inter-regional level within Scotland. At the fourth, purely local level, accessibility depends mainly on the road system, though a few locally significant rail routes are still in existence, while in the islands and peninsulas of the north and west, local air and sea routes are of some importance. Small areas, even within the central part of Scotland are relatively inaccessible but the degree of inaccessibility tends to rise north-westwards and southwards from this area to such a degree that increasingly large blocks of territory are truly remote from all means of mechanised transport.

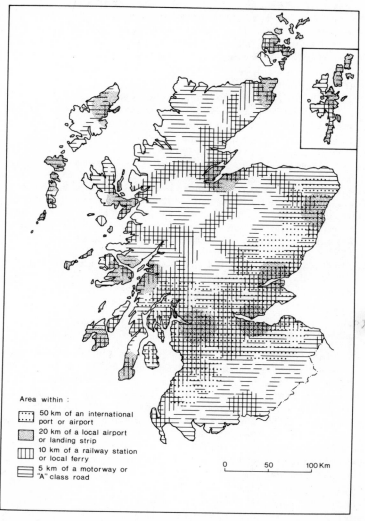

Area within :

⬚ 50 km of an international
    port or airport

▦ 20 km of a local airport
    or landing strip

▥ 10 km of a railway station
    or local ferry

▤ 5 km of a motorway or
    "A" class road

0   50   100 Km

Figure 17.   Accessibility to transport nodes
and routeways

The accessibility map (Fig 17) inevitably reflects many aspects of the physical maps of Scotland, since many of the physical characteristics of Scotland exert controls on the transport systems as they do on other aspects of man's development. The map also bears a close resemblance to the map of population distribution since the development of transport systems is both a cause and a result of population concentrations.

Within Scotland there already exists some degree of complimentality rather than competition between the different transport systems. In general however the different means of transport are competing for similar traffic on both international and internal routes. As a result the operation of the complete transport system is far from rational. Although considerable efforts are now being made, the drive towards a more rational operation faces severe handicaps. The existing route patterns developed under very different conditions in the past. There is argument as to whether economic or social considerations should be of paramount importance. Above all however there is the multiplicity of bodies, public and private, large and small, involved in the transport business. Even within the different sectors, only in the case of the railways does a single body wield nearly complete control over all aspects of operation.

Road Transport

The road network is far and away the most extensive transport system in Scotland and one which is still being extended. Apart from the extent of the network, road transport routes also possess the advantages of being accessible to a wide range of individually owned vehicles at any point on the network. Although the road network is dense in Scotland as a whole, especially in comparison with other transport routes, there are significant regional variations. Local road networks are much denser in the coastal lowlands and in the central isthmus of Scotland. Physical restrictions and lack of population in the more mountainous areas result in a skeletal network of inter-regional roads rather than a local network.

Even within the lowland areas, the nature of the terrain may impose tortuous or circuitous road routes, especially is this so as a result of the presence of

92

water bodies.   In the case of the islands, the break in
the network from this cause is complete, but even on the
mainland the deep estuary and fiord-like inlets which
break the landmass of much of the country into distinct
peninsulas, impose considerable problems.   One of the major
modifications to the road network of Scotland since 1945
has been the progressive reduction in the number of ferries
forming important links in the system (Plate 5A).   In spite
of much discussion, especially in relation to Skye and
Bute, none of the main islands are yet linked to the mainland by road bridges.   Within the island groups however
some linkages have occurred, such as the causeways in the
Outer Hebrides linking Benbecula with the islands of both
North and South Uist.   On the mainland, significant new
road bridges and roads have now replaced ferries across
most of the major inlets, although tolls are levied in
many instances.   The Forth and Tay road bridges now
provide a direct road route from Edinburgh through
Dundee to Aberdeen.   The Erskine bridge now provides
for the first time a road link across the Clyde estuary
west of Glasgow.   A bridge now crosses Loch Leven at
Ballachulish on the main holiday route to the north west
while further north a new road link has rendered redundant
the notorious bottle-neck of the Strome ferry across Loch
Carron.   Road plans for the Moray Firth area envisage
the bridging of the Beauly and Cromarty Firths.
        Although Scotland possesses a fairly comprehensive
road network, many of the roads are of a very modest
standard.   In view of the steady increase in both the
number and size of road vehicles, this gives rise to very
considerable demands for road improvement.   Table 3
illustrates the rise in the number of vehicles using, and
the increasing expenditure on, roads since 1964, compared
with the reduction in the status of many of the roads
themselves.
        Improvements to the standard of existing roads and
substantial new road building is most evident in two main
areas, the increasingly heavily used inter-regional trunk
routes linking Dundee, Edinburgh, Glasgow, the Lower Clyde,
Ayrshire and Carlisle, and ring-road by-pass routes in the
major urban areas especially Glasgow and Edinburgh.   Motorway and near-motorway routes have been, or are being,
constructed between Carlisle and Glasgow (A74/M74),

Greenock and Edinburgh (M8), Edinburgh and Dundee (M90), Glasgow and Stirling (M80), Edinburgh and Stirling (M9) and Glasgow and Ayr.   Urban motorway systems are under active construction, especially in Glasgow with its inner ring road and river side expressway linking with new bridge and tunnel crossings of the Clyde (Plate 5B).

	1964	1967	1972	1974
Road Length (Km)	45,915	46,454	47,902	48,265
Trunk	3,132	3,175	3,204	3,251
Principal	24,288	7,274	7,371	7,314
Others	18,496	36,005	37,328	37,600
Licensed Vehicles (000s)	900	1,035	1,181	1,274
Cars	611	769	938	1,018
Goods	–	125	124	133
Others	–	141	119	123
Expenditure on roads (£m)	34.1	57.25	76.13	82.00
Trunk	–	18.44	30.41	26.26

Table 3.   Roads and road transport in Scotland 1964–74
Source :   Abstract of Regional Statistics and Regional
            Statistics

     These areas stand in marked contrast to the rest of Scotland.   Reclassification in the mid-nineteen sixties reduced drastically the lengths of road in Scotland considered adequate for principal status.   North of a line from Dumbarton to Aberdeen and south of a line from Ayr to Dunbar (except for the A74/M74), the standard of even the 'A' class roads declines markedly in terms of widths, gradients and directness.   North of the Great Glen all but a few of the 'A' class roads are single track with passing bays.   Even these roads are now carrying a sufficient level of traffic, especially as a result of summer tourist movements, to warrant considerable improvements.   Already some high quality new road links have been built to connect the isolated strands of the road network in remote parts of Scotland.   These new double-track roads still stand in marked contrast to the unimproved old roads which they

connect.   The Shieldaig-Torridon link in Wester Ross and
the Inverailort-Ardmorlich link in Moidart are good examples.
Few of the main roads in Scotland are now devoid of at least
short stretches of substantially widened and realigned
carriageways, and increasing traffic is likely to demand
many more improvements, some indeed are already planned or
actively in hand.

The Scottish road system is used by a wide variety of
vehicles for a wide variety of purposes over a wide variety
of distances.   Few of the movements are subject to official
schedules.   Some indication of the busiest sections of the
network and of the overall growth in road vehicles has
already been given, but few other generalisations can be
made with any confidence about the use of the system.   From
table 3 it can be seen that the increase in the number of
licensed vehicles in Scotland since 1964 is accounted for
almost entirely by the increase in the number of cars.
Cars are the most complex of all road vehicles in terms of
usage, length of journey and patterns of movement.   Certainly over this period figures reveal that the numbers of
coaches and buses licensed in Scotland declined, as did the
number of passengers carried and the total distance
travelled by such vehicles.   This might suggest some reduction in heavy passenger vehicle movements.   On the other
hand the increase in tourist traffic in particular over this
period means that the number of cars, coaches and buses
licensed in Scotland bears little relation to the number of
passenger vehicles using Scottish roads.   Goods transport
by road is also complex, although the private car plays a
less important part.   Local distribution and collection
services, feeder services to and from trunk road and other
transport terminals as well as trunk road movements themselves, all intermingle.   Again, as the heavy traffic
flow on the A74/M74 illustrates, a great many of these
traffic movements occur with vehicles licensed outside
Scotland.

In spite of shortcomings in the road system, for
almost all movements of people and goods within Scotland,
the distances involved and the comprehensive nature of the
network give road transport the edge in cost and efficiency
terms over other means of transport.   Only where stretches
of water impose breaks on the road routes or where large
regular flows of goods or people occur between two nodal
points, do other forms of transport really compete.   Since

road transport is to a great extent under fragmented control and indirectly financed with a large element of private individual movements, great difficulties face the planned integration of this very dynamic sector into a rational overall transport system.

Rail Transport

Compared with the road network, the rail network of Scotland is skeletal and unlike the slow increase in the total length of roads, the total length of railway line has been reduced by a third since 1964 (Table 4). The rail network is only accessible at specified stations, and the closure over this same period of many station access points, even on routes which remain open, further emphasises the severity of the pruning which the railway system has undergone to better fit it for present needs.

The Ayrshire and Clyde lowlands are the only areas which possess a local passenger rail network of any density. The lines for the most part radiate from Glasgow. In the other main urban areas of Scotland, including Edinburgh, the local services which still exist operate almost exclusively on sections of inter-city trunk routes. This trunk route network is limited to the links between Glasgow and Edinburgh and between those cities and Dundee, Aberdeen and England (via Carlisle and via Berwick). Apart from these trunk routes, a handful of long, circuitous often single-track lines extend the network to Stranraer, Oban, Mallaig, Kyle of Lochalsh, Wick and Thurso.

The rugged nature of much of Scotland clearly poses severe problems to rail transport, but railway engineering feats of the past, such as the Forth and Tay bridges and the routes over the Beattock and Drumochter passes and Rannoch Moor, illustrate that many of these physical problems can be overcome (Plate 5A). The cost however is only justified if there is enough potential traffic. Even in the heyday of rail transport in Britain a hundred years ago, potential traffic in Scotland was never sufficient to justify the construction of a dense rail network. It is the very limited potential rail traffic in the late twentieth century which accounts for the reduction of the network to its present skeletal form. Much of the pruning of the network has involved the removal of competitive installations developed by rival rail companies in earlier years. It has proceeded hand-in-hand with a heavy

investment in the modernisation of the track, rolling-stock
locomotives and operational systems.   In spite of this heavy
expenditure and rationalisation, Table 4 illustrates the
stagnation in railway business since 1964.

	1964	1969	1974
Route length (Km)	4,729	3,216	3,012
Electrified	128	188	375
Track length (Km)	9,931	6,668	5,900
Electrified	285	399	785
Sidings	2,520	1,412	1,179
Locomotives	1,147	498	457
Steam	497	-	-
Diesel	650	498	457
Multiple units	777	831	748
Diesel	502	501	411
Electric	275	330	330
Passenger journeys (millions)	73.0	68.4	69.1
Freight traffic (million tonnes/km)	2,135	1,680	1,969
Coal and coke	690	515	449
Iron and steel	436	415	498
Receipts (£ 000s)	46,623	35,834	49,162
Passenger train	19,733	18,511	30,709
Freight train	22,890	17,323	18,453

Table 4.   Rail transport in Scotland 1964-74
Sources: Digest of Scottish Statistics and
           Scottish Abstract of Statistics

Considerable efforts have been made to increase the
volume of regular, substantial point to point passenger
and goods traffic on which economically viable railway
operations depend.   The containerisation of miscellaneous
goods traffic in particular and the introduction of freight-
liner express goods services has helped the railways to
retain some freight business in the face of severe competition
from other forms of transport.   Nevertheless, excluding
the routes to England from Glasgow via Beattock (now
electrified) and from Edinburgh via Berwick, the only internal
rail routes which are economically highly competitive with

97

other means of transport are the Glasgow—Edinburgh
passenger route and a few short specialised heavy mineral
freight routes in Central Scotland.   Most of the trunk route
system, if not highly competitive, is at least economically
viable.

The justification for the retention of other elements
of the rail network rests less on economic and more on
social grounds.   In spite of tourist traffic and some key
goods movements (e.g. timber to the Corpach pulp mill), the
long lines to remote western and northern coastal towns and
island ferry ports do not pay their way.   Indeed, the local
fight to prevent the closure of the line from Dingwall to
Kyle of Lochalsh has been almost continuous since 1964.
These lines are, nevertheless, essential lifelines for many
communities in remote parts of Scotland where any form of
public transport would be uneconomic.   As long as they
continue to carry a reasonable volume of traffic and fulfil
the transport needs of such communities, a strong case
exists for the continued subsidy of such lines.   For very
different reasons, a strong case also exists for the continued subsidy of local commuting lines, mainly those in
the Glasgow area.   Such lines tend to operate at a
financial loss not becuase of lack of traffic, but because
of the concentration of very heavy traffic flows at very
short peak periods.   Much expensive equipment lies idle
for much of the time.   However, commuter traffic in
urban areas places such severe strains on urban transport
systems as a whole, that subsidy is accepted as a norm.
Although the highly efficient, largely electrified Glasgow
suburban train services are a doubtful economic proposition,
their essential place in the urban transport system as a
whole is indicated by the fact that it is in relation to
this sector of the rail network that the construction of
new lines or the reopening of abandonned lines is being
seriously considered.

Water Transport

Water transport in Scotland has three main roles.
Firstly the internal movement on river, loch and canal
of freight and passengers;   secondly the extension of the
outer strands of the road and rail network to the islands
and peninsulas;   and thirdly the coastwise and inter-

national movement of people and freight to and from the main ports.

Inland water transport on lochs and rivers is of very little significance, except for a few isolated local movements in remote areas and to cater for tourist interests. Of the artificial waterways, the Forth and Clyde, Monkland and Union canals, of great passenger and commercial significance in the nineteenth century, are no longer navigable. (Plate 5B). Pressure from recreational interests may however encourage the reopening of parts of the network not yet infilled. Increased traffic on the two remaining canals, the Crinan and the Caledonian, since 1962 is also largely accounted for by the increase of pleasure vessels, although local freight traffic has increased on the Caledonian Canal.

Scheduled ferry services from mainland road and rail terminals such as Oban, Mallaig, Ullapool, Thurso and Aberdeen, play an essential part in passenger, mail and freight movements to and from the islands of the west and north. In spite of supplementary tourist traffic, most of these services are heavily subsidised as essential transport links for such communities. So fragmented are the land areas of the island groups and parts of the mainland west coast that the private boat frequently replaces the private car as a means of local travel.

The coastwise and international movement of freight is far and away the most important role played by water transport in Scotland, both in terms of volume and economic value. At this level however, Scottish water transport is part of a larger United Kingdom whole. Much Scottish freight, estimated in 1964 at about eighteen per cent, and almost all Scottish international passengers, travel overland to and from English ports. Scottish ports in return handle some freight of English origin or destination. The growth of the Scottish ports at the international level is inextricably linked with the urban and industrial development of their hinterlands. As a result the Clyde (mainly Glasgow and Greenock) and the Forth ports (mainly Leith and Grangemouth) and to a lesser extent Aberdeen and Dundee, dominate the port business of Scotland.

The steady increase in the volume of traffic handled by the major Scottish ports since 1962 is clearly illustrated in Table 5. The balance of inward and outward and foreign and coastwise traffic however varies markedly from

	Inward				Outward			
	1962	1967	1972	1974	1962	1967	1972	1974
Scotland: total	9,475	17,860	24,132	26,782	4,617	6,336	8,007	8,531
Foreign	6,245	12,367	16,785	19,696	2,749	2,178	2,870	2,879
Coastwise	3,230	5,493	7,347	7,086	1,867	4,158	5,137	5,652
Clyde ports: total	5,046	10,167	13,719	15,658	1,600	1,225	1,813	1,692
Foreign	3,382	8,383	11,253	13,467	843	773	1,274	977
Coastwise	1,663	1,783	2,486	2,192	757	450	539	715
Forth ports: total	2,977	4,119	5,971	5,544	2,917	3,318	3,497	4,209
Foreign	2,236	2,773	3,917	4,087	1,812	1,113	1,199	1,468
Coastwise	741	1,346	2,054	1,457	1,046	2,206	2,298	2,741
Aberdeen: total	1,022	1,126	1,259	1,343	84	125	169	130
Foreign	327	389	392	385	28	75	54	28
Coastwise	695	737	867	958	56	50	115	102
Dundee: total	430	725	998	1,047	15	12	44	17
Foreign	299	313	332	303	6	6	14	4
Coastwise	131	413	666	744	9	6	29	13

Table 5. Scottish port freight traffic 1962–74 (ooo's tonnes handled)
Sources: Digest of Scottish Statistics, Scottish Abstract of Statistics, Digest of Port Statistics

port to port. The volume of foreign import traffic greatly exceeds that of export traffic in all cases. The volume of inward coastwise traffic also exceeds that of outward coastwise traffic except in the case of the Forth ports. The volume of coastwise traffic also assumes greater significance than that of foreign traffic in the smaller ports of Aberdeen and Dundee. In terms of value there is much less discrepancy between inward and outward traffic.

A breakdown of the commodities involved in the port traffic provides some explanation of these patterns. Unprocessed food, industrial raw materials and fuel loom large in the import figures, whereas processed commodities with considerable added value dominate the export figures. The Clyde and to a lesser extent the Forth ports handle the greater part of these high value but comparatively light export commodities.

Since the mid-nineteen-sixties substantial sums have been spent on port improvements. On the east coast this has occurred especially in association with the development of closer economic links with Europe and the exploitation of North Sea oil. On the Clyde it has occurred especially in association with the changing scale and pattern of world ocean shipping movements. These latter trends have resulted in the dramatic rise of Greenock to parity with Glasgow as a port. In 1962 Greenock handled just about £30 million of trade compared with Glasgow's near £200 million. By 1972 Greenock handled £204 million of trade compared with Glasgow's £260 million. The trend towards a concentration of world trade on deep water ports equipped for bulk and container handling is likely to encourage the concentration of world traffic on the lower Clyde, with the east coast ports specialising in more local coastal and European trade.

Air Transport

In spite of the short distances involved, air transport plays an important part in passenger and freight movements within Scotland. This results largely from the speed and convenience of this form of transport between points separated by both land and sea. Although the network allows, and is utilised, for local movements between airports

101

on the mainland, internal services are primarily designed
to link the main western and northern islands with the main
centres of Glasgow, Edinburgh, Inverness, Aberdeen and Wick.
On a very local level within the Orkney and Shetland islands,
very short distance inter-island services also operate.
These services are based on small aircraft utilising landing
strips rather than airports.   These internal services rely
heavily on subsidies, the volume of passenger and freight
traffic being small.

      Although these internal services are vital to many
isolated small communities, air transport has a larger
significance in relation to links with the rest of Britain
and foreign countries.   The airports at Glasgow (Abbotsinch)
and Edinburgh (Turnhouse), and to a lesser extent those at
Aberdeen (Dyce) and Inverness (Dalcross), are nodes on the
internal British air network.   Between the main airports,
this network operates in competition with long distance
rail and road transport for both passengers and freight.
In spite of rail and road improvements, partly stimulated
by this competition from air transport, air traffic between
Scotland and the main centres of England continues to
expand.

      Prestwick is the major Scottish node on the inter-
national air network, except for a few European links from
Abbotsinch and Turnhouse.   Prestwick however is a British
rather than a purely Scottish international airport. Much
Scottish international traffic operates to and from international terminals in England, just as Prestwick handles
much English traffic.   Flows between world centres on a
scale sufficient to sustain direct air links require
concentrations of traffic on a British rather than a
Scottish scale.

      The upward trend in air transport to and from Scottish
airports since 1964 is illustrated in Table 6.   It can be
seen that freight traffic as well as passenger movement is
important.   Indeed both Prestwick and Abbotsinch airports
now handle substantially more freight by value than the
sea ports of Aberdeen and Dundee.   Light machinery and
precision instruments form a particularly large part of
the freight carried by air to and from Scotland.

	1964	1969	1974
Air movements (000's)	92.2	176.0	314.9
Passenger movements (000's)	2319.1	3202.0	4392.5
Prestwick	368.3	480.2	564.3
Glasgow. Abbotsinch	1173.8	1630.7	1971.2
Edinburgh. Turnhouse	454.2	614.4	810.2
Aberdeen. Dyce	77.6	130.0	460.0
Inverness. Dalcross	43.6	89.5	146.9
Wick	46.9	63.4	68.5
Orkney. Kirkwall	44.1	74.7	100.4
Shetland. Sumburgh	17.8	26.0	160.2
Stornoway	32.6	41.2	47.6
Benbecula	30.8	30.4	42.0
Islay. Port Ellen	15.4	16.2	16.3
Tiree	6.4	5.2	4.9
Mail carried (000's tonnes)	3.4	3.7	4.0
Freight carried (000's tonnes)	13.4	39.9	47.7

	Inward 1968	Outward 1968	Inward 1972	Outward 1972
Value of foreign freight carried (£ million)				
Abbotsinch	20.1	6.2	42.4	28.0
Prestwick	36.8	34.3	47.0	33.9

Table 6.   Scottish air transport 1964-74
Sources: Digest of Scottish Statistics and
Scottish Abstract of Statistics

THE ENERGY INFRASTRUCTURE

The availability of energy has played, and continues to play, a key role in the economic and social development of Scotland.   The fact that energy consumption has risen steadily in recent decades is itself an indication of the continuing economic growth of the country.   There are however a number of different primary sources of energy, and the importance of each in the total energy balance is constantly changing, with far reaching geographical repercussions. Some of these changes between 1963 and 1974 are illustrated in Table 7. The most significant trend revealed by these figures is the almost complete reversal of the roles of coal and petroleum in the energy equation during the nineteen-sixties. The significance of this trend is heightened by the fact that coal is largely home produced, the industry is a large employer of labour and is nationalised. Petroleum on the other hand is largely imported (although there is the future potential of North Sea supplies), the refining industry is only a small employer of labour and is in large measure operated by international private companies. Other sources of primary energy in Scotland are on a much smaller scale. Hydro-electric power has a limited future potential and is unlikely to expand its share of the energy supply market. The future of nuclear power is in theory rather more promising, as is that of natural gas as a result of the exploitation of North Sea supplies.

Fig 18 shows the location of the main sources of primary energy in Scotland. Although there are marked regional variations in terms of endowment, this places only limited direct restrictions on economic development. This apparent anomaly arises from the fact that modern energy supplies can be fairly easily and cheaply transported. Gas, electricity and petroleum are much more flexible than coal in terms of transport because of movement by wire and pipeline. In consequence a marked trend away from the direct use of coal to the use of more flexible energy sources in Scotland is evident.

Of much greater geographical significance than the location of primary energy sources is the planning of a balanced energy policy for the future. This is a process of great complexity but one which has immense employment and other implications. Of particular importance are the questions of the short and long term future roles of coal and other limited fossil fuel resources such as petroleum and natural gas, in relation to the future roles of nuclear and to a lesser extent hydro-electric power; the balance to be struck between the conservation of home energy supplies and foreign imports; and the priorities to be established in relation to economic expansion and environmental conservation.

Fuel	1963 Total	%	1969 Total	%	1974 Total	%
All fuels	6,658	100	7,654	100	8,142	100
Fossil fuels	6,043	91	6,795	89	7,330	90
Coal	4,288	64	3,548	46	2,746	34
Coke	27	–	30	–	45	–
Petroleum	1,725	26	3,212	42	3,978	49
Natural Gas	3	–	5	–	561	7
Nuclear electricity	150	2	363	5	335	4
Hydro-electricity	385	6	369	5	449	6

Table 7.   Primary sources of energy in Scotland 1963-74
(in million therms heat value)
Source: Scottish Abstract of Statistics

Coal

Coal has been mined in Scotland since at least the
thirteenth century and at the height of production before
1914 Scotland exported coal on a large scale (Plate 6A).
Although production has declined from this peak and con-
traction is still a major characteristic of the industry,
very substantial reserves of coal remain.   The location
of the coalfields played a key role in the location of
industry and urban growth in Scotland from the late eighteenth
century onwards, and present day production is largely from
the same historically important areas (Fig 18).   Except
for a few locally important small mines, most of Scotland's
coal (99 per cent) is produced from the National Coal Board's
mines and opencast workings in the central belt.   Since
1945 the western coal basins of Ayrshire and Lanarkshire
(central) have tended to decline in significance, while
the eastern basins of Fife and Lothian have tended to
increase in relative importance.   However the Scottish
share of the total United Kingdom production has also
tended to decline, reflecting the disadvantages which the
Scottish industry as a whole has faced in a wider context.
Partly as a result of difficult geological conditions,

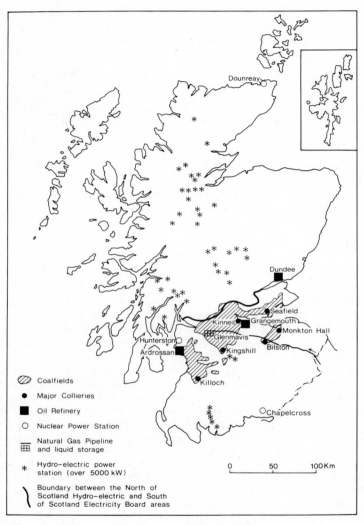

Figure 18.   Location of major energy sources

(faulting and distortions of the coal seams), and partly as a result of a higher proportion of older, small-scale labour-intensive pits, Scottish coal has been consistently more expensive per ton than English coal since 1945. The effect of rationalisation of production since the national-isation of the industry in 1947 has therefore been especially severe in Scotland.

Until the end of the nineteen fifties, the rational-isation of the British coal industry was set against a background of a steady or expanding demand for coal. After 1958 however the demand for coal turned sharply downward, intensifying the changes associated with rationalisation. Mechanisation and increased efficiency resulted, in com-bination with falling production, in substantial colliery closures and reductions in manpower. Substantial problems of unemployment and social decay, especially in some of the small pit villages in Ayrshire and Lanarkshire, have inevitably arisen and largely account for the designation of parts of the coalfields as Special Development Areas (see Chapter 2).

In spite of reorganisation, coal has continued to lose ground in almost all sectors of the energy markets in Scotland (Table 8). Between 1961 and 1974 the traditional markets for coal, with the exception of the electricity industry and coke ovens, declined sharply. The reasons are not hard to find. The continued implementation of legislation designed to reduce smoke pollution decimated the industrial and domestic markets already turning to cheaper, cleaner, more easily transport-able and more flexible fuels. The railways moved out of the age of steam into the diesel and electric era. Coal gas began to give way to cheaper supplies of more efficient and safer natural gas. Even in the electricity production market, alternative primary sources and the increasing use of oil rather than coal in conventional thermal electricity power stations, reduced the potential rise in demand for coal.

In Scotland in the late twentieth century coal is a costly, bulky, inconvenient source of energy in spite of substantial reserves. Even the case for promoting the use of coal in order to reduce the demand for costly petroleum imports loses force in the face of potential home supplies of petroleum from the North Sea. The

future of coal mining in Scotland in the next twenty or
thirty years therefore depends very much on decisions made
in relation to a planned energy policy and the social
argument in favour of retaining some coal mining as a
source of employment. In the long term coal may even be
more important as an industrial raw material than as an
energy source.

	1961	1966	1974
Total consumption	17,437	13,923	11,067
Industrial	3,852	2,494	687
Domestic	3,925	2,738	1,411
Coke ovens	1,688	1,518	1,295
Gas supply	1,655	959	84
Electricity supply	3,713	4,912	6,890
Railways	1,036	200	-

Table 8.   Major markets for coal in Scotland 1961-74
(000's tonnes)
Source :   Scottish Abstract of Statistics

Petroleum

The dramatic rise in the importance of petroleum as an
energy source in Scotland in the second half of the twentieth
century is almost entirely based on imports rather than home
production.   The production of oil from crushed shale in
West and Mid Lothian which lasted from the early nineteenth
to the mid-twentieth centuries, was minute compared with
the quantities of refined products now derived from imports
of crude petroleum.   The previous existence of the shale
based industry is not without significance however in that
it supported the early development of the refining industry
at Grangemouth (Fig 18 and Plate 6B).   The Ardrossan and
Dundee refineries are on a much smaller scale.
The exploitation of North Sea reserves (Fig 19) is not
likely to alter the dominant position of Grangemouth as the
major centre of the Scottish petroleum industry since it
is the refinery centres rather than the productive oil
fields or shore terminals which are of major locational
significance for employment and economic growth.   Because

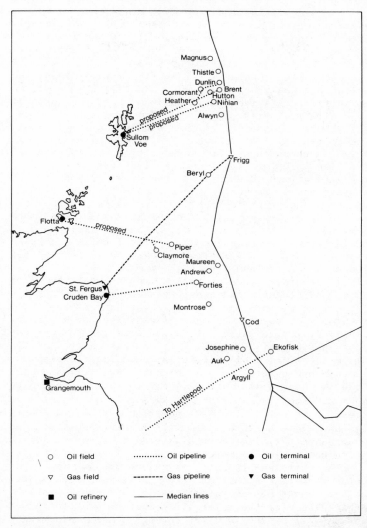

Figure 19. North Sea oil developments to 1975

of the low levels of direct employment and the ease of
transporting refined products, even the refinery centres
are less significant than the coal mines were in the past
as attractors of population and industry.   The Scottish
refinery industry only employs about two and a half
thousand workers in spite of producing about fifty per
cent of Scotland's primary energy.

The refinery capacity of Scotland, in spite of considerable expansion between 1961 and 1974 (Table 9), was
not sufficient to meet the demand for petroleum products,
especially fuel oils, in 1974.   Scotland therefore is
still a net importer of refined products as well as of
crude petroleum.   Although known North Sea reserves are
estimated to be capable of supporting an annual production
of at least 100 million tonnes by 1980 (ten times the
present Scottish consumption), the reserves seem to be
relatively poor in heavy oils suitable for fuel oil
production but rich in light oils suitable for the production of motor spirit.   The future character of the
petroleum industry in Scotland, although likely to
display a net export balance, is also likely to display
a complex balance of imports and exports of specialised
products.   Petroleum from the North Sea may not therefore
entirely replace crude petroleum imports, but the export
of refined products and possibly some crude also will be
of great benefit to the country's foreign exchange balance.
Except by increasing the pace of expansion it may have
relatively little influence on the existing refinery and
supply pattern of Scotland.   It may have a greater impact
on the location of oil terminals, changing the emphasis
from western centres such as Finnart and Bowling on the
Clyde to eastern and northern centres such as Cruden Bay
and the Orkney and Shetland Islands.   Oil terminals
however have only a limited impact on a region's economic
growth.   Some North Sea oil will also probably be piped
as crude to refining centres outside Scotland closer to
the larger consuming markets.

The petroleum industry is unique amongst the major
energy concerns in that it is not a nationalised under-
taking.   Central government does have a considerable
stake in some of the major oil companies and controls
many aspects of the industry through general planning
legislation.   However the development of a balanced
national energy policy is made more complex by the fact

that this expanding, competitive sector of the energy supply industry is primarily the concern of profit-making international private companies.

	1961	1966	1974
Total refinery throughout	3,489	4,654	8,056

	Production			Consumption		
	1961	1966	1974	1961	1966	1974
Aviation, motor industrial and white spirits	744	869	1,364	771	934	1,251
Kerosine and burning oils	164	170	476	304	313	514
Gas and diesel oils	701	1,058	1,994	778	1,195	1,964
Fuel oils	1,375	1,902	2,973	1,073	2,618	4,349
Other products	4	656	1,249	686	1,418	1,845
Total	3,489	4,654	8,056	3,562	6,480	10,023

Table 9. The Scottish petroleum industry 1961-74 (Production and consumption in 000's tonnes)

Source : Scottish Abstract of Statistics

Gas

The gas industry of Scotland, like that of Britain as a whole, has traditionally been based on the conversion of coal and the use of by-product gas from coke ovens. Traditionally too the production units have tended to be small and located close to the consumer as evidenced by the ubiquitous local gas works. This character of the industry is reflected in the 1961/62 figures in Table 10. By 1966 the gas industry had clearly undergone major changes. In spite of an almost fifty per cent increase in output, gas works and coke oven production was virtually unchanged while the bulk of the increased production was obtained from the by-products of oil refineries. At the same time, Table 10 indicates a major change in the fuels used at the gas works; substantial falls in the use of

111

both coal and coke and a dramatic increase in the use of oil. By 1974, in spite of a further increase in gas output, gas works production had been decimated, and the amounts of both coal and oil used in gas production had in consequence been greatly reduced.

Production (in million therms)	1961/2	1966/7	1974/5
Produced at gas works	162	176	54
Purchased from coke ovens	34	20	-
Purchased from oil refineries	10	100	15
Natural gas	2	6	567
Total	208	302	636
Fuel used (000's tonnes)			
Coal	1,620	825	25
Coke	61	17	-
Oil	22	260	123
Consumption (in million therms)			
Domestic	98	158	270
Industrial and farm	50	62	221
Commercial	31	38	60
Public administration and lighting	5	4	9
Total	184	262	560

Table 10.   The Scottish gas industry 1961-75
Source   :   Scottish Abstract of Statistics

By 1974 too, coke ovens had ceased to be a significant source of gas, while even the utilisation of waste gas from oil refineries had declined. The second revolution in the Scottish gas industry within a decade was the result of a change from secondary to primary sources of gas. By 1974 natural gas was providing over seventy per cent of the country's gas compared with less than two per cent only ten years earlier.

These developments introduced substantial changes in

the pattern of the gas supply industry. The decline in
the significance of the gas works and the rationalisation
of the remaining gas works greatly reduced the number of
separate production points. Although not a large employer
of labour, this trend resulted in a decline in the industry's
labour force from nine and a half thousand in 1961 to seven
and a half thousand in 1972. The same trend, together with
the greatly increased importance of natural gas, has led
to an expansion of the gas pipeline network though remoter
parts of the country still depend on bottled gas. Continuing discoveries of natural gas reserves in the North
Sea (Fig 19), now estimated to be capable of supplying more
than Scotland's requirements for the immediate future, are
likely to intensify the changing pattern of the gas supply
industry. They are also likely to provide surplus gas
for export to England, thus reversing the import flow from
England on which the original trends in favour of natural
gas were based.

The increase in the consumption of gas in Scotland
between 1961 and 1975 was largely accounted for by large
increases in the demands of the domestic and industrial
markets (Table 10). The expansion of the pipeline grid
and supplies of gas from the North Sea could lead to
further substantial increases in the consumption of gas
at the expense of other energy sources, especially
electricity and petroleum if their costs continue to
increase relatively faster than those of gas. Policy
decisions in relation to the balance of Scotland's energy
industry are thus likely to be of paramount importance in
relation to the future of the gas industry.

Electricity

Electricity is the most flexible form of energy
available at present in Scotland, a fact which explains
its increasing share of the total energy markets. It can
be used for lighting, heating or driving machinery of all
kinds; it is easily distributed by means of the wires
which, together with their associated installations, have
become such a universal feature of twentieth century
landscapes; it can meet with much less difficulty than
other energy sources (except perhaps gas) sudden and rapid
fluctuations in demand; it can be produced from a wide
variety of different sources.

The considerable increase in the demand for electricity
from almost all consumers in Scotland between 1961 and 1975
is shown in Table 11, which also illustrates the extent to
which during the same period the installation of new
generating capacity more than kept pace with rising demand.
The Scottish electricity grid is connected to the English
grid, and considerable exchanges occur between the two
systems.   Over the year however imports and exports just
about cancel each other out, and Scottish plant produce
about as much electricity as is consumed in Scotland.   In
spite of the increase in production, the labour force in
the electricity industry as in most of the energy industries,
declined substantially in this period, from about twenty
five thousand in 1961 to only seventeen and a half thousand
in 1972.

    Scotland's electricity is derived from three main
sources, fossil fuel based thermal power stations, nuclear
fuelled thermal power stations and hydro-electric power
stations.   The relative importance of each of these
sources in each of the two electricity board areas is
summarised in Table 12.   Some of the information in this
table clearly reflects the distribution of each type of
generating plant as shown on Fig 18.

    The major part of Scotland's electricity production
is derived from the traditional fossil fuel based thermal
power stations, the proportion in fact rose from sixty
five per cent in 1961 to over seventy per cent in 1974.
Coal is still the chief fuel used, although oil and some
lesser fuels are making increasing inroads into this
last major expanding market for coal in Scotland.   The
coalfields, and within them coastal and riverside sites
with plentiful water supplies, still therefore exert a
powerful influence on the location of thermal electricity
power stations.   The major new additions to Scotland's
electricity generating capacity in the nineteen sixties
were the three giant thermal power stations of Kincardine,
Longannet and Cockenzie, all located on the Forth and
on productive coalfields. (Plate 6B).   Since the South
of Scotland Electricity Board's area contains all the
main coalfield areas of Scotland, it is not surprising
that the North of Scotland Hydro-electric Board should
control a very small proportion of Scotland's total
thermal electricity generating capacity.   Since the

114

late nineteen sixties however oil has been gaining over coal as a thermal power station fuel, even to the extent of the conversion of some existing coal fired power stations.

Sales (in million units)	1961	1966/7	1974/5
Domestic	3,828	7,278	8,629
Farm	319	448	267
Commercial	1,639	2,736	3,111
Industrial	3,840	5,203	5,347
Public lighting	158	203	234
Traction	81	83	146
Total	9,876	15,943	17,734

Generation and demand (in million kwh)

	1961	1966/7	1974/5
Generated by Electricity Boards	10,089	17,237	26,997
Purchased (mainly from BNFL)	1,240	1,543	1,582
Transmission losses	364	654	860
Total available	10,965	18,126	27,719
Demand from consumers	11,265	17,949	27,176
Net surplus	- 300	177	543

Table 11.   Electricity sales, generation
            and demand 1961-75
Source :   Scottish Abstract of Statistics

Some large new thermal power stations, based on oil, are now planned for the north east of Scotland.   In spite of the concentration of conventional thermal generating capacity in the coalfield areas, the transmission and distribution system is such that all but a very few isolated communities (served largely by small diesel generating plant) are accessible to the electricity grid.

Nuclear electricity power stations operate in exactly the same way as other thermal power stations, except for the fuel used to convert water into steam to drive the generators.   Nuclear fuel being virtually self-replacing

115

results in very low running costs, though the capital cost of the power station is much higher than a coal or oil based power station. In overall cost terms, nuclear power stations have not yet quite attained parity with other thermal electricity power stations, and this largely accounts for the limited installed capacity of nuclear plant in Scotland. Apart from small amounts from experimental plant at Dounreay and Chapelcross in the extreme north and south of the country respectively, Hunterston is the only source of nuclear generated electricity in Scotland. Expansion is likely to be delayed until clear cost advantages of nuclear over conventional thermal generating plant become apparent.

Hydro-electric power stations are based on a different technology, using running water rather than heated water (steam) to drive the generators. Most of the early schemes in Scotland at the beginning of the twentieth century were associated either with isolated industrial plant in remote areas (e.g. the aluminium works at Foyers, Kinlochleven and Fort William), or very small public supply schemes for isolated local communities (e.g. Fochabers and Dingwall). Between the wars however a number of larger public supply schemes were introduced in Galloway, on the Clyde and in the Tummel Valley. After the establishment of the North of Scotland Hydro-electric Board in 1943, much more comprehensive development of the water power resources of the Highlands occurred. By British standards the hydro-electric power resources of Scotland are large (though they are small by world standards), and especially in the north, play a major role in the total pattern of electricity supply. At first sight (Fig 18), the location of the main sources of hydro-electric power seem to happily complement the location of the coalfields, thus providing a source of electricity in areas remote from thermal power stations. Although of undoubted benefit to existing local communities and enterprises, hydro-electric power stations have not, since 1943, proved powerful attractors of new economic developments in their immediate vicinity. Hydro-electric power fulfils a more important role in the electricity supply pattern of Scotland as a whole.

Thermal power stations are extremely inflexible in the sense that they cannot be rapidly switched on and off in response to fluctuating demand patterns. Since a hydro-electric power station can be run up to full production in a matter of minutes, and can equally quickly be shut down, it is particularly suited to satisfy short peak demands in an integrated electricity supply system (i.e. a grid fed by both thermal and hydro-electric power stations).

	South of Scotland Electricity Board Area			North of Scotland Hydro-electric Board Area		
	1961	1966/7	1974/5	1961	1966/7	1974/5
Nuclear	–	339	384	–	–	–
Other thermal	1,832	2,473	5,630	133	373	307
Hydro	123	123	124	884	1,347	1,752
Diesel	–	–	–	45	49	87
Total	1,955	2,934	6,138	1,062	1,769	2,146

Table 12.   Installed capacity of generating plant in Scotland 1961-75 (in Megawatts)

Source :   Scottish Abstract of Statistics

Since 1950, the new hydro-electric power stations in the Highlands have been increasingly designed to fulfil this role.   The Sloy power station on Loch Lomond for example was designed with only a ten per cent load factor.   This in effect meant that instead of a small installation designed to generate electricity continuously from the available water resources, a large installation was built on the assumption that it would concentrate electricity production from the available resources into only two and a half hours in each twenty four.   The opening of the Cruachan power station on Loch Awe in Argyllshire in 1965 marked a new phase in the use of hydro-electric power stations in an integrated electricity supply system.   The Cruachan power station, fitted with turbines which can be reversed and used as pumps, uses thermal electricity at off peak periods to pump water up into a small storage reservoir high above the power station.   This water is then used at peak demand periods to generate electricity. This pumped storage system removes the necessity for large

117

expensive high-level water catchment and reservoir
installations, a severe limiting factor to the introduction
of new conventional hydro-electric power stations in
Scotland.   As long as it remains economically viable
pumped storage offers the prospect of hydro-electric
generation at least maintaining its present share of the
expanding electricity generating capacity of Scotland.

THE WATER SUPPLY INFRASTRUCTURE

     Water is an essential requirement of human life and
of a wide range of human activities.   It is a commodity
with which Scotland is well endowed.   The natural rainfall of the country produces an average daily runoff of
about two hundred thousand megalitres of water, enough
to provide every inhabitant of Scotland with forty thousand
litres a day.   Since the daily per capita demand for water
is only just over four hundred litres there appears to be
a substantial excess of supply over demand.   However the
figures for the daily per capita demand are based on
domestic and industrial consumption of water, far from the
complete story of water use.
     A large part of the natural run-off is essential for
the maintenance of the natural water habitats and functioning of streams, rivers and lochs.   Such natural water
bodies also fulfil important functions for man, from
enhancement of the scenery through recreational usage to
flood control and sewage disposal.   Severe reductions of
river flows or loch levels would seriously limit the
effectiveness of these important functions of natural
water bodies.   Already the volume of sewage disposal
expected of Scottish rivers is excessive, especially in
the case of rivers like the Clyde which traverse densely
populated areas.   Severe pollution problems have resulted
most notably in the lower courses and estuaries of such
rivers.
     Other demands are made on water which only temporarily
remove water from the natural cycle.   The production of
hydro-electric power, the cooling and steam requirements
of thermal power stations and some industrial processes
and the maintenance of artificial (canal) water courses
all require large volumes of water on a temporary basis.
Water may be used many times over for such purposes, and

118

may even subsequently be purified for consumptive use.
Nevertheless these requirements must be met at any one
time from the total available water supply.

The water supply industry of Scotland is primarily
concerned with the satisfying of the domestic and industrial
demands for potable water.   In 1971 the total consumption
of potable water in Scotland was running at an average of
2085.0 megalitres per day.   A further 44.6 megalitres per
day of other water was also consumed, making a total daily
demand on the supply system of 2130.5 megalitres.   The
sources of supply from which this demand was met were
capable of a yield of 2,622.5 megalitres per day, a margin
of supply over demand of 492 megalitres per day.   Clearly
only a very small part of the total water available in
Scotland is tapped by the water supply industry.   Thus
although the demand on the industry is forecast to double
by the end of the century, no great overall problem of
water shortage is likely to emerge in the foreseeable
future (though new sources of supply will obviously have
to be developed.)

There are however likely to be, indeed there are
already, local problems of water shortage.   The location
of the main centres of consumption by no means coincides
with the main centres of supply.   As a result the construction of reservoirs in areas of high rainfall, linked
by pipeline to centres of population, is already a feature
of the water supply pattern of Scotland at all scales,
from the urban centre of Glasgow provided from Loch Katrine
forty miles away, to the isolated village fed from a small
reservoir in the local hills.   It is the lack of integration between the large and small local supply networks
which gives rise to the major supply problems.   Before
1968 responsibility for water supply was in the hands of a
multiplicity of local bodies who developed separate and
often quite small supply schemes.   Although by 1971 over
ninety-eight per cent of the population was connected to
a water supply system, some of the isolated systems depended
on limited reservoir or river catchment areas which tended
to run short of water in periods of drought.   Many of the
islands and areas in the east of the country have suffered
from such short term shortages with increasing frequency
since the mid-nineteen sixties as increasing demands have
been made on limited local supplies.   Even parts of the
wetter west, notably the lower Clyde area, have also

suffered temporary shortages. Unlike the electricity
network there is no national water grid by means of which
local shortages can be compensated with surplus supplies
from other areas, nor is such a national grid deemed
feasible or necessary. However inter-regional linkages
have become more common following the rationalisation of
the supply system which saw responsibility for water supply
given to thirteen large water board area authorities after
1968 and to the new first tier local authorities after
1975. The installation in the early nineteen seventies
of a master pipeline through to eastern Scotland from
Loch Lomond is a notable example of the more integrated
approach to water supply undertakings now emerging and
likely to become more common in future.

4 RURAL SCOTLAND by I. R. Bowler

Rural Scotland is passing through a period of rapid change owing to mounting pressures on the limited land surface, pressures which emanate from the urban population's increasing demands for food, timber, water, outdoor recreation and land for building. Fortunately, Scotland is better placed than other parts of the United Kingdom to absorb the effects of these demands, since only 2.8 per cent of its area is in urban use, compared with 11.5 per cent of England and Wales (Plate 7B). Nevertheless, two types of change in the use of rural land in Scotland can be recognised: change within existing land uses, such as alterations within agriculture from one type of production to another, and change in the amount of land allocated to different land users, such as the transfer of agricultural land to recreational use.

THE STRUCTURE OF LAND OWNERSHIP

In rural areas in particular the system under which the land is held is of great importance, since the individual, from crofter to laird, makes the decision on how the land is to be used. The land holding system of Scotland is peculiarly its own, being based on a modification of the feudal system. Norman feudalism was introduced to Scotland in the twelfth and thirteenth centuries and was grafted onto the traditional clan organisation. Under the feudal system the Sovereign is theoretically the source of all land rights in the kingdom, and crown vassals hold land from the Crown. Initially clan chiefs occupied this role, but through time the clan system has devolved to create a multiplicity of feudal superiors (landowners). Superiors can feu their land to sub-vassals or feuars, who continue to pay feu duty to

121

their superiors. These feuars are permitted however to sell or lease their lands on terms that do not conflict with their feu-charters. Nevertheless, powers of direction can be used by superiors over the land-use decisions of their feuars, and consequently the influence of large land-owners is more pervasive than in England and Wales.

The pattern of land holding that has evolved has produced a ragged mosaic of boundaries of estates, forestry plots and individual farms. Nevertheless it is possible to recognise three major categories of landowner, although they disguise an underlying complexity in the landholding system. The categories are estate owners (lairds), owner-occupiers and the State, each category varying in its spatial distribution.

Estate owners

Large estates are found throughout Scotland, but are characteristic of both the west Highlands, and the lowland areas of Fife and the Lothians. Estate owners can be individuals or limited companies, and in the former case it is usual for land to be handed down within families for generations. Extensive areas of Scotland are held in private ownership in this way, for example by the Duke of Buccleuch (200,000 ha), the Duke of Sutherland (100,000 ha), the Countess of Seafield (86,400 ha) and Lord Lovat (80,000 ha). However, private estate owners are giving way to limited companies. In part this reflects the purchase of blocks of land by industrial and property companies as a hedge against inflation, or as a method of avoiding certain tax liabilities. In part too it reflects the efforts of individuals to avoid the full weight of death duties by forming limited companies out of their assets.

Fragmentation of estates is also progressing under the pressure of tax demands, with owners feuing land between farming, forestry and sporting interests. One consequence of fragmentation has been the steady decrease since 1950 in the proportion of farms and land held under tenancy agreements. Tenanted farms have been either feued to sitting tenants, amalgamated with other holdings at the conclusion of a tenancy, or taken in hand to enlarge the estate farm. Although changes in the basis of enumeration make comparison through time problematic,

122

the agricultural census data reveal a decrease in the proportion of tenanted holdings from 73 per cent to 50 per cent between 1951 and 1974. A lower proportion of the land area is held by tenant farmers, but it declined by a similar amount over the same period, to 42 per cent in 1974. In England and Wales a much lower proportion of holdings are tenanted (35 per cent in 1974).

A distinction must be drawn within this category of tenant farmers however, between crofters and non-crofters. Broadly speaking, a crofter is the tenant of a holding in the seven Crofting Counties (Argyll, Inverness, Ross and Cromarty, Sutherland, Caithness, Orkney and Zetland), of less than twenty hectares of arable land and/or less than £50 annual rent. While rented small-holdings are present in all parts of Scotland, they have been recognised as a special case only in the north west Highlands and Islands. Crofts are registered with the Crofters Commission, which conveys security of tenure and rights of common pasture to the occupier. Forty per cent of registered crofts are on the mainland, 45 per cent on the Islands and 15 per cent on Shetland. The number of crofts declined by only 7.5 per cent between 1959 and 1972, so that they still remain a significant element in the land-holding structure of the Crofting Counties. Other tenanted holdings are particularly characteristic of the Lothians, Angus and Morayshire where large estates are located.

Owner-occupiers

The distribution of owner-occupied farm holdings is the inverse of tenanted holdings (Fig 20), the highest proportions being in the counties of Kirkcudbright, Lanark and Kinross. However, owner-occupation may refer to a large home farm or an estate, so blurring the distinction between estate owners and owner-occupiers. Nevertheless, owner-occupiers have a greater freedom of action in farming than tenants and are not dependent upon estate owners for the provision of fixed equipment such as buildings, or for other farm improvements.

Production co-operatives comprise a growing, but still restricted form of land holding. The resources of several holdings are combined, either wholly or in part, with a view to reducing the costs of producing certain agricultural

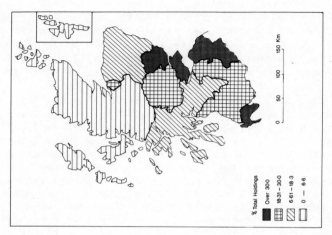

% Total Holdings
Over 66·9
49·11 – 66·9
31·31 – 49·1
0 – 31·3

a.   Owned holdings

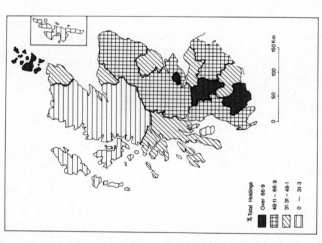

% Total Holdings
Over 300
18·31 – 30·0
6·61 – 18·3
0 – 6·6

b.   Large holdings (over 1200 SMD)

Figure 20.   Ownership and size of landholdings 1971

commodities.   Co-operatives have been formed under the
stimulus of Government grant aid mainly in the east of
Scotland in the arable farming areas of Aberdeen and
Angus.   Most groups have been concerned with the joint
production of potatoes, sugar beet, cattle or grass.

The State

The State has become a major landowner in Scotland,
holding over 950,000 ha through bodies such as the Forestry
Commission, the Department of Agriculture and Fisheries for
Scotland (DAFS), the Nature Conservancy and the Ministry
of Defence.   The Forestry Commission was established by
the Forestry Act of 1919, and has subsequently purchased
over 460,000 ha on the open market to build up reserves
of timber.   Forestry Commission land is widespread, but
with concentrations in south-west Scotland, Argyll and
the north-west Highlands (Fig 24).

The Department of Agriculture and Fisheries for
Scotland by contrast inherited its commitment through the
land settlement estates created by the former Congested
Districts Board between 1897 and 1912 and through land
acquired by the Secretary of State under the Small Land-
holders Acts 1886-1931, and the Land Settlement Acts
1919-34.   The DAFS is also responsible for managing land
owned by the Forestry Commission which is either unplantable,
or is pending planting.   86.3 per cent of the total land
under management is leased, nearly 50 per cent as crofts in
the Highlands.

The Nature Conservancy and the Ministry of Defence are
also large landowners, and together control nearly 38,000 ha.
The estates of the Nature Conservancy have been purchased
since 1949, and are distributed throughout the Highlands
(Fig 26).   Ministry of Defence lands are more widely dispersed, serving as training areas for personnel and as air
and sea bases.   A number of other State bodies also hold
land, such as British Rail, the National Coal Board, the
Water Boards and the British Airports Authority.   They
exercise a localised rather than a general influence on
land use changes in rural Scotland.

AGRICULTURE

The size of farms

The distribution of farms of different sizes is
highly variable within Scotland and is a factor that has
considerable bearing on changes in the agricultural sector.
There are approximately 38,000 agricultural units although
73 per cent of the agricultural area is farmed by only 12
per cent of the holdings. The concentration of land in
large units is more exaggerated than in England and Wales,
but the considerable areas of rough grazing attached to
many farms in Scotland overemphasises the difference.
With rough grazing discounted, the dominance of large farms
is reduced, but not eliminated.

Large farms are found throughout Scotland, but are
most prevalent in the east of Scotland on the lowland
areas from Berwick to Angus, and along the coastlands of
the Moray Firth (Fig 20, Table 13). These areas were
amongst the first to experience the full impact of the
Improvement Movement between 1750 and 1850, during which
landowners reorganised their estates to form commercial
rather than subsistence farming units. The traditional
joint- or multiple-tenancy farms were swept away and
replaced by single farms, individually tenanted and dispersed among a pattern of rectangular fields. The present
pattern of farm and field boundaries date in large part
from this era, when the agricultural landscape of much of
Scotland was virtually remade.

Small farms are numerically dominant, so that agriculture is characterised by small units of production. A
considerable proportion are part-time holdings, being
occupied either by retired farmers or by those with
ancillary forms of employment. Their distribution
exhibits a distinct clustering in the north-west Highlands
and, to a lesser extent, in north-east Scotland (Table 13).
The majority of smallholdings are tenanted and have been
created by three separate processes. Firstly, joint-farms,
and tacksman's farms with sub-tenants, were let as
commercial farms early in the eighteenth century. The
displaced tenants were settled by the landowner, either on
small-holdings or in planned villages, or they became
squatters at the moorland edge. Those that left

126

agriculture found employment in the growing industrial
towns.   Secondly, crofting townships were created in
the Highlands by landowners to resettle the displaced
tenants of joint-farms during the Improvement Movement.
The reorganisation of agriculture was retarded in the
Highlands by remoteness and the continuation of the clan
system, while the character of the Improvement Movement
underwent changes. ✓

Region[b]	0-275 SMD[a]	276-600 SMD	601-1200 SMD	above 1200 SMD	Total Holdings
Highlands	81.4	9.2	5.8	3.6	9,909
North east	43.1	28.8	18.9	9.2	11,134
East central	22.3	21.3	25.8	30.6	4,790
South east	26.7	18.3	24.4	30.6	3,056
South west	26.7	21.2	31.7	20.4	9,171
Scotland	45.2	20.1	19.9	14.8	38,060

a.   SMD or Standard Man Days are the annual requirements of
     normal labour for the normal production of the unit. Less
     than 275 SMD indicates part-time holdings, while more than
     1200 SMD indicates commercial holdings.
b.   Highlands: Argyll[c], Inverness[c], Ross & Cromarty[c],
                   Sutherland[c], Zetland[c].
     North east: Aberdeen, Banff, Caithness[c], Kincardine,
                   Moray, Nairn, Orkney[c].
     East central: Angus, Clackmannan, Fife, Kinross, Perth.
     South east: Berwick, East Mid and West Lothian, Peebles,
                   Roxburgh, Selkirk.
     South west: Ayr, Bute, Dumfries, Dunbarton, Kirkcudbright,
                   Lanark, Renfrew, Stirling, Wigtown.
c.   Crofting counties.

Table 13.   Business size of farms in Scotland
             by region 1971
             (percentage of holdings in each region)
Source :   D.A.F.S. Agricultural Statistics

The earlier evolutionary disbandment of joint-farms became
increasingly revolutionary in nature, culminating in the
Highland Clearances of the early nineteenth century.   In
the Highlands enclosure was used to create extensive,
commercial holdings for sheep farming, and tenants of
joint-farms were resettled in small unenclosed crofts,

either on patches of arable land in the glens, or in coastal areas. (Plate 9). Common grazings were attached to each of the new crofting townships. Enclosure in the Highlands was further complicated by the rising population of the late eighteenth century and by the lack of alternative employment for the displaced population. Crofts, therefore, were envisaged at the outset as part-time holdings, to be supplemented by employment in activities such as fishing. Enclosure policy varied between estates, so that the distribution of land ownership was crucial to the detailed pattern of land settlement that emerged. Finally, statutory small-holdings were created through the land resettlement schemes of the Congested Districts Board and the DAFS as previously described.

Farm size structure is changing slowly however, through the gradual amalgamation of small farms into larger units. Small farms are unable to provide a sufficient livelihood for their occupiers owing to relatively high production costs and the absence of the economies of scale available to larger farms. Changes in the basis of the agricultural census makes measurement problematic, but an annual reduction in the number of full-time farms of just under one per cent is accepted as a rough estimate. The rate of change has accelerated in recent years, and is highest amongst the smallest holdings. Only farms larger than 120 hectares (crops and grass) in size have shown a net increase in their number over the past two decades. The rate of change is greatest for tenant farms, since landowners are able to effect amalgamations at the conclusion of tenancies. Between 1962 and 1968 the mean size of tenanted holdings increased by 12.5 per cent, while that of owner-occupied holdings increased by only 1.6 per cent.

Farm size structure has been subject to Government legislation for nearly a century, although historically such legislation has tended to preserve the distribution of small-holdings. The original Crofters Holdings Act of 1886 for example gave legislative protection to crofters. Subsequent legislation removed many of the problems of arbitrary eviction, rack-renting and compensation for improvements made to the croft, but did nothing to solve the long-term problem of the small size of the holdings. Structural change has been inhibited by the insistence of crofters on their rights of tenure, even when absent

from the croft, and by the essentially communal nature of
the township system whereby a conservative minority can
obstruct the proposals of a progressive majority.   The
rigid structure of crofting has proved resistant even to
the efforts of the Crofters Commission in amalgamating
holdings.   The 1973 Crofting Reform (Scotland) Bill
aimed to enable crofters to become owner-occupiers and
was designed, in part, to allow the freer interchange
of land between individuals.   In addition, the informal
combination of crofts, illegal before 1961, has reduced
the 18,320 registered holdings to 15,443 working units.

Small farms have been maintained also by the provision
of grants and subsidies under the 1959 Agriculture (Small
Farms) Act.   Holdings of between 8 and 40 hectares, and
between 275 and 500 SMD have been eligible for assistance
in becoming properly equipped and stocked.   Working
capital and supplements to existing field husbandry grants
were offered until 1970, although they continued the
existence of basically uneconomic holdings.

More recently, Government policy has been reorientated
to encourage a more rapid rate of farm amalgamation.   Grants
were made available under the 1967 Agriculture Act to assist
with the costs of amalgamation schemes, while annuities or
lump sums were provided for farmers who permitted their
holdings to be amalgamated.   However, only 288 amalgamation
schemes had been approved in Scotland by 1972, and little
impact has been made on the rate of farm amalgamation.

Types of farm

Agriculture remains Scotland's largest single industry,
although it exhibits considerable internal diversity.   Nine
basic types of farm can be recognised: hill sheep; upland
(cattle and sheep); rearing with arable; rearing with
intensive livestock; arable, rearing and feeding; cropping;
dairying; intensive (livestock or horticulture); and
crofting.   Individual types of farm predominate in certain
regions, although every region contains the full range of
farm types (Fig 21, Table 14).   In general, regional
variations in type of farming result from the interaction
between the physical environment in the form of topography,
climate and soil, and economic factors such as commodity
prices, production costs and distance from markets.

Within each region, inter-farm differences generally reflect variations in the size of holding, and characteristics such as the age of the occupier, the type of tenure, and whether or not the farm is a full-time holding. (Plate 7A).

	1	2	3	4	5	6	7	8
Highlands	23.0	35.2	12.6	1.2	3.8	7.8	14.4	2.0
North east	0.3	23.9	33.9	6.1	10.1	13.3	8.2	4.2
East central	4.7	13.2	7.9	1.3	4.5	45.6	10.4	12.4
South east	7.4	22.4	14.7	1.9	4.6	27.3	11.6	10.1
South west	5.7	27.3	4.7	1.2	1.0	2.8	50.5	6.8
Scotland	5.6	24.0	16.1	2.8	5.1	16.6	22.9	6.9
Percentage of total area	41.5	30.4	6.9	1.1	2.0	7.9	9.6	0.6
Percentage of crops and grass area	2.3	23.1	16.7	2.2	5.8	24.3	23.9	1.7

1. Hill sheep: 2. Upland: 3. Rearing with arable: 4. Rearing with intensive livestock: 5. Arable rearing and feeding: 6. Cropping: 7. Dairying: 8. Intensive.

Table 14.   Distribution of farm type in Scotland by region 1971 (percentage of full-time holdings in each region)

Source :   D.A.F.S. Agricultural Statistics

Scottish agriculture is dominated by the production of livestock and livestock products to a greater degree than is the rest of the United Kingdom. The two categories together account for nearly 80 per cent of the value of agricultural output. Indeed, the contribution made by fatstock, especially fat cattle and calves, has tended to increase through time at the expense of farm crops and other livestock products. The increasing value of output has lagged marginally behind the United Kingdom as a whole; thus Scotland contributed approximately 11.1 per cent to the total output of the United Kingdom in 1971, compared with 12.2 per cent in 1951.

Hill sheep farming.

Hill sheep farming is practised on 5.6 per cent of

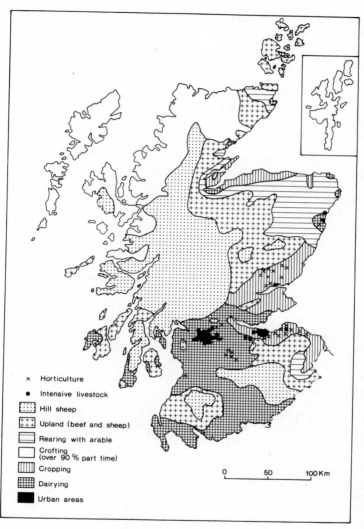

Horticulture
Intensive livestock
Hill sheep
Upland (beef and sheep)
Rearing with arable
Crofting (over 90 % part time)
Cropping
Dairying
Urban areas

0   50   100 Km

Figure 21.   Type of farming

131

full-time holdings, and yet occupies 42 per cent of the agricultural area (Table 14). Such extensive farming is associated with the highest and poorest land and, apart from forestry, is the most economic use of most hill areas. Although hill sheep farms are found throughout Scotland, they are most prevalent in the Highlands. High rainfall and windspeeds combine with low temperatures, a short growing season and acid soils to produce a pattern of land use dominated by rough grazing. Improved pasture and tillage together account for less than two per cent of the total area under hill sheep farming. Oats is the major crop, although rape is grown where fields are sufficiently sheltered (Table 15).

Breeding ewes in pure-bred, self-maintained flocks form the major enterprise. In the Highlands and south-west Scotland the small but hardy Scottish Blackface breed predominates. On the grass moorlands of south-east Scotland and in Caithness by contrast, the Cheviot breed is more numerous and has become slightly more popular during the past twenty years. Output from the flocks is comprised of wool, store ewe lambs, wether (male) lambs and draft ewes.

Beef breeding is the main subsidiary enterprise using hardy breeds such as the West Highland and Beef Shorthorn crosses, but with the Galloway breed popular in the Southern Uplands. Beef breeding has experienced a revival in recent years after a long period when cattle were a declining element in hill farming. All other enterprises are relatively insignificant, since the cost of producing animal feed does not warrant the fattening of lambs or cattle on a large scale.

The output per hectare of hill land has remained low, and an above average number of hill sheep farms have small business sizes, despite occupying a large area of land. The low volume of output is caused by the poor stocking capacities of the rough grazing that dominates land use. Between four and six hectares of heather and sedge-grass moorland in the Highlands are required to support one ewe and her lamb, while comparable figures for the agrostis-fescue pastures of the Border uplands are 0.8 to 1.2 hectares. The limited area of improved inbye land around the farmstead thus assumes critical importance in the operation of hill sheep farms. It is the source of winter

132

Type of farm[a]	Percentage crops, grass and rough grazing			Percentage tillage						Number of holdings
	Rough grazing	Pasture	Tillage	Wheat	Barley	Oats	Turnips & Swedes	Potatoes	Other	
1	98.3	1.6	0.1	0	7.2	29.0	11.9	2.5	49.4	1,213
2	77.2	19.3	3.5	0.3	27.8	40.3	17.2	0.9	13.5	5,179
3	26.9	45.9	27.2	2.6	50.3	26.4	14.8	2.3	3.6	3,466
4	37.2	34.7	28.1	0.04	68.1	14.2	8.3	2.9	6.5	610
5	11.3	44.0	44.7	6.0	53.2	22.2	11.7	4.4	2.5	1,103
6	8.1	29.9	62.0	10.1	58.2	9.9	5.7	10.6	5.5	3,590
7	25.4	56.4	18.2	4.0	61.3	14.9	8.7	5.0	6.1	4,943
8	13.9	33.7	52.4	5.3	46.4	3.5	1.7	5.9	37.2	1,482
Total full time holdings	69.9	18.9	11.2	6.3	53.7	17.4	9.3	6.5	6.8	21,586
Total part time holdings	77.8	17.9	4.3	0.9	30.1	45.2	10.6	5.3	7.9	16,474

a.   See Table 14.

Table 15:   Land use in Scotland by type of farm 1971
Source :   D.A.F.S. Agricultural Statistics

feed for the younger breeding ewes, and for the cattle of the subsidiary beef breeding enterprise. The limited extent of inbye land, however, forces between 62 and 73 per cent of farmers to away-winter their young ewes on lowland farms.

The product prices received by hill sheep farmers are dependent on the demand from farms at lower altitudes for store lambs and draft ewes owing to the vertically integrated nature of sheep production in Britain. Upland farms take pure-bred draft ewes for cross-breeding, and store lambs for fattening. The returns to sheep farming on lower land have been depressed for many years, and product prices on hill sheep farms have been similarly effected. Direct Government grants on hill sheep, hill cows, winter keep, farm buildings and amenities have been provided for decades in order to supplement incomes. To-day they form the net income of most hill sheep farms (Table 16). Rising production costs pose a further problem, particularly with the high proportion of costs attributable to farm labour.

A solution to the problem of low income has been sought by increasing the output of hill sheep farms, and it has required changes in land use within agriculture. A persistent problem of hill areas has been the selective grazing of sheep which tends to eliminate the palatable species from the rough grazing. The ranker grasses, such as nardus and molinia, are encouraged, so that rotational moor burning is required to remove the unwanted herbage. The overall carrying capacity of the hills has declined in the long-term as a result of this practice, while the problem has been exacerbated by the lower stocking densities of cattle which previously grazed off the coarser grasses. Improvement of the lower rough grazing and inbye land therefore has been encouraged by Government grant aid on items such as drainage, ploughing, liming and reseeding.

Improvement to pastures has been allied to changes in stock and pasture management practices. Supplementary feeding of concentrates to ewes has been introduced to improve lambing rates, together with controlled mating with quality rams. An increasing proportion of store lambs are fattened off the improved pastures, while controlled grazing through fencing has ensured the more efficient use of available pasture. In addition, more

134

frequent use has been made of cattle to graze off the
rank grasses on accessible rough grazing.   The lower hill
land therefore has become of increasing importance,
particularly with the trend to overwintering the ewe flock
on the home farm in preference to away-wintering.

SMD Group [a]	Type of farm [b]						
	1	2	3	4	5	6	7
250 - 599	1,168	1,461	1,799	2,095	958	1,176	1,187
600 -1199	1,681	2,585	2,146)	4,048	2,019	2,536	2,255
Above 1199	2,973	2,936	4,665)		3,221	5,621	5,027
Direct Government grant as percentage of net farm income	126	112	58	18	34	NA	11

a.   See Table 13.   b.   See Table 14.

Table 16.   Average net income per holding in Scotland
              by type and size of farm 1970/71 (£'s)

Source :   Scottish Agricultural Economics 1973

Upland farming

        Upland farming occupies an irregular band of lower
hill land at altitudes between 150 and 300 metres.   It
is the most prevalent type of farming in Scotland and is
the dominant type in the central Highlands and Orkney
(Fig 21).   A greater proportion of farmland is in pasture
and tillage compared with hill sheep farms, although rough
grazing again forms the major land use (Table 15).   Crops
of oats, barley and rape are consumed by stock on the farm
as winter feed.
        Sheep remain the major enterprise although cross-bred
store lambs are produced.   Rams of the long-wool breeds,
such as the Border Leicester, are crossed with pure-bred
Blackface or Cheviot ewes.   The progeny are termed Greyface and Halfbred sheep respectively, and are associated
with higher lambing rates and greater productivity per
ewe and per hectare.   A proportion of store lambs are
fattened off turnips or rape to produce higher net farm

135

incomes than experienced on hill sheep farms (Table 16).
However, more emphasis is placed on the breeding and
rearing of beef stores (cattle sold for fattening at
about 18 months) than on higher land.   Aberdeen-Angus
and Beef Shorthorn breeding herds predominate on better
land, but earlier-maturing cross-bred stores are produced
for fattening on lowland farms.   The average size of herd
is 23 cows, reaching a maximum of 43 cows in south-east
Scotland.

Direct Government grants provide the net income of
most Upland farms (Table 16), and again increases in output have been sought as a solution to the problem of low
incomes.   Higher stocking densities of beef cows have
been made possible by improvements to hill pastures, a
trend stimulated by the Hill Cow subsidy.   Much of the
pasture improvement has been carried out on middle-hill
land using Government grants.   At the same time, however,
bracken incursions into the rough grazing and upper
pastures has reduced their carrying capacity, particularly
in the south-west Highlands and on the Galloway hills.

Rearing with arable farming

North-east Scotland has a system of farming which
closely integrates animal and crop production.   The
system exploits the area's capacity to produce crops
which historically distance has made difficult to market.
Crops are converted into livestock which are then
slaughtered for sale.   The system is locally important
also in the upper Tweed Valley, in Caithness and Orkney
(Fig 21).

Cattle are reared and fattened off grass in the summer,
and off barley, hay or silage in yards during the winter.
Turnips and oats previously filled this role, but they have
been replaced by barley with its higher feeding value.   A
proportion of the store cattle originate in local breeding
herds but the remainder are purchased as stores either
from Ireland, or from hill farms throughout Scotland.
Most of the cattle are crossbreeds rather than pure-bred
stock.   42 per cent of fat cattle slaughtered in Scotland
are produced in the north-east region.

Crossbred ewes are also purchased and crossed with
Suffolk rams to produce a heavier store lamb for fattening.

136

It is the third stage in the vertically integrated or stratified system of sheep production, since it utilises ewes produced by Upland farms. Additional Greyface store lambs are purchased through market centres such as Oban, Inverness, Stirling, Lanark and Newton Stewart. For Halfbred store lambs favoured markets are Thurso, Lairg, Inverness and Dingwall. Store lambs are fattened off rape, turnips or grass.

The land use pattern reflects the system of farming. A regular cropping rotation is practiced, often with oats, roots and barley followed by a 3-4 year grass ley. 46 per cent of the area under rearing with arable farming is pasture, the majority being rotational grasses. The systematic renewal of grassland enables high stocking densities of sheep and cattle to be maintained. Half the tillage area is under barley, while turnips and swedes are also important elements of land use (Table 15).

Rearing with intensive livestock, and arable rearing and feeding farming.

Rearing with intensive livestock farms, and arable rearing and feeding farms are located intermittently throughout north-east Scotland and the Tweed Valley. The former farm type is associated with smaller holdings which produce pigs and poultry. Livestock production takes place in buildings, so that the tillage area is predominantly in barley. The latter farm type has a considerable proportion of its area in crops, the surplus to feeding requirements being sold off the farm.

Crop farming

Cropping farms comprise 17 per cent of all holdings in Scotland and 24 per cent of the area in crops and grass. They predominate in the lowland areas of east-central Scotland around the Firths of Moray, Tay and Forth, and in the lower Tweed Valley (Fig 21). Cropping farms occupy the most favourable agricultural land in Scotland and are characterised by their large size and favourable net incomes (Table 16).

The majority of land is in tillage, producing cash crops such as wheat, potatoes and barley. Nearly half

137

of Scotland's barley crop originates on these farms, while
they are the major source also of seed potatoes for export
to England, South Africa, Spain and Cyprus. Sugar beet,
once of local importance in Fifeshire, is no longer grown
in quantity owing to the closure of the sugar beet factory
at Cupar in 1972. However, canning and quick-freezing
factories have been established in the areas of crop farming during the 1960s, and their location is now an
important factor in the distribution of crops such as peas,
carrots and beetroot. Such is the scale of operation,
however, that many crops are concentrated in the hands of
a few producers under contract to a processing factory.
For example, 89 per cent of pea production is in the hands
of sixty-eight producers. Many crops now require
specialised, expensive machinery for their production, and
only large producers have the resources to invest in items
such as mobile pea viners and web-type carrot and beetroot
harvesters. Hedges and fences have been removed to
provide the large fields needed for economic use of the new
machinery, and this has had important consequences both
for the landscape of lowland areas and for wildlife.

Nevertheless the majority of cropping farms have
subsidiary cattle or sheep fattening enterprises at some
time of the year. Sheep occupy the areas of rotational
grass in the summer months, so that Half-bred ewe flocks
are characteristic of the Lothians and the Tweed Basin.
The fattening of beef stores in yards uses surplus crops
during the winter.

Dairy farming

Until the twentieth century, the Scottish dairy
industry was principally a farm-cheese economy, with
liquid milk produced only near the major towns to satisfy
local demand. However foreign competition in the butter
and cheese markets, a rising demand for liquid milk in
the urban centres, and the operation of milk marketing
boards after 1933, led to the present day emphasis on
liquid milk production. The milk marketing boards
reduce the problem of distance to market by charging a
uniform transport rate over zones of varying width,
measured from the main markets. A flat rate is payable
by producers in Orkney and the islands of Argyllshire,

138

while rates taper with distance from markets for other producers. The distribution of dairy farms, therefore, is more widespread than might be expected. In addition, milk processing factories have been established in remoter areas to absorb production that is surplus to the demand for liquid milk. They are located mainly in south-west and north-east Scotland (Fig 23).

Dairying remains the traditional type of farming in south-west Scotland where it is practised on 51 per cent of holdings (Fig 21, Table 14). The mild winters and moderate rainfall favour the production of grass rather than crops, and permanent pasture is the dominant land use. The limited tillage area is in barley for use as feed on the farm. However increasing use has been made of grass silage as winter feed to combat the problem of hay-making in the moist climate. Dairying is locally important to the west of Edinburgh, where it merges with crop farming, and in the vicinity of the larger settlements in the north and north east of Scotland.

There are few major subsidiary enterprises with dairying, although poultry, potatoes or sheep can be of importance on individual farms. Seed and early potatoes for example are produced on the sandy soils of raised beaches in Ayrshire and Wigtownshire. However, dairy farming has been traditionally dissociated from beef production in Scotland, both as an enterprise and as the source of beef calves. In England and Wales 66 per cent of beef animals originate in the dairy herd, whereas in Scotland the figure is approximately 33 per cent. In part this stems from the dominance of the Ayrshire breed of cow in Scotland. The breed was developed for milk production, and does not give a good beef calf. More recently however, dual-purpose Friesian cows have become more popular with the development of subsidiary beef enterprises on dairy farms.

Intensive farming

Intensive farming includes horticultural, pig and poultry production. It has a limited extent and is generally practised on small but highly capitalised holdings. Horticulture is highly localised in the upper Clyde Valley, the Lothians, Strathmore and the Carse of Gowrie. This distribution was determined in the nineteenth century

and has not altered materially in recent decades. The
largest concentration of glasshouses in Scotland developed
in the shelter of the Clyde Valley around Lanark although
the area under glass is now in decline. Historically,
the Clyde Valley supplied the urban markets of the Central
Lowlands with a variety of horticultural products but with
the increased efficiency of national marketing this is no
longer a locational factor. Indoor production now
specialises in tomatoes, although crops of cut-flowers and
lettuce are grown both under glass and outdoors. Glass-
house crops account for approximately 30 per cent of the
value of Scottish horticultural production.

Musselburgh is the centre of the Lothians horticultural
area, traditionally supplying Edinburgh with perishable
crops. Today production is concentrated on outdoor
vegetables, their growth being favoured by low rainfall,
high sunshine hours and a low incidence of late frosts.
A wide variety of crops is grown in the open, including
cabbage, brussels sprouts, beetroot, leeks and lettuce.
Although the total range of crops is smaller than in
England and Wales, the area under vegetables has increased
in recent years. Favourable conditions in Strathmore and
the Carse of Gowrie have permitted the development of soft
fruit production in the form of raspberries, strawberries
and blackcurrants. Their combined value exceeds that of
vegetable production, while 85 per cent of the United
Kingdom's raspberry production comes from Scotland. Raspberries are grown on large farms however, and 54 per cent
of the crop is in lots greater than 12 hectares in size.
Processing of the crop for jam is carried out in centres
such as Dundee, Forfar and Montrose. The majority of
the strawberry crop is also located in the counties of
Angus and Perth, and being later than the English crop,
a large proportion can be marketed fresh.

Intensive pig units are found to the north and east
of Glasgow, although major concentrations occur in
Aberdeenshire and Midlothian too. Poultry are less
frequently found as subsidiary enterprises than formerly,
while specialised battery units with over 100,000 birds
are becoming more prevalent. The major concentrations
of poultry are in the counties of Fife, Kinross and West-
lothian, although egg production is an important element
in the agricultural output of Orkney.

Crofting

Attention has been drawn already to the distribution
of small, tenanted crofts on the north-west coast of
Scotland and on the Islands. Crofting is a modified
survival of the original farming system, contributing only
7 per cent of the total value of Scottish agricultural output, but supporting 40 per cent of the rural population of
the Crofting counties. It continues to present a very
special and somewhat intractable problem. Fundamentally,
most crofts are too small to exist as viable farming units
and only 3 per cent are of a size in excess of 275 SMD,
thus emphasising their part-time nature (Plate 8A). Supplementary employment is found in forestry, weaving, road
maintenance, and local services such as shops and the Post
Office.

Poor soils, high winds and rainfall limit both the
extent of arable land and the range of crops that can be
grown. Rough grazing is the major land use and 2.2 million
hectares are held in common by townships. The division
of the common grazing into soumings (grazing rights) is no
longer so precisely implemented as in the past, but it
remains an important factor in the operation of the croft.
The fragmented areas of enclosed arable land are used to
produce animal feed, mainly oats or hay, while small areas
of potatoes are grown for consumption by the crofter. The
tillage area has contracted by 32 per cent since 1960 with
the gradual changeover to grassland farming. The Crofters
Cropping Scheme has fostered this trend by providing subsidies for the conservation of grass for winter keep.

The major enterprises are the breeding of beef and
sheep stores for sale to mainland fatteners. Stock are
kept on the common grazing, and Scottish Blackface sheep
have been used increasingly at the expense of beef cattle.
Only where croft size is larger, as on Tiree and North
Uist, have beef cattle numbers increased. Marketing of
the livestock remains a major problem, while inaccessibility
and the poverty of natural resources serve to depress the
returns from farming. The absence of alternative employment has perpetuated the outmigration characteristic of
the Crofting Counties, so that 20 per cent of crofters are
absentees. Consequently pastures have become infested
by bracken, heather and gorse through neglect and the
tillage area has continued to decline. Recently, encouragement has been given to the non-agricultural use of crofting

land.   Between 1965 and 1969 for example, 2080 hectares of
crofting land was transferred to forestry use.

Regional agricultural trends

        Crop and livestock patterns within Scotland reflect
variations in the distribution of farm types (Figs 22 and
23).   Wheat, for example, is concentrated in the cropping
areas of east-central and south-east Scotland, potatoes
are characteristic of land use in the counties of Perth,
Angus, Kincardine and Fife, rotation grass is most prevalent
in north-east Scotland, and dairy cows are concentrated in
south-west Scotland.   However, barley is widely distributed,
reflecting its value as a source of animal feed on many types
of farm, and beef breeding cows are similarly dispersed
throughout Scotland.   However, the relatively limited area
of crops and grass in the Highlands exaggerates the density
of beef cows.
        Scottish agriculture has continued to change over the
past two decades in response to technological developments,
market forces and government policy.   Several of the
changes have been described already, but Table 17 summarises
the broad trends for the major crop and livestock enterprises.   Two groups of trends can be recognised: increasing
crop areas and livestock numbers, and stable or decreasing
crop areas and livestock numbers.   Barley, wheat, pigs and
beef cattle fall into the first group.   Barley, with an
increase of over 300 per cent between 1951 and 1971, has
experienced the same rapid expansion in area and output as
in England and Wales.   It has replaced oats as the main
feed grain owing to its superior yield, suitability for
combining, and higher feeding value.   Breeding, store and
fat beef cattle numbers have also expanded between 1951
and 1971, young cattle by 245 per cent.
        Breeding ewes, dairy cows, poultry, oats, rotation
grasses, potatoes, turnips and swedes form the group with
stable or decreasing crop areas and livestock numbers.
Breeding ewes increased in number between 1951 and 1965-66,
but then declined substantially in the face of falling
relative profitability.   The extent of rotation grass
contracted after 1963, following the trend in Scotland to
longer leys and a smaller tillage area.   The trend is
reflected in the falling contribution of farm crops to
the total agricultural output of Scotland.   Dairy cows

142

decreased in number by 12 per cent between 1957 and 1971 as producers moved into beef production. The profitability of beef rose following increases in guaranteed prices and in the hill and beef cow subsidies.

	Figure as a percentage of 1951 figures				Coefficient of localisation[a]	
	1956	1961	1966	1971	1961	1971
Increasing crop areas and livestock numbers						
Barley	106	173	361	416	0.30	0.22
Wheat	113	135	94	129	0.43	0.41
Beef cows[b]	-	139	169	209	0.24	0.19
Male cattle 1-2 years	133	189	188	208	0.18	0.16
Male cattle under 1 year	143	220	301	345	0.14	0.10
Sows & gilts in pig	106	111	109	151	0.19	0.28[c]
Stable or decreasing crop areas and livestock numbers						
Oats	91	70	44	31	0.15	0.19
Turnips & swedes	96	83	61	49	0.19	0.23
Potatoes	94	79	71	57	0.36	0.38[c]
Dairy cows[b]	-	99	92	88	0.38	0.41
Breeding ewes	104	117	117	102	0.32	0.34
Fowls	92	93	90	97[c]	0.21	0.29[c]
Rotation grass[d]	-	106	104	90	0.06	0.09
Tillage	95	88	87	85	0.16	0.20

a. As the coefficient approaches zero it indicates an even spread throughout Scotland; as it approaches unity it indicates a spatially concentrated distribution. (see Chisholm M. Rural settlement and land use p. 93 (1962) Hutchinson.
b. As a percentage of 1957 figures.   c.   1969.
d. As a percentage of 1959 figures.

Table 17.   Agricultural trends in Scotland 1951-71
Source :   D.A.F.S. Agricultural Statistics

These aggregate trends have not acted uniformly within Scotland (Figs 22 and 23). Regions have varied in the relative rates of increase and decrease in the area under crops and livestock numbers. A coefficient of localization can be used to summarise changes in the relative distribution of individual enterprises (Table 17). By comparing the coefficients for 1961 and 1971, an indication is given of the degree of change in the spatial concentration

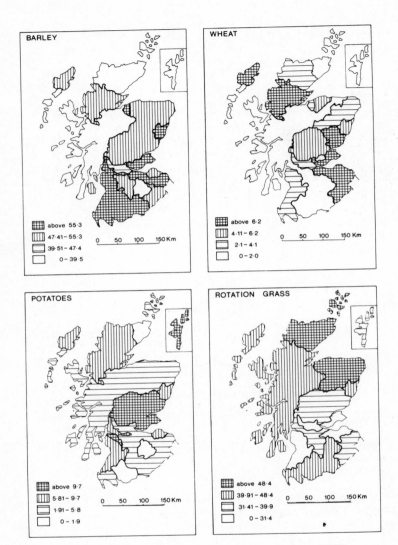

Figure 22A.   Land under various crops 1971
(percentages of tilled land)

144

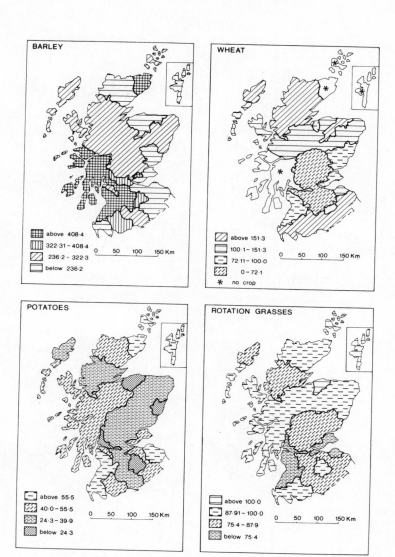

Figure 22B. Changes in crop areas 1961-71 (1971 figures expressed as a percentage of 1961 figures)

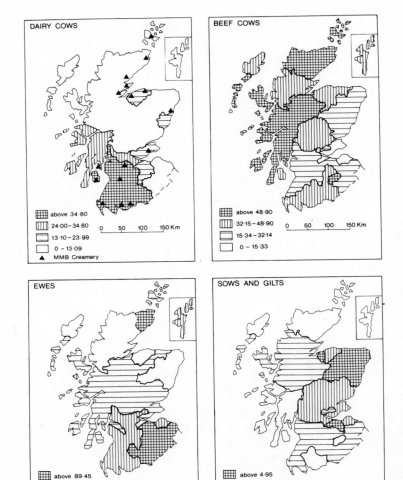

Figure 23A.   Distribution of livestock 1971
(Numbers per 100 ha of crops and
grass, crops and rough grazing in the
case of ewes)

146

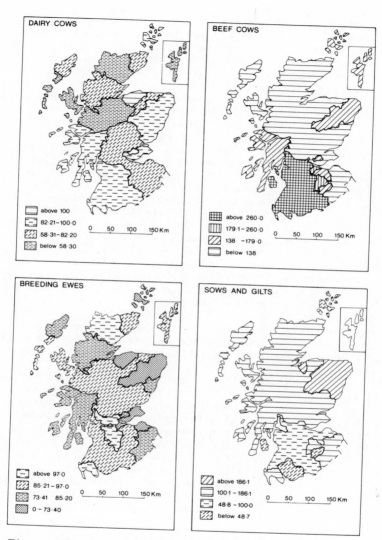

Figure 23B. Changes in livestock numbers 1961–71 (1971 figures expressed as a percentage of 1961 figures)

or dispersion of each enterprise. The figures confirm
the distinction drawn already between enterprises increasing and those decreasing in importance. For the former
group, a more dispersed pattern of production has emerged,
with an increasing number of farmers participating in the
enterprises. Dispersion has been greatest for the barley
and beef enterprises, although wheat also shows the same
tendency. For beef production, dispersion has been greatest for beef breeding and least for the fattening of beef
stores, and it has reduced the pre-eminence of north-east
Scotland in the beef enterprise.

The rate of change toward spatial concentration has
been greatest for the pig and poultry enterprises, although
dairy cows, sheep and field crops show similar tendencies.
Areas which have had a traditional association with these
enterprises are having that association consolidated. The
poultry flock, for example, has become more concentrated
in east Scotland, in the counties around the Firth of
Forth. In the case of oats, the acid soils of hill areas
in south-east Scotland and in the central Highlands provide
the last refuges of this once widespread crop. Only the
pig breeding enterprise runs contrary to the general trends,
having rising numbers of sows and gilts in pig, yet becoming
more concentrated in its spatial distribution. The
development of the enterprise in large, intensive units, in
its traditional area of production in north-east Scotland,
has been favoured by the operation of a bacon factory at
Dyce.

Scottish agriculture therefore is becoming more
regionally specialised in its pattern of production, although
the trend is not uniform for all commodities. Barley,
wheat and beef are the major exceptions. The trends are
facilitated by changes in the structure of agriculture.
All enterprises are increasing in size as farmers create
economies of scale through larger units of production
(Plate 8B). In addition, individual producers have
continued to reduce their range of enterprises to one or
two chosen lines of production, so intensifying the trend
towards spatial concentration.

FORESTRY

The present ownership, distribution and utilisation
of Scotland's forests are of relatively recent origin and

historically there has been no attempt to conserve and manage the natural forest. Indeed, the history of Scottish forestry is one of continuous exploitation and depletion, so that while one third of Britain's forest resources are in Scotland, few European countries have such a small forestry sector. The exploitation of the natural woodland has been stimulated by a succession of economic opportunities and military crises. Economic incentives for deforestation were provided by salt making on the eastern coastlands in the twelfth and thirteenth centuries, by sheep farming on the Southern Uplands in the fifteenth century, by charcoal production for iron smelting in the seventeenth and eighteenth centuries, and again by sheep farming in the Highlands in the nineteenth century. More recently, the timber demands of two world wars completed the virtual destruction of the natural forest, and the further depletion of privately owned woodland. Today, semi-natural forests survive only as isolated patches in locations of low grazing potential, or where recent attempts at conservation have been successful. Such remnants are no longer of commercial value, and are discounted from the following discussion together with all scrub woodland.

Ownership

The process of reafforestation has its origins in the late seventeenth century, with small-scale planting of woodland around the residences of the large landowners for ornament or game coverts. The Improvement Movement of the late eighteenth century added more extensive plantations to estates in the east of Scotland, with the use of Scots pine, larch and exotic hardwoods such as beech and sycamore. The woodland served as shelter for stock, or again as ornament.

However, the most dramatic rise in the area of private woodland occurred after 1950, with annual planting rates reaching 4 - 6000 hectares (Table 18). Productive private woodland now comprises approximately 31 per cent of the total woodland area. The present emphasis is on production for timber from commercially managed 'high forest', although the tax benefits that accrue to forest owners are major factors in recent developments. For income tax, losses on investment during the early years of a forest can be offset against the owner's income from other sources. Standing timber remains exempt from capital gains tax,

although the land does not. For estate (death) duty, the
land qualifies for the same 45 per cent abatement of duty
as does agricultural land, and no duty is payable on the
timber until it is felled or sold.

	Planting in Scotland (hectares)		Increase in total area of Forestry Commission land (hectares)
	Private	Forestry Commission	
Before 1918	1,376	–	–
1919–29	1,942	971	116,345
1930–39	1,457	3,278	104,731
1940–49	911	3,378	111,084
1950–59	4,209	12,190	213,469
1960–69	6,070	12,103	159,930

Table 18. Average annual forestry planting rates in
Scotland 1919–69

Sources : Martin P.C. The hills – farming or forestry?
Occasional paper 1. Economics Department,
East of Scotland College of Agriculture
(1970)

and Anderson M.L. (in Taylor C.J. ed.)
A history of Scottish forestry (1967)
Edinburgh

In addition, the Forestry Commission has offered technical
advice and financial aid to private owners since 1947.
The Dedication of Woodlands Scheme at present provides a
planting grant for forestry land under the management
supervision of the Commission. Annual management grants
are also paid for new and established woodland, and the
majority of private woodland is under this form of management. Planting grants are available under the Approved
Woodlands Scheme, although there is limited Forestry
Commission involvement in management decisions. Similar
provision is made for small blocks of woodland under the
Small Woods Scheme, and the various incentives have
attracted investment companies into private forestry in
recent years.

The main impetus for reafforestation, however, has
been provided by the Forestry Commission through its own

forestry programme.   The Commission was established by
the Forestry Act of 1919, after the First World War had
revealed the strategic vulnerability of the United Kingdom
in timber resources.   The original objective of the
Commission therefore was to create a strategic reserve of
standing timber to meet requirements in the event of further
military emergencies.   A forested area of 0.7 m hectares
was proposed for the United Kingdom.   However, the planting targets of the Commission have been altered on several
occasions since that time, being increased to 2 m hectares
after the Second World War.   The annual planting rate
accelerated accordingly, reaching a maximum in 1954
(Table 18).   National targets were again increased in
1967, and in Scotland the annual area planted had risen
to over 19,000 hectares by 1972, compared with approximately 11,000 hectares in 1962.   However, the Commission
experienced increasing difficulty in acquiring new land,
partly as a result of purchases by private forestry
interests, and in 1972 projected levels of planting were
reduced.   In addition, the role of the Commission has
been broadened through time to include the maintenance
of rural employment, the fostering of industries ancillary
to forestry, the encouragement of outdoor recreation,
profit making, and the production of timber rather than
the creation of a standing forest reserve.

Distribution

        Private woodland occurs on estates of varying sizes,
but is located predominantly on the upland margins in
eastern areas of Scotland.   Forest blocks are small in
size, having an average extent of less than twenty hectares
in the north of Scotland.   However, the entry of investment companies into forestry has increased the scale of
operation, especially within the upland area.
        The transfer of land to forestry is, on the one hand,
a function of the policy of individual landowners, and on
the other the ability of the Forestry Commission to purchase land on the open market.   The criteria used by the
Commission in acquiring land include the potential
economic return, the amount of land in the property that
is surplus to planting need, the maintenance of local
employment, and, more recently, recreational capability.
Land purchases have to meet with the approval of the
DAFS, and this ensures that where possible better

agricultural land remains unplanted. Consequently, rough grazing has been the major source of land for planting, although exposure to wind and soil quality act as limiting factors. Unplanted land suitable for agriculture is rented as grazing land, or as complete farms, through the DAFS.

The process of purchasing land on the open market has resulted in a fragmented pattern of forest properties. However, land purchases have been so extensive that the Commission is now the largest single landowner in Scotland, while the woodland area is mainly State-owned, rather than in private ownership as in the past. The recent transfer to Edinburgh of the headquarters of the Commission underlines the importance of Scotland in British forestry. The location of Commission properties is unevenly distributed within the upland area, and the greatest increases have been in the south and west of Scotland. However, the largest properties are located in the north-west Highlands (Fig 24), in the forests of Shin (31,786 ha), Affric (27,896 ha) and Skye (20,441 ha). High altitude, exposure and infertile soils limit the area that can be planted, and only 32 per cent of the land in the forest of Shin, for example, is in forest. In practice the pattern of afforestation is fragmented along the sides and floors of the glens, and planted blocks rarely exceed 800 ha in size. The recent difficulty of acquiring new land has forced the Commission to purchase properties whose plantable area is small, thus increasing production costs. The other major concentrations of Commission land are in Argyllshire (Glenorchy 20,989 ha) and in south-west Scotland (Glen Trool 22,503 ha). Extensive forest blocks are characteristic of south-west Scotland and the Borders, owing to the more subdued relief and the lower proportion of unplantable land. Finally, the smallest blocks of forestry land occur in east and south-east Scotland as a result of severe competition with agriculture for available land.

Utilisation

The commercial 'high forest' is comprised of large stands of fast growing, mainly exotic, softwood species. Scots pine (Pinus sylvestris) and Sitka spruce (Picea sitchensis) together account for nearly 60 per cent of the forested area, despite the wide range of species

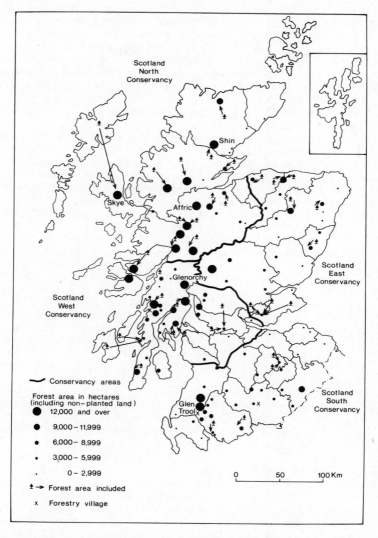

Figure 24. Location of Forestry Commission forests 1972

which can grow successfully in Scotland. In part this reflects the industrial demand for a large volume of softwood with a uniform character. Private estates have favoured the Scots pine, and it remains the only indigenous conifer of major importance. Although slower in growth than other species, it is tolerant of the drier conditions in the east of Scotland where private woodland predominates. Private estates are also the location of the high forest comprised of hardwood species.

By contrast, the Forestry Commission has favoured the Sitka spruce which thrives on the peaty soils and heavy rainfall of its properties in west and south-west Scotland. The species produces a large volume of timber in a relatively short time, and is tolerant of a wide variety of poor sites. However, the Scots pine is used in many Border forests, and on drier sites in the eastern Highlands. The Norway spruce (Picea abies) which was popular until the post-war era, has given ground to the Sitka spruce, while the Lodgepole pine (Pinus contorta) is reserved for the poorest sites, especially on peat areas in the north of Scotland.

The 'high forest' produces small roundwood (thinnings) 20-30 years after planting, and row cutting is now favoured in place of the selective thinning of plantations. Further thinnings are taken at 5-10 year intervals, until the site is clear-felled after 50-80 years to produce saw-log timber. The larger thinnings are used to produce posts, stakes, fencing, pit props and fish boxes. The smaller thinnings are consumed for pulp and paper, while the largest logs serve as telegraph poles and timber for the construction industry. The pulp and paper mill at Corpach, near Fort William, is a major consumer of softwood, although additional hardwood chips are imported from Canada. Chipboard factories at Irvine (Ayrshire) and Annan (Dumfriesshire) consume local production in the south of Scotland, while many small sawmills, dispersed throughout Scotland, process local timber supplies.

However, the utilisation of State-owned forests is undergoing change following redirection in national forest policy in 1964. Increasing emphasis has been placed on forestry as a recreational resource, although the first National Forest Park was created in Argyll as early as 1936. Car parks, picnic areas, camp sites, access roads, nature trails and information centres are rapidly becoming an integral part of the forest landscape.

Forestry and agriculture

Over the last decade there has been a net loss of over 20,000 hectares of agricultural land per year. Forestry has been the major recipient of such land, although mainly from the rough grazing category (Table 20). The transfer of rough grazing to forestry has not been without its problems in upland areas. Firstly, the lower rough grazing in hill sheep farming districts, and middle-hill land in upland farming districts, have been purchased by the Forestry Commission and private owners. Hill farms have thus been denied such land for the purposes of farm amalgamation, although the unplanted land in valley bottoms and hill tops has been made available to neighbouring farms for renting. Both agriculture and forestry give low returns on investment in such areas, and although both enterprises are maintained by government support, there is no integration of agricultural and forestry policy, and no agreement on the basis on which the relative economic value of the alternative uses might be calculated.

A second clash of interests stems from the considerable amount of planting in the past which was in linear blocks along middle-hill land without access through to the unplanted higher rough grazing. Consequently, the grazing above the tree line is effectively sterilized for sheep farming. Closer attention is now paid to the integration of agriculture and forestry than in the past, and agriculture benefits from provision of shelter for crops and livestock on many exposed uplands. The construction of approximately 6000 miles of forestry roads has also brought improvement to upland pastures through greater accessibility.

Thirdly, the presence of forestry plantations has excluded the practice of moor burning in the management of rough grazing. The benefits gained through the provision of shelter are offset by the increased problems of pasture management. Nevertheless, increased densities of stock on hill land have raised the number of hill cows and maintained the number of hill sheep. In a general sense, therefore, the process of afforestation has not been to the detriment of agriculture. However, instances of mistaken planting at particular locations serve to maintain the antagonism between agricultural and forestry interests.

The case for afforestation has increasingly emphasised

the social and recreational advantages of forestry. Forestry provides more employment per hectare than the hill sheep farming that it replaces. Approximately 11,000 people are directly employed in the forestry sector: 4000 by the Forestry Commission, 4000 by private estates, and 3000 by the timber trade. A ratio of 1 to 4 or 5 has been suggested between those directly employed in forestry and those in the wood-using industries. This results in an average ratio of one man to 100 hectares of planted land for those directly employed on Commission holdings, although the ratio varies between forests. Variations are created by the size of the forest unit, since small blocks require a higher labour input per hectare. In addition, the terrain influences the degree of mechanisation that is possible, while further factors are the volume of timber to be cut, and the sizes of the sawmill and nursery associated with each forest. On private estates the average ratio is one man to 73 hectares, but the increasing mechanisation of forestry in general is leading to a dwindling labour force.

Forestry has already reversed the trend of rural depopulation in many areas of the Crofting Counties, where planting has been social rather than economic in its justification. Forestry workers maintain or swell local communities, so continuing the viability of schools, bus services, shops and social services. This has been the case particularly since 1960, when the Forestry Commission abandoned its policy of establishing separate villages for its workers, in favour of adding houses to existing settlements. However, the forestry villages of Ae (Dumfriesshire), Glen Trool (Galloway) and Dalavich (Argyll) bear testimony to the earlier phase of Commission policy (Fig 24).

OUTDOOR RECREATION

The growth in demand for rural land for outdoor recreation reflects the increasing time spent on leisure activities in general, arising from greater affluence and education, shorter working hours, longer paid holidays, and more widespread car ownership.

On the basis of their demands on rural areas, recreational uses can be broadly divided into three types: passive enjoyment of rural beauty; informal activities

156

requiring access to the countryside at large, and organised sports which often require special facilities.

Passive enjoyment of rural beauty

Informal picnicking and pleasure driving are the most important recreational uses of rural areas, although the degree of participation is influenced by possession of a private motor vehicle. Both tourists and day-trip recreationists contribute to the pattern of demand in Scotland. There are two facets: the pleasure drive, and the visit to a site of recreation (honeypot). (Plate 10B). In pleasure driving, the mobility of the recreationists creates a pattern of widely dispersed use over areas where visual amenity is the main attraction. Demand is restricted to scenic views from the roadway, and no direct access to the land is required.

However, limited access is necessary at sites of recreation. The site can be a picnic area, a beauty spot or scenic viewing point, a water resource, an historic building, or a small town in a rural setting, such as Callendar, Strathaven or Penicuik (Fig 25). These sites are often incidental to the pleasure drive, rather than the primary objective. Visitors do not move far from their cars, and the concentrated pattern of recreation results in conflict with existing land uses, and in congestion of the site and its access roads. The pressure on resources is revealed by wear and tear on paths, pollution of water supplies, disturbance of wild-life, accumulation of litter, and by wild camping and caravanning at the roadside by tourists. Sensitive areas are Torridon, Loch Lomondside, and Glencoe.

For the day-trip recreationist, accessibility is of equal importance to visual amenity in influencing the location and extent of demand. The majority of trips and sites of recreation are contained in a radius of 30-40 miles from the main urban areas (Fig 25), although trips to the coast outnumber those to the country. Most coastal settlements near urban areas participate in day-trip recreation: Rothesay, Dunoon, Ayr and Largs for Glasgow; Dunbar, North Berwick and Gullane for Edinburgh. Recreational facilities are contained mainly within the urban area, but conflict with the conservation interest exists on stretches of coast around the resorts, as at Gullane.

157

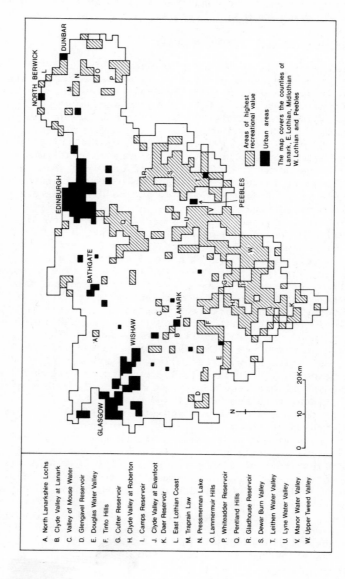

A. North Lanarkshire Lochs
B. Clyde Valley at Lanark
C. Valley of Mouse Water
D. Glengavel Reservoir
E. Douglas Water Valley
F. Tinto Hills
G. Culter Reservoir
H. Clyde Valley at Roberton
I. Camps Reservoir
J. Clyde Valley at Elvanfoot
K. Daer Reservoir
L. East Lothian Coast
M. Traprain Law
N. Pressmennan Lake
O. Lammermuir Hills
P. Whiteadder Reservoir
Q. Pentland Hills
R. Gladhouse Reservoir
S. Dewar Burn Valley
T. Leithen Water Valley
U. Lyne Water Valley
V. Manor Water Valley
W. Upper Tweed Valley

Areas of highest recreational value

Urban areas

The map covers the counties of Lanark, E. Lothian, Midlothian W. Lothian and Peebles

Figure 25. Recreation environments in Central Scotland 1970

The sites of recreation used by tourists are dispersed throughout the wilderness area of Scotland, a dwindling asset owing to the inroads made by forestry and hydro-electricity schemes in addition to the localized pressure exerted by tourists. As tourist pressures increase, so do the demands for new routes and wider roads. For the most part, pressure to widen the single-track roads of the Highlands has been resisted. It poses the essential dilemma in coping with the demand for outdoor recreation in rural areas, namely altering the countryside to meet the rising demand, while at the same time protecting the landscape from harm and loss of amenity. The attractive quality of the wilderness area, for example, is given a measure of protection by the sparse network of roads. New routes would fragment the wilderness area into smaller blocks, while the inevitable increase in the number of visitors would destroy the fragile qualities of isolation and remoteness.

Tourism has a wider effect on the rural area than at sites of recreation. Approximately 11 per cent of all holidays in Britain are taken in Scotland, and 22 per cent of all main caravan holidays. Between 1965 and 1970, spending by tourists rose from £82 m to £164 m, and it has become an important element in the economy of many rural areas. The Highlands and Islands are the major areas of attraction to tourists, and in 1968 the average number of visitors per night during the holiday season was estimated to be 130,000. Visitors concentrate especially at Oban, Inverness, Fort William, Ullapool and Gairloch. The tourist trade spreads its influence beyond these holiday centres, and is a significant source of income in crofting communities. Crofts are rented to holiday-makers, and crofters provide bed-and-breakfast facilities for those touring by car. The contribution that tourism can make to solving the problems of the crofting areas has been recognised by the Highlands and Islands Development Board. Grants and loans have been provided to foster the development of hotels, and to assist crofters in building additional croft accommodation, chalets and caravan sites on crofting land. The Scottish Tourist Board gives similar financial assistance throughout Scotland.

Informal activities requiring general access to the countryside

General access to the countryside is required by a small proportion of those taking outdoor recreation, while in Scotland there is a long tradition of public access to open land. Walking is the most popular activity, with camping, rock climbing and pony-trecking other minority interests. These activities are space-consuming, but, at their present level of demand, they are readily integrated with existing forms of land use.

However, formal provision of access to the countryside has been made in the four National Forest Parks, which together cover over 99,000 ha (Fig 26, Table 19). The Parks were created by the Forestry Commission out of existing plantations and unplanted land, before the recent upsurge in demand for recreation. The public have right of access to the Parks which contain lochs, mountains and farmland, in addition to woodland. The Glen Trool Forest Park, for example, still has 40 per cent of its area in farms. Picnic areas, camping sites and walking routes are provided within each Park, and encouragement is given to pursuits such as sailing and canoeing. With the exception of Glen More, all the Parks are now within the day-use zone of the major urban areas, although the Parks also serve long-stay visitors and tourists during the summer months. Recreational facilities are also provided in a further forty-six individual forests which are scattered throughout Scotland. They have more recent origins, and reflect the Forestry Commission's policy of increasing the recreational value of their properties (Fig 26).

Formal provision of facilities to meet the rising demand for outdoor recreation has been made by the creation of Country Parks. Four have been authorised by local authorities since 1968: Culzean (Ayrshire), Muirsheil (Renfrewshire), Palacerigg (Dunbartonshire) and Almondell (Midlothian) (Fig 26). They are designed to relieve the recreational pressure on farmland near to urban areas, and to divert recreationists from overused sites. Consequently, the Country Parks have been located in rural areas reasonably accessible to centres of population. This avoids the need to travel far, and helps to reduce congestion on the main day-trip routes. Culzean

Plate 9 Coastal Villages

A. Shieldaig, Wester Ross. A small coastal village on Loch Torridon, combining the resources of both sea and land. Tourism is now also a vital source of income.

B. Diabeg, Wester Ross. A small crofting/fishing village. Many small villages were founded on such limited coastal sites as people were cleared from the land to make way for sheep after the mid-eighteenth century.

Plate 10 The Changing Rural Economy
A. Lochinver, Sutherland. Fishing boats unloading in the late evening in 1961.
Many small fishing fleets and ports have ceased operation.

B. Pitlochry, Perthshire. Tourists at the hydro-electric power station and dam
on the River Tummel. A growing army of tourists congregate at such sites in the
season.

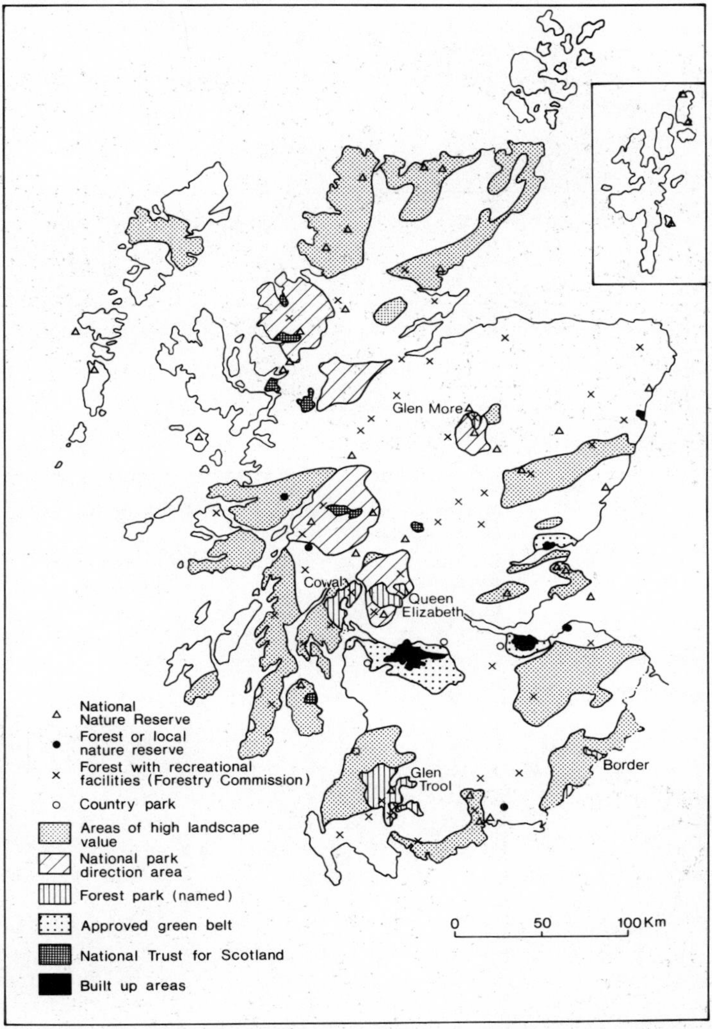
Glen More
Cowal
Queen Elizabeth
Glen Trool
Border
National Nature Reserve
Forest or local nature reserve
Forest with recreational facilities (Forestry Commission)
Country park
Areas of high landscape value
National park direction area
Forest park (named)
Approved green belt
National Trust for Scotland
Built up areas
0
50
100Km

Figure 26. Recreation and conservation areas 1972

Country Park on the Ayrshire coast, for example, contains a large house open to the public, and 220 hectares of open farmland and woodland under more regulated access. The retention of some degree of farming and forestry fosters the feeling of being in the countryside, and not just in an urban park.

National Park Direction Areas			National Forest Parks		
Name	Area (hectares)	Date	Name	Area (hectares)	Date
Glen Nevis-Glencoe	165,120	1947	Argyll (Cowal)	25,200	1936
Loch Torridon – Little Loch Broom	129,000	1947	Glen Trool	52,000	1947
Loch Lomond-Trossachs	82,560	1947	Glen More	5,000	1948
Glen Affric-Strathfarrar	67,080	1947	Queen Elizabeth (Loch Ard-Lomond)	16,900	1953
Cairngorms	46,440	1947			

Table 19. National Park and Forest Park Areas in Scotland 1972

Sources : Forestry Commission Annual Reports & National Parks in Scotland Cmd 7235 (1947)

Organised sports

Organised sports play a minor role in total leisure activity, but they require access to land and water which have special qualities. Such sports are water-skiing (Loch Earn), sailing (Loch Lomond), snow skiing (Glen Coe, Glen Shee, Glen More), golf (numerous courses in east-central Scotland) and game fishing (the Tay and many other rivers). The demands of these sports tend to be localised, but conflict with other land uses is created by the development of large concentrations of active participants. One such concentration has emerged since 1957 with the development of Aviemore as a centre for winter sports, and more recently for summer activities. The ecological damage to the Spey valley region is only beginning to be appreciated, but it is readily apparent in the mechanical wear and tear on the soil and vegetation in the vicinity of the ski-lifts

and tows in Coire Cas.   Damage caused to the mountainside
at altitudes over 600 metres is thought to be irreversible.
        Recent changes in outdoor recreation have affected
specific sites and major routeways.   However, deer forests
and grouse moors are the traditional uses of land for
sporting recreation, and they extend over a considerable
area of rural Scotland.   The major development of deer
forests occurred during a recession in hill sheep farming
in the second half of the nineteenth century.   As
sporting rents outstripped grazing rents, the poorer farms
in inaccessible mountainous terrain were amalgamated to
produce extensive moorland areas, over which deer could be
stalked to the exclusion of other uses.   A maximum of 1.52 m
hectares of deer forest was reached prior to the First World
War, although statistics are no longer kept to record the
present situation.   However, there are approximately 183
separate deer forests located on estates in the central
moorlands of the northern Highlands, and they contain nearly
185,000 red deer (Cervus elaphus).   The migratory habits
of the deer extend their seasonal range over 2.7 m hectares,
although only 0.6 m hectares are not jointly used by hill
sheep under the present system of management.
        Areas of sheltered low ground for overwintering are
crucial to the seasonal migrations of the deer.   Conflict
with forestry interests has arisen owing to the afforestation,
since 1957, of approximately 92,000 hectares of low ground.
Traditionally deer forests and forestry have been mutually
exclusive land uses, but sympathetic afforestation of low
ground in recent years has ensured the sufficiency of winter
grazing.   In addition, the operations of the Red Deer
Commission have reduced the damage done by deer to farming
and forestry.
        Considerable supplementary employment is associated
with the deer forests, both in the management and stalking
of the deer, and in the provision of services to shooting
parties in the hunting lodges.   Today, the sport of
stalking stags for trophies is giving way to the business
of killing hinds to supply venison to the growing market
in West Germany.   On such poor land, meat production
compares favourably with returns from hill sheep farming.
        Grouse moors occupy between 0.5 m and 1.2 m hectares
of heather moorland in the eastern Highlands, at altitudes
of between 250 and 600 metres.   Their origins were also
in the late nineteenth century, and they were extended
under the Victorian patronage of the Highlands.   The

163

management of game birds has tended to decline with the
fragmentation of the large estates, although the sport
has revived in the last ten years with leases being taken
by industrial interests and syndicates.   The grouse moors
are jointly occupied by sheep, but a carefully managed
rotation of moor burning is required to provide the red
grouse with the young heather shoots that are the basis of
their diet.   The sport remains exclusive to the wealthy,
as does deer stalking, but it provides an important
additional source of employment and income on estates.

Conservation

Finally, attention must be drawn to the increasing
area of rural Scotland that is devoted to the interests
of conservation.   Conservation in Scotland has a long
history, but its scope and objectives have been widened
in recent years.   This is a reflection of the increasing
concern in society for the natural environment.   There
are three main categories of land used for conservation
purposes: National Park Direction Areas, National Nature
Reserves, and National Trust properties.
Scotland has no National Parks of the type found in
England and Wales.   However, 490,000 ha of land in the
Highlands, designated as National Park Direction Areas in
1947, remain under special planning controls (Fig 26, Table
19).   The controls act in a negative way to preclude
undesirable landscape changes, but no positive management
of resources is practised.   Similarly, Areas of Outstanding Natural Beauty conserve the landscape in prescribed
districts.
By contrast, positive conservation of resources is
practised on the thirty-eight National Nature Reserves
established by the Nature Conservancy and on its Sites
of Special Scientific Interest.   The Conservancy was
constituted by Royal Charter in 1949, and has subsequently
purchased 21,600 hectares of land, mostly as extensive
estates.   It has management agreements with the owners
of a further 52,000 hectares of land.   The properties
are located mainly in the north-west and central Highlands
(Fig 26), and they contain examples of the different types
of ecosystem found in Scotland.   Public access is permitted
to most reserves, but the primary interest of the Conservancy
remains in the management and conservation of wildlife and
landscape for its scientific, amenity and sporting value.

Smaller wildlife refuges and nature reserves are also operated by bodies such as the Scottish Wildlife Trust.

The third type of prescribed area is associated with the National Trust for Scotland. The Trust was founded in 1931 as a voluntary society, and has since purchased eighty properties which extend to 32,000 ha, and combine farmland, woods, exotic gardens and moorland. The more extensive properties are located in the north-west Highlands. The primary concern of the Trust is the preservation of countryside and buildings of natural beauty, or of historic and scientific interest.

RURAL LAND USE PLANNING

Recent trends in rural land use have revealed many areas of potential conflict, for example, the threat to the rural environment of mechanised agriculture, with the undue enlargement of fields and the removal of hedges and copses, and of large-scale forestry developments, or the loss of agricultural land to other uses (Table 20). However, the present scale and intensity of competing demands in Scotland has permitted the joint-use of resources in most situations of potential conflict.

Nevertheless, there are economic pressures on most land-use systems to increase production or reduce costs, and they foster a trend away from the joint-use of land. Amenity and ecological dangers have been recognised in specialised land-use systems, while there is also an inevitable increase in conflict between specialised land uses.

The present system of land ownership and management is not conducive to controlling these mounting pressures. There is no overall authority to co-ordinate the proliferation of policies and interests. The Highlands and Islands Development Board, for example, has wide powers over rural resource use, but only in the Crofting Counties. Even so, the situation is complicated by the Crofters' Commission which has more limited powers, but is responsible for the same rural area. The Countryside Commission for Scotland has operated since 1967, but only with advisory powers in reconciling conflicts of interest in rural areas. General powers of land use control lie mainly with local planning authorities, under the terms of the 1968 Town and Country Planning Act. In addition, nearly

one third of Scotland is subject to specific land-use con-
straints within Green Belts, National Park Direction Areas,
Areas of Outstanding Natural Beauty, National Nature Reserves,
and National Forest Parks.   Even in these areas, however,
changes in agriculture and forestry lie outside the powers
of regulation.   Consequently, the attention of planning
authorities has tended to be focussed on urban issues,
although recent demands for recreational facilities are
changing the attitudes of planners to rural areas.

Net annual average transfers to:	1951-5[a]	1956-9[a]	1961-5	1966-70	1971-74
Forestry	0.24	0.32	17.16	17.85	24.72
Urban and industry	1.33	1.05	1.90	2.35	1.25
Recreation	0.16	0.28	0.24	0.20	0.33
Water and mineral exploitation	0.12	0.08	0.32	0.20	0.37
Armed services	(0.08)[b]	(0.08)[b]	0.25	(0.04)[b]	0.01
Miscellaneous	(1.46)[b]	4.40	(1.94)[b]	0.52	0.64
Total	0.32	6.07	17.73	21.08	27.32

a.   excludes rough grazing   b.   gain to agriculture

Table 20.   Transfers of agricultural land to other
           uses in Scotland 1951-74 (000's hectares)
Source : D.A.F.S. Agricultural Statistics

     A recent Select Committee of the House of Commons
recognised these problems in considering the use of land
resources in Scotland.   The advantages of continuing the
joint or multiple-use of land were acknowledged, although
a preference was indicated for the concurrent use of land,
rather than the subdivision of properties for specialised
use.   The Select Committee proposed three types of co-
ordinating body to ensure the rational allocation of
resources.   Proposals were made for a Land Use Council to
consider the strategy of resource use, a Land Use unit to
provide research support for the Council, and Countryside
Committees within local planning authorities.   Inevitably,
the mounting pressures on rural Scotland will require both
more statutory control of land use than in the past, and
a method of regulating the allocation of land that is not

based purely on economic advantage. The alternative is a decline in the amenity value of the countryside, and an increasing level of disharmony in the allocation of rural resources.

5 INDUSTRIAL SCOTLAND

Industry is popularly associated with that group of economic activities which involve manual and mechanised labour in factory premises. However any attempt to provide a precise definition is fraught with difficulties. Factory premises vary in scale from the large integrated steel works or car assembly plant to the individual cottage with a weaver's loom or potter's wheel. Most factories employ a considerable number of office staff, whose activities are similar in kind to those of other office staff in banking or other establishments with no associated factory premises. Other industries, such as the forestry industry or construction industry, are not strongly associated with any fixed premises but are essentially associated with dispersed outdoor locations. In view of all these problems, no single set of industrial definitions is entirely satisfactory. However, the Standard Industrial Classification, last revised by the then Board of Trade in 1968, provides a widely accepted set, and this, in spite of its shortcomings, provides the most satisfactory basis for a discussion of Scottish industry (see summary in Table 21).

The Standard Industrial Classification is based on identifying and grouping types of industrial activity. Of the 183 separate categories of activity, 123 are grouped into the 17 classes of the Manufacturing sector. The type of product produced in the factory or workshop provides the basis of the definition. The type of product is also the basis of definition used to distinguish the 8 categories of activity grouped into the 2 classes of the Primary sector. In this case however, the product is collected from the natural environment rather than produced in a factory where some kind of processing is involved. The definition of the single category in the single class of the Construction sector is based not so much on the nature of the product as on the process involved in its production.

Roads, bridges, houses, factories etc. are very different
kinds of phenomena, but they are all constructed in situ.
The lack of product-based subdivisions of the Construction
sector makes it very difficult to make valid comparisons
between the Construction sector and any of the classes within
the Primary, Manufacturing and Service Sectors. The 50
categories grouped into the 7 classes of the Service sector
give rise to further problems of comparison. Except for
the gas, electricity and water industries, service
industries do not generally produce any tangible product
measurable in physical or financial terms. The subdivisions
of the Service sector, based on functions, are broadly
comparable with the subdivisions of the Manufacturing sector
based on factory products, but the lack of tangible,
measurable output and the very different kind of activities
involved, means that apart from employment levels, very few
common points of reference exist on which to base meaning-
ful comparisons of the two sectors.

THE STRUCTURE OF SCOTTISH INDUSTRY

Employment figures provide a starting point for the
examination of the relative importance of different types
of industry in Scotland, whether it be in the Primary,
Manufacturing, Construction or Service sectors. From
Table 21 it can be seen that the service industries in
1971 accounted for over half the labour force, with only
just over a third employed in manufacturing industry and
less than a fifth in the construction and the primary
industries together. Employment was similarly very
unevenly divided between the twenty seven main classes of
industry. If each class had contained an equal share,
each would employ 3.7 per cent of the total labour force.
This share was in fact exceeded by five of the seven classes
in the Service sector and by the one class in the Construction sector, but by only three classes in the Manufacturing
sector (III Food, drink and tobacco, VII Mechanical
engineering and XIII Textiles). However, such inequal-
ities are built into the classification system that without some other point of reference the relative size of
the industrial classes in employment terms is of interest
but not greatly significant.

One such point of reference is provided by the growth

| Class | Description | Total | Employment 1971 | | | Employment change 1966-71 | |
			000's	Percentage	Order	Percentage change	Order
	PRIMARY SECTOR	95.5		4.7		-27.6	
I	Agriculture, forestry and fishing		55.3	2.7	11	-25.2	25
II	Mining and quarrying		40.2	2.0	16	-30.7	26
	MANUFACTURING SECTOR	698.7		34.6		- 7.6	
III	Food, drink and tobacco		108.3	5.4	7(1)	+ 4.2	7(4)
IV	Coal and petroleum products		3.3	0.2	26(16)	+74	1(1)
V	Chemicals and allied industries		28.3	1.4	21(11)	- 6	11(8)
VI	Metal manufacture		45.8	2.3	14(6)	-11.2	17(12)
VII	Mechanical engineering		101.6	5.0	8(2)	-21.0	23(15)
VIII	Instrument engineering		18.9	0.9	24(14)	+35	3(2)
IX	Electrical engineering		50.2	2.5	13(5)	+13	5(3)
X	Shipbuilding and marine engineering		44.8	2.2	15(7)	- 6.5	12(9)
XI	Vehicles		37.1	1.8	17(8)	-12.5	19(13)
XII	Metal goods not elsewhere specified		29.1	1.4	20(10)	- 4.3	10(7)
XIII	Textiles		76.0	3.8	9(3)	-22.7	24(16)
XIV	[a]Leather, leather goods) and fur)		37.0	1.8	18(9)	+ 4.0	8(5)
XV	Clothing and footwear)						
XVI	Bricks, pottery, glass, cement etc.		22.5	1.1	23(13)	-12.5	19(13)
XVII	Timber, furniture etc.		25.7	1.3	22(12)	- 0.4	9(6)
XVIII	Paper, printing and publishing		54.0	2.7	12(4)	- 8.0	14(11)
XIX	Other manufacturing industries		16.2	0.8	25(15)	- 7.9	13(10)
	CONSTRUCTION SECTOR	158.7		7.9		-14.5	
XX	Construction		158.7	7.9	4	-14.5	22
	SERVICE SECTOR	1,064.9		52.8		- 0.4	
XXI	Gas, electricity and water		30.1	1.5	19	-11.2	17
XXII	Transport and Communication		140.2	6.9	5	-10.2	16
XXIII	Distributive trades		242.3	12.0	2	-14.1	21
XXIV	Insurance, banking, finance and business services		66.3	3.3	10	+49.0	2
XXV	Professional and scientific services		291.5	14.4	1	+13.3	4
XXVI	Miscellaneous services		166.4	8.2	3	- 8.1	15
XXVII	Public administration and defence		128.1	6.3	6	+12.5	6
	Total	2,018.0		100		- 5.8	

[a] Negligible in Scotland

Table 21. Employment and employment trends in Scottish industries 1966-71

Source : Scottish Abstract of Statistics

or decline of employment over a period of time. The trends for the period 1966 to 1971 are also illustrated in Table 21. During this period employment in Scotland as a whole fell by over five per cent. Only the service industries enjoyed a fall of less than this overall average, while in the manufacturing industries the fall was only just greater than this figure. Well above average falls however occurred in the construction industry and above all in the primary industries. Primary industry lost more than twenty five per cent of its labour force in six years. Clearly the overall balance in employment terms during this period tilted towards the service industries, especially at the expense of the primary industries.

Within the 27 industrial classes however, some markedly divergent trends were recorded. Three classes in the Service sector, (XXIV Insurance, banking, finance and business services, XXV Professional and scientific services and XXVII Public administration and defence), recorded actual increases in employment, though all other service classes lost a greater percentage of their employment than Scotland lost as a whole. Five classes in the Manufacturing sector, (IV Coal and petroleum products, VIII Instrument engineering, IX Electrical engineering, III Food, drink and tobacco and XV Clothing and footwear), also recorded increases in employment. Four others, (V Chemicals and allied industries, X Shipbuilding and marine engineering, XII Other metal goods, and XVII Timber, furniture etc.,), declined by less than the overall decline in the Manufacturing sector, two of them (XII and XVII) by less than the decline in total employment. All other manufacturing and both primary industry classes recorded a substantial relative decline in employment terms. Employment change is only one indicator of an industry's growth potential, nevertheless an examination of the employment trends in combination with actual employment totals in the 1966-71 period produces some interesting results.

Of the ten industrial classes which recorded growth in this period relative to the overall employment trend in Scotland, only four were amongst the ten largest employers of labour in 1971. These were the three classes in the Service sector and the Food, drink and tobacco class in the Manufacturing sector. This suggests that the pre-eminence of these industries in Scotland in employment

171

terms was considerably reinforced between 1966 and 1971.
On the other hand, five of the remaining six growth classes
were amongst the ten smallest employers of labour in 1971.
Together with the heavy decline in employment suffered
over this period by some industries with a large labour
force, this suggests powerful forces operating to bring
about a redistribution of employment. Thus, in the
Service sector considerable decline characterised some
big employers of labour like XXIII Distributive trades
and XXII Transport and communication and these classes
lost a great deal of ground relatively to some of the
smaller employers of labour such as XIV Insurance, banking
finance and business services. Large employers of labour
in other sectors which declined substantially in the same
way were XX Construction industry, both classes in the
Primary sector and three classes in the Manufacturing
sector (VII Mechanical engineering, XIII Textiles and
VI Metal manufacture). Small employers of labour
outside the Service sector which significantly improved
their relative status by enjoying a large relative growth
of employment were six classes of manufacturing industry
(IV Coal and petroleum products, VIII Instrument engineering,
IX Electrical engineering, XV Clothing and footwear,
XVII Timber, furniture, etc. and XII Miscellaneous metal
goods). It is interesting to note that by this measure
of growth at least, X Shipbuilding and marine engineering,
long regarded as the epitome of industrial decline in
Scotland, more or less held its own in this period, while
XI Vehicles, generally regarded as a growth leader, did
not fare particularly well. Part of the explanation for
this lies in the inclusion of a number of different
categories of industries in each class, e.g. the growth
industry of motor vehicle construction is more than cancelled
out by the declining rail vehicle category within the overall class X Vehicles. More importantly however, a part
of the explanation lies in the inadequacy of employment
size and change as measures of an industry's importance
and growth potential.

Unfortunately no other measurements exist which
enable other aspects of importance, growth and decline to
be compared across the whole range of industry. Some
limited information is however available (Table 22).
Standardised comparative information about the actual

172

value of output is confined to the Manufacturing sector, surveyed by the 1968 Census of Production. Although limited to the Manufacturing sector it provides some indication of the extent to which a different order of industrial significance emerges if the classes are ranged on the basis of output rather than employment. By comparing the Manufacturing sector in Tables 21 and 22, it can be seen that in only two of the seventeen classes does the ordering diverge markedly. Class V Chemicals and allied industries is very much more significant in output terms (4th) than in employment terms (11th), while class XV Clothing and footwear is markedly more significant in employment terms (9th) than in output terms (13th).

The Index of Industrial Production (supplemented by other sources for Agriculture, forestry and fishing) provides a wider comparative coverage, excluding only the last six classes of the Service sector, from which production trends can be tentatively established (Table 22). It is immediately apparent that a number of industries with modest labour requirements and a heavy decline in their labour force between 1966 and 1971 nevertheless increased production at well above the average rate over the same period. In the Service sector XXI Gas, electricity and water and in the Primary sector I Agriculture, forestry and fishing clearly exemplified this increasingly non-labour intensive characteristic, as did three classes in the Manufacturing sector (V Chemical and allied industries, VI Metal manufacture and XI Vehicles). The Construction sector, in spite of considerable labour shedding, also substantially increased production. Other classes, notably III Food, drink and tobacco, large employers of labour with an above average increase in employment also had an above average increase in production. On the other hand it is clear, in spite of some amalgamation of the figures, that all classes which displayed a declining production performance also declined in employment terms, although in some the decline in production was rather more severe than the decline in employment (X Shipbuilding and marine engineering and XVI Bricks, pottery, glass, cement etc.).

One other measure of growth and decline in the Manufacturing sector is provided by the statistics on new factory building over the not directly comparable period 1962-71 (Table 22). It can be seen that there is a considerable degree of correlation with the trends identified on the basis both of employment and output

173

Class	Description	Value of Output 1968		Index of Industrial Production 1971		New Factory Space 1962–71	
		As a percentage of the Scottish Total	Order	As a percentage of 1966	Order	As a percentage of the Scottish Total	Order
	PRIMARY SECTOR						
I	Agriculture, forestry and fishing			119[a]	2		
II	Mining and quarrying			87	15		
	MANUFACTURING SECTOR	100		101		100	4420m²
III	Food, drink and tobacco	22	1	110	6(3)	18	1
IV	Coal and petroleum products	1	16	115	3(1)	6	16
V	Chemicals and allied industries	8	4	109	7(4)	6	9
VI	Metal manufacture	7	6	90		9	8
VII	Mechanical engineering	16	2		12(9)	2	3
VIII	Instrument engineering	2	13	90		9	14
IX	Electrical engineering	5	7			1	4
X	Shipbuilding and marine engineering	4	8	109	12(9)	8	15
XI	Vehicles	4	8	92	7(4)	4	5
XII	Metal goods not elsewhere specified	9	3	90	11(8)	7	11
XIII	Textiles	–	17			–	6
XIV	Leather, leather goods and fur	2	13	90	12(9)	3	17
XV	Clothing and footwear	3	11			3	12
XVI	Bricks, pottery, glass, cement etc.	5	11	84	16(12)	5	13
XVII	Timber, furniture etc.	5	4	106	9(6)	6	10
XVIII	Paper, printing and publishing	8	4	102	10(7)		7
XIX	Other manufacturing industries	2	13	114	4(2)	12	2
	CONSTRUCTION SECTOR			111			
XX	Construction			111	5		
	SERVICE SECTOR			–			
XXI	Gas, electricity and water			125	1		
	SCOTLAND	100		103	1	100	4420m²

a. Estimated on a different basis.

Table 22. Scottish industry: Output, production trends and new factory space 1962–74

Source : Scottish Abstract of Statistics. Census of Production 1968

change in only four classes: III Food, drink and tobacco
and IX Electrical engineering, well above average growth
by all measures;   XVIII Paper, printing and publishing,
slight growth by all measures;   XVI Bricks, pottery, glass,
cement etc. decline by all measures.   Below average levels
of new factory building place V Chemicals and allied
industries, X Shipbuilding and marine engineering, XII
Miscellaneous metal industries, XV Clothing and footwear
and XVII Timber, furniture etc. in the declining sector,
although at least one other measure suggests some relative
growth.   On the other hand VII Mechanical engineering and
XIII Textiles appear to have enjoyed more growth on this
measure than either employment or output trends would
indicate.   Some of these variations in the pattern which
emerges with the new factory space index are largely
explained by the different factory size/output/employment
ratios of the various industries, and this index is
perhaps of rather less significance than either of the
other two.

    Table 23 attempts to summarise some of these con-
clusions about growth and decline in the different branches
of Scottish industry.   All but two of the industrial
classes can be fitted into one of three groups;   growth,
stagnation and decline.   The two unplaced classes displayed growth characteristics in some respects but declining
characteristics in others.   By taking into account the
importance of each industry in terms of employment and,
where applicable, output, the industries can be tabulated
in such a way as to indicate a decreasing influence on
the growth and increasing influence on the decline
tendencies of Scottish industry as a whole.   Thus the
biggest growth impetus to Scottish industry over the
period in question resulted from the growth in XXV
Professional and scientific services, followed by that in
XXVII Public administration and defence.   Conversely,
the biggest handicap to overall industrial growth was the
decline in XXIII Distributive trades, followed by that in
XX Construction.   In the manufacturing sector, III Food,
drink and tobacco, IX Electrical engineering and VI Metal
manufacture were the main growth stimuli, while VII
Mechanical engineering and XIII Textiles were the main
handicaps to growth.   Stagnating and small growing or
declining industries towards the middle of the list in
Table 23 had comparatively little influence on the overall

Overall trend	Relative size (Employment)	Relative size (Output)		Industry	1971 Employment — Percent	Order	Output value — Percent	Order
GROWTH	Large	-	XXV	Professional and scientific services	+10	8		
	Large	-	XXVII	Public administration and defence	- 2	12		
	Large	Large	III	Food, drink and tobacco	+42	5	+75	2
	Large	-	XXIV	Insurance, banking, finance and business services				
	Medium	Medium	IX	Electrical engineering	-25	19	-50	14
	Medium	Large	VI	Metal manufacture	-37	23	-12	8
	Small	Large	V	Chemicals and allied industries	- 8	16	-12	8
	Small	Small	XIX	Other manufacturing industry	-33	21	-37	13
	Small	Small	IV	Coal and petroleum products	-50	25	+12	5
	Small	Small	XVII	Timber, furniture etc.	-33	21	-12	5
	Small	Small	XIV	Leather, leather goods and fur }	0	11		
	Small	Small	XV	Clothing and footwear	-25	19	-25	8
	Small	Small	VIII	Instrument engineering	+29	6	+12	12
STAG-NATION	Large	-	XXVI	Miscellaneous services	+ 1	10		
	Large	-	XXII	Transport and communication	- 3	13		
	Large	Large	XVIII	Paper, printing and publishing	- 4	14	0	7
	Medium	Medium	XXI	Gas, electricity and water	-12	17		
DECLINE	Small	Small	XVI	Bricks, pottery, glass, cement etc.	-21	18	-12	8
	Medium	Medium	XII	Metal goods not elsewhere specified	-46	24	-50	14
	Medium	Medium	X	Shipbuilding and marine engineering	+144	1	+112	1
	Medium	Medium	II	Mining and quarrying	+11	7		
	Large	Large	XIII	Textiles	+38	5	+25	3
	Large	Large	VII	Mechanical engineering	- 4	14	+25	3
	Large	-	XX	Construction	+39	4		
	Large	-	XXIII	Distributive trades	+ 3	9		
MIXED	Large	-	I	Agriculture, forestry and fishing	+69	2		
	Medium	Medium	XI	Vehicles	-51	26	-62	16

Figure 23. Scottish industry: overall trends and relative significance

Sources : Scottish Abstract of Statistics. Census of Production.

Plate 11 Historic Manufacturing Industrial Sites

A. The Carron Iron Works. Founded near Falkirk in 1759, the Carron Works played a key role in the development and the location of the Scottish iron and steel industry.

B. New Lanark. The mill, founded on a water power site in 1785 was purchased by Robert Owen in 1799 and together with the village, developed as a model for the growing industrial communities of Scotland.

Plate 12 Industrial Landscapes
A. A Sand and Gravel Quarry near Muir of Ord, Ross and Cromarty. A tied industry, depending on the raw materials it exploits.

B. Hillington Industrial Estate, Glasgow. Founded in 1937, the Estate contains standard factory units which can be easily converted for use by a succession of footloose industrial concerns.

trends.

The analysis of the industrial structure of present-day Scotland can be given greater meaning by comparing the relative importance of each industrial class in Scotland with its relative importance in the United Kingdom as a whole. This comparison is made in percentage employment and output terms in Table 23. As far as employment is concerned, six of the industrial classes were markedly more significant in Scotland than they were in the United Kingdom as a whole in 1971. The growth or decline trend in these regionally important industries with employment levels more than fifteen per cent above the United Kingdom average naturally had a more significant impact on the overall trend of Scottish industry than on the trend in the United Kingdom as a whole. It is therefore significant that three of them were large employers of labour which suffered a substantial decline in employment in the period 1966-71 (I Agriculture, forestry and fishing, XX Construction and XIII Textiles), while a fourth (X Shipbuilding and marine engineering) was a medium employer of labour also suffering some employment decline over this period. Only one of the industries regionally over-developed in Scotland (III Food, drink and tobacco) was a large employer of labour enjoying employment growth.

On the other hand nine industrial classes were markedly under-represented in Scotland in 1971 in employment terms compared with their importance in the United Kingdom as a whole. Of the four of these which displayed some relative employment growth between 1966 and 1971, only one was a large employer of labour (XXIV Insurance, banking, finance and business services); one was a medium employer (IX Electrical engineering); and two were only small employers (XV Clothing and footwear and IV Coal and petroleum products). Two others were relatively stagnant small employers of labour (V Chemicals and allied industries and XIX Other manufacturing industry. The remaining three consisted of two declining medium employers (XII Miscellaneous metal goods and XI Vehicles) and one declining small employer of labour (XVI Bricks, pottery, glass, cement etc.).

These comparisons reveal a serious imbalance of industry in Scotland. Large employers of labour in the declining sector tend to be over represented and are counterbalanced by only a few at present under-represented medium and small employers of labour in the growth sector. However,

177

by definition, the declining industries become less and less, and the growth industries more and more, significant in the overall pattern of Scottish industry year by year. Assuming, and it is a large assumption, that no major change occurs in the relative growth and decline trends of each class of industry, then the overall structure of Scottish industry as far as employment is concerned, must improve. On the other hand, the present imbalance in the structure will only improve if the growth industries, especially those at present under-represented, grow faster in Scotland than in the United Kingdom as a whole, and fast enough to offset the proportionately larger loss of employment in Scotland from the over represented declining industries. There is very little evidence to suggest that this process is yet taking place.

On the basis of the 1968 Census of Production a similar examination can be made of the balance of manufacturing industry in Scotland relative to that of the United Kingdom on the basis of output (Table 23). Output in Scotland in 1968 was more than twenty per cent above the United Kingdom average in four industrial classes. Two of these over-represented industries were large producers in the declining sector (VII Mechanical engineering and XIII Textiles), one a medium producer in the declining sector (X Shipbuilding and marine engineering), and only one a large producer in the growth sector (III Food, drink and tobacco). Apart from the inclusion of mechanical engineering this is a very similar pattern to that revealed on the basis of employment. Of the five under represented industries whose output was more than twenty per cent below the United Kingdom average, two were medium-output growth industries (IX Electrical engineering and XI Vehicles), and two were small output growth industries (XV Clothing and footwear and XIX Other manufacturing industry). Only one of the five, with a medium output, was in the declining sector (XII Miscellaneous metal goods). This is a rather different pattern from that revealed by a study of employment characteristics; in output terms the bulk of the under represented industries were clearly in the growth sector. The fact that most of the under-represented industries in output terms are in the growth sector while the bulk of the over represented industries are in the declining sector, suggests that Scotland is at present more unfavourably placed in output terms than in employment terms compared with the United Kingdom as a

178

whole.   Although the continuing decline of the declining,
and growth of the growth, industries in Scotland is tending
to produce a better internal pattern of industry in output
terms, there is no evidence to suggest that this process
is operating at a sufficiently fast rate to produce year
by year an improvement in Scotland's position relative to
that of the United Kingdom as a whole.

Regional variations within Scotland

Within Scotland, the distribution of industry is
extremely uneven.   Figure 27 shows the relative size
and broad structural breakdown of the employed population
in the eight planning regions in 1971.   Obviously the
regional distribution of employment bears a very close
relationship to the regional distribution of the population.   Thus it is not surprising that the West Central
(Glasgow) region accounts for very nearly fifty per cent
of the workforce and the East Central (Edinburgh) region
for a further twenty per cent, while the Border and South
West regions have less than five per cent between them.
Another interesting aspect of regional industrial
variations revealed by Figure 27 is the variation in the
proportion of the total regional employed population
accounted for by each of the Primary, Manufacturing,
Construction and Tertiary sectors.

Primary industries account for about five per cent
of the total Scottish employment, but this proportion
varies regionally from nearly fifteen per cent in the
Borders and South West to less than two per cent in the
West Central region.   Away from this latter region and
the neighbouring Falkirk-Stirling region, the relative
importance of the agricultural, forestry, fishing, mining
and quarrying industries loom larger in the regional
economies than in the Scottish economy as a whole.

About thirty five per cent of the Scottish employed
population is engaged in manufacturing industry, but
regionally the proportion varies from over forty per cent
in the West Central to under fifteen per cent in the
Highlands region.   This regional variation does not
entirely compliment the pattern revealed by variations
in primary industrial employment.   Certainly both the
West Central and Falkirk-Stirling regions have a larger
proportion of their work force engaged in manufacturing

179

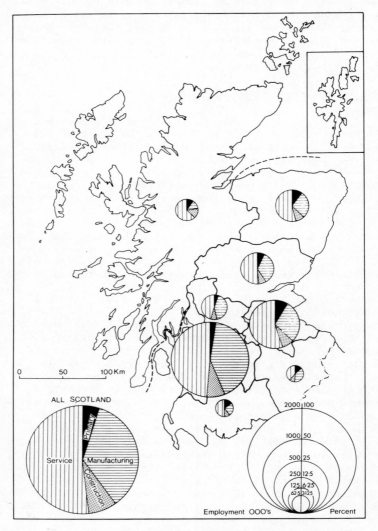

Figure 27.   Regional patterns of employment 1971

than does Scotland as a whole, but so too does the Borders
region which has a high level of primary industrial
employment.   Since Tayside also has about the same proportion of its employed population in manufacturing
industry as Scotland as a whole, manufacturing industry
tends to loom large in the regional economies in the
crescent between the East Central region on the one hand
and the South West, Highlands and North East regions on
the other.

The construction industry is much more evenly distributed, with most regions having roughly the same
proportion (eight per cent) of their total employees in
this sector as does the country as a whole.   The Highlands
region is the one exception, with nearly fourteen per cent
of its employed population engaged in construction industries.
Since the proportion in the North East region is also
slightly higher than the overall Scottish proportion, the
construction industries assume above average significance
in the northern half of Scotland.

Just over fifty per cent of Scotland's work force is
engaged in service industries, but regionally the proportion
rises to nearly sixty two per cent in the Highlands and
over fifty five per cent in the East Central region, the
only two regions in which service employment assumes greater
significance than in the country as a whole.   The proportion falls to just below fifty per cent in the West
Central and Falkirk-Stirling regions, but it is the Borders
region which has the least well developed service industrial
employment, accounting for only just over forty per cent
of the region's work force.

These broad regional industrial variations revealed
in terms of employment statistics are just one crude
indicator of the very complex pattern of regional variations which industrial Scotland presents.   Within the
Manufacturing sector for example regional specialisms
abound.   The West Central region possesses almost the
whole of Scotland's steel and marine engineering industries,
the East Central region the major part of the malting and
brewing industries, and Tayside almost the whole of the
jute industries.   Other regions, although not possessing
all Scotland's capacity, are nevertheless dominated by one
or two manufacturing industries;   the woollen textile
interests of the Borders region, the whisky industry of
the North East and the aluminium industry of the Highlands
region for example.   These and other regional patterns

181

arise essentially from the impact of differing industrial
location factors which have operated in the past and which
continue to operate with varying intensity in the various
parts of Scotland today.

INDUSTRIAL LOCATION

It is a comparatively simple matter to isolate in
theory the factors which may contribute to the development
of a particular industrial activity in a particular area.
It is quite another matter to evaluate the significance
of each factor at each of the formative stages in the
evolution of an industrial pattern in an area the size of
Scotland.   There is a danger of over-emphasising those
aspects of the picture which can be apparently simply
explained, thereby greatly over-simplifying the total
explanation.   Accepting this reservation, an examination
of the influence of various locating factors on the development of Scottish industry provides some explanation of the
very varied regional industrial patterns of present-day
Scotland.

A distinction is often drawn between tied industries,
whose potential location alternatives are limited by
special requirements such as raw material or power resources
or local market outlets, and footloose industries, where
such limiting requirements are so insignificant as to give
almost complete freedom of choice in terms of location.
Infrastructural developments in relation to power and water
distribution, and transport and communications, have
greatly increased locational flexibility by loosening many
of the direct ties between the location of an industry and
the location of its basic requirements.   Raw materials,
power, finished products, the work force and capital can
now be moved over considerable distances easily and
cheaply.   However the discussion on the infrastructures
of Scotland in an earlier chapter revealed a by no means
even distribution of power and transport facilities, while
regional variations of natural resources and population
also still persist.   No Scottish industries are completely
footloose in the sense that they could literally be
located anywhere in the country and function equally well;
all kinds of regional variations continue to exert an
influence on the location of industry.

182

The location of primary industry

Primary industries are still very strongly influenced by the location of raw materials, since they are concerned with the direct exploitation of such resources. Based on land resource exploitation, the agricultural and forestry industries are easily the most widespread industries in Scotland. The variations of resource endowment, together with a wide range of other factors do nevertheless introduce considerable regional variations both in intensity and type of activity. These have already been discussed in chapter 4. The mining and quarrying industries are much more localised in their occurrence since the concentrated resources on which they depend are much more limited in their distribution. The resources themselves are also irreplaceable once exploited, which means that the location of activity changes quite rapidly. (Plate 12A). Variations in the quality and quantity of the mineral resources also influence the continuing viability of the industry, in association with changing markets and evolving methods of exploitation. Some of these influences have already been discussed in relation to the coal and oil industries in chapter 3, and they also apply to other branches of the mining and quarrying industries of Scotland. Apart from the still widespread quarrying of sand, gravel and stone (especially granite and sandstone), for the construction industry, most such industries have greatly declined or vanished. Formerly important centres of mining and quarrying, such as the slate quarries of Ballachulish and Aberfoyle, and the lead and barytes mines of Leadhills and Wanlockhead, have now ceased operation, either because of exhaustion of the resources or low qualities and quantities for modern markets and exploitation techniques. Scotland possesses many mineral resources, including precious metals such as gold and silver, but they are insufficiently concentrated to support continuous mining enterprises on a commercial scale.

The fishing industry also has a limited location pattern, but in part for a different reason. The industry is largely concerned with the exploitation of the resources of the sea, and hence is strongly tied to a coastal location. However, although the resources do vary from place to place around the Scottish coast, and some local specialisation occurs, the most significant factors in the development of the present pattern of fishing activity are the economies

of scale to be gained from the concentration of activity
on a few landing sites. The rise of Aberdeen, Peterhead
and Mallaig to pre-eminence is associated particularly
with the concentration there of the shore facilities, and
market transport links required by large-scale commercial
herring fishing and deep-sea fishing for demersal fish
such as haddock, cod and whiting. Inshore and shallow
sea fishing, especially for herring, is less demanding in
terms of capital investment, and many smaller ports are
important centres of this branch of the industry. These
smaller ports however are more dependant on the resources
of their local seas or the landings of foreign vessels.
Variations in the movements of fish, especially herring,
thus introduce fluctuations in the fortunes of such ports
from year to year, or to the demise of formerly important
fishing ports. (Plate 10A). The almost complete disappearance of herring shoals from the seas off the south
west of Scotland, especially the renowned waters of Loch
Fyne, in the present century, and the diminution of North
Sea shoals in the nineteen sixties provide examples of the
vulnerability of small local fishing ports to changes in
the resource base. Most vulnerable are the many, often
single small-boat fishing activities associated with
almost every small harbour and landing site around the
Scottish coast. Small enterprises are also handicapped
by limited market outlets, unless the luxury demand for
a local product is sufficient to offset high transport
cost. The rise in the shell fish, above all lobster,
industry on the west coast in the nineteen sixties
associated with continental markets and air transport
is a graphic example.

The vulnerability of inflexible primary industries
to resource exhaustion and commercial change, together
with the fact that many smaller settlements in remoter
parts of the country depend very heavily on such industries
for their livelihood, has led to considerable government
intervention in the present century. Such intervention
may have the result of either maintaining a local primary
industry in operation long after it has ceased to be
economically viable (agricultural enterprises are often
maintained in this way), or of supporting the development
of replacement manufacturing or service industries. In
both cases this process leads to a locational pattern of
industry inexplicable in contemporary economic terms, but
one clearly associated with the location of formerly

184

significant centres of primary industry (e.g. Leadhills, Ballachulish).

The location of manufacturing industry

The exhaustion of the resource base inevitably leads to the abandonment of primary industry, but manufacturing industry is not subject to immediate collapse once the reason for its initial location ceases to operate. (Plate 11). This inertia factor greatly complicates the explanation of the location of manufacturing industry in Scotland. Because of the capital installations, a skilled labour force and very often a regional reputation (Harris tweed, a Clyde-built ship), manufacturing industry may continue in a particular location almost indefinitely. The locational explanation of manufacturing industry is therefore continually involved with causative factors operating at various times in the past, as well as those influencing new developments at the present time.

The influence of raw materials

Manufacturing industry is not tied to the exact place in which its raw materials are produced. Nevertheless most manufacturing industry is drawn to some extent by the location of its raw materials, the closeness of the location correspondence depending on the nature of the industry and its raw materials. Those branches of manufacturing industry engaged in the first stages of bulk raw material processing tend to be most closely linked to the areas where their raw materials are produced. In Scotland, this association can be seen in the case of the many fish and food processing industries found in or near the fishing ports and small agricultural towns; in the case of the whisky industry associated with the location of water of special quality; in the case of the brick and refractory materials industries of Central Scotland; in the case of the widespread distribution of the saw-milling industry; and in the case of the woollen textile industries of the Borders and scattered locations in the Highlands. The location of the woollen textile and perhaps the whisky industry, is today explained at least in part by the inertia factor, the regional name, accumulated skills and capital equipment being rather more significant than local raw material supplies. In other Scottish industries local raw material supplies have almost entirely been exhausted but the inertia factor still maintains a locational pattern associated with their former occurrence. The iron and steel industry is still heavily concentrated in the Clyde valley east of Glasgow, where it grew up in the nineteenth century in association with local supplies of iron ore and coal. The former is no longer produced locally (although scrap iron is), while the latter is very much in decline.

Another very significant but slightly less direct link between location of manufacturing industry and source of raw materials is illustrated by the concentrations of large elements of manufacturing industry in or near the major Scottish ports. These areas are those in which bulk imported raw materials are most readily available. Since a very large proportion of the raw materials for Scottish manufacturing industry are now imported, the attraction of a port location for a wide range of activities is very strong. Often these port industries represent an expansion of originally local raw material-based industries, such as the grain milling and food processing interests around the Forth ports, the steel industry associated with the Clyde ports, or timber using industries. In other instances the link with original local industries is less direct, and the present industrial pattern reflects a change of activity based on a new imported raw material. The jute industry of Dundee largely replaced an earlier linen making tradition, traces of which still persist in Tayside, and is itself being partly replaced by synthetic fibre industries. The cotton industry of Paisley is the last substantial remnant of a major imported raw material-based industry which largely replaced the earlier local linen industries of West Central Scotland in the eighteenth and nineteenth centuries. The import of non-indigenous raw materials also created completely new manufacturing industries in or near ports. Food industries, such as sugar refining and confectionery manufacture, the tobacco industry, many non-ferrous metal industries and the chemical industries display a marked concentration in the Clyde and Forth areas largely for this reason.

The raw materials of many manufacturing processes are the products of other manufacturing industries. This is just one of the many linkage factors which encourage the development of concentrations of a wide range of industries in small areas. Most more sophisticated manufacturing, and particularly assembling, industries

186

draw on one or more semi-finishing industries for their
raw materials. The clothing industry requires threads
and woven cloth produced by the textile industry, the
engineering industries require semi-finished steel. There
is therefore a tendency for such industries to locate in
reasonable proximity to industries producing their basic
materials, industries which may themselves be quite strongly
tied to their raw material source. This natural tendency
towards the development of concentrations of varied
manufacturing industry around key raw material-based semi-
finishing activities has played a major part in the location
of manufacturing industry in Scotland. It provides a
large part of the explanation for the development of the
mixed industrial complexes in association with the location
of basic food processing, textile and iron and steel
industries. It has also been used, with limited success,
in efforts to stimulate the growth of manufacturing industry
in areas where few other favourable factors for such
developments exist. The pulp mill at Corpach near Fort
William, established in the late nineteen-sixties is a
good example. Located in an area with little manufacturing industry, but in proximity to local timber supplies,
it was hoped that it would provide semi-finished products
which would attract further manufacturing industries to
develop. However, the availability of semi-finished
materials has not proved a strong enough advantage to offset other disadvantages which the Fort William area
possesses for most manufacturing industries.

The influence of power supplies

The location of the power source does not exert a
very strong influence on the location of new manufacturing
industry in Scotland today, since power is relatively
cheap and easy to move in bulk over the kind of distances
involved in Scotland. Prior to the industrial revolution
manufacturing industry was on a very small scale and the
demands for power were limited. Indeed the lack of
technology in relation to industrial power supplies was
itself a limiting factor to the scale of industrial units.
The development of industrial power technology however,
in the two hundred years after about 1700, led to a very
different situation. During this period, the location of
large scale power sources exerted an almost complete control
on the location of manufacturing industry in Scotland.

Many traces of this influence still remain and thus contribute to the explanation of present day locations. (Plate 11).

Few manufacturing industries resisted the increased scale of activity and commercial prospects which first water power and then steam power opened up in the eighteenth century. The craft industries of remoter parts, and a few specialist industries such as the cottage-based Harris tweed and some elements of the whisky industry, are the only true relics in locational and scale terms of the pre-industrial revolution widespread distribution of small scale units of manufacturing industry. Mill sites were the first power points to attract food, timber and above all textile enterprises, particularly mill sites on the upland margins in the Borders and to the north and south of the Central Lowlands. A little later the coal-fields of Ayrshire, Lanarkshire, Fife and the Lothians and areas accessible to them by canal and later rail, attracted all kinds of manufacturing industry, but especially metal industries, to very limited parts of Scotland. The concentrated pattern of manufacturing industry produced by these two power revolutions still persists. Later revolutions, such as hydro-electric and nuclear power developments and oil, have had markedly little influence on the location of manufacturing industry. The most recent examples of significant new industrial developments tied to the location of the power source are the works associated with aluminium production at Foyers (now closed), Kinlochleven and Fort William. Located in proximity to sources of hydro-electric power in the early twentieth century, they have conspicuously failed to provide the key industrial foci for growth that both mill sites and sources of coal provided in the two previous centuries. In the twentieth century power is transported to already established industrial locations rather than encouraging manufacturing industry to thrive where it is produced.

The influence of markets

The distribution of manufacturing industry is also influenced by the locational pull of the market. Industries which produce perishable or general goods for public consumption, such as the food, clothing and household article industries occur widely in association with

188

almost all centres of population, the range and scale of
such industrial enterprises displaying a close relationship
with the size of the immediate consumer market. Many
manufacturing industries are also, as already mentioned,
themselves markets for the produce of other industries, and
the location of key consuming industries, such as the
assembling of cars, television sets or complex machinery
of any kind, is another powerful cause of regional concentrations of a wide range of manufacturing industry.
Most of the branches of the engineering industry in Scotland
display this kind of locational relationship with their
industrial markets. Marine engineering is located in
proximity to the ship assembling yards, notably on the
Clyde, textile machinery manufacture occurs in all the main
textile producing regions, while the bolt, screw, wire and
all kinds of tool-making industries are in their turn
located in proximity to the engineering industries. Most
recently this association has been demonstrated by the search
for, and exploitation of, North Sea oil. Engineering and
other oil related industry has been attracted to east coast
locations, that part of Scotland closest to the new market
for their products. This kind of market association has
also been used to encourage the growth of manufacturing
industry in regions of Scotland suffering from economic
stagnation. The introduction of vehicle assembly plant
at Bathgate and at Linwood in the nineteen sixties for
example, was designed to provide a growth focus for a
whole range of smaller industries producing the various
components required by such markets. The limited success
of these attempts to stimulate industrial growth would
suggest that the locational pull of the market for most
manufacturing industries is not particularly strong.
Certainly, since most manufacturing industries reduce the
bulk and add to the value of their materials, it is
theoretically more economic to transport the finished
product than the raw material. More important though is
the extent to which developments in transport have altered
the meaning of proximity in locational terms.

The influence of transport

   Modern transport has greatly enlarged the distances
over which the advantages of industrial linkage can be
obtained. Scotland's industrial raw materials and markets
are no longer confined to the country's internal resources.

189

However, proximity to means of transport is vital. Regional
disparities in the transport infrastructure of Scotland have
already been discussed in chapter 3, and they have a considerable influence on the location of manufacturing industry.
Isolation, or even access to only limited transport routes,
is a serious handicap to the continuing viability of manufacturing industry. Only the Central Valley, Ayrshire and
limited locations on the east coast are really accessible
to a wide range of internal and external transport routes.
Thus the largely historical advantages of these areas for
the development of manufacturing industry are maintained
and reinforced by the present day advantages of accessibility
in relation to modern transport facilities. In the past,
the development of these transport services themselves
gave rise to important elements of manufacturing industry,
such as the shipbuilding activities of the Clyde and the
railway works of Glasgow.

The influence of labour supply

    At various formative stages in its development, Scottish
manufacturing industry made heavy new demands for general
and skilled labour. This demand was satisfied by the
movement of people to the areas in which industry was expanding, thus playing a large part in the redistribution
of the Scottish population since 1801 discussed in chapter
2. In times of prosperity and growth, concentrations of
manufacturing industry provide high levels of employment,
which tends to prevent the attraction of new enterprises
as a result of availability of labour. However in less
prosperous times, such as those generally obtaining in
Scotland since the mid-nineteen twenties, concentrations
of manufacturing industry tend to generate unemployment
or an excess of semi-skilled and skilled labour. In
theory it might be expected that this would provide an
attraction for new manufacturing industry. In practice,
the general industrial stagnation of which unemployment
is one symptom has seemed, in the Scottish experience, to
cancel out this attractive factor. Without government
intervention it is likely that excess labour generated
by recessions in Scottish manufacturing industry would,
like its predecessors, have moved to areas of natural
industrial growth, mostly beyond the borders of Scotland,
rather than have attracted new manufacturing industry to
Scotland. However, since the mid-nineteen thirties

190

central government has adopted an increasingly powerful
policy of directing new industry to areas with an excess
labour force (see chapter 2). As a result areas which
suffer high rates of unemployment, reflecting in part
decreasing locational advantages for manufacturing industry,
are singled out as key areas for new developments. Scotland
as a whole, but especially Glasgow and Clydeside, is thus
being strongly promoted as an area for new manufacturing
industry largely because of its high rate of unemployment.
This kind of policy, providing new work for the work force
in areas of declining industry, of considerable significance
in Scotland, has the effect of fossilising existing dis-
tributions of manufacturing industry, though it changes the
character of that industry.

The influence of capital

As outlined in chapter 2, the chief methods by which
the location of industry policy in Britain operates are
through various measures of relief from the full costs of
development offered to firms establishing or extending
manufacturing industries in designated areas. In effect,
a designated region becomes a highly attractive location
for new industry as a result of availability of capital.
The internal accumulation of capital in earlier times played
a key role in the development of new industries in Scotland,
while the capital tied up in established premises and equipment is a factor of importance in the continuation of
industrial enterprises. Since 1934, however, it has been
the designation of particular areas for government aid that
has been the most significant capital incentive to new
manufacturing industrial developments in Scotland (see
chapter 2).
A great deal of this industry has been rather small
scale, very often branch factories of non-Scottish firms.
Much of it has been in the light engineering and textile
fields and located on small standardised factory estate
premises or in the New Towns. Although not a few such
enterprises have been comparatively short-lived, a steady
succession of small firms has provided continuity of
activity in spite of high turnover. (Plate 12B). This
very flexible pattern of miscellaneous, often short-term,
manufacturing industries may, in the long run, provide a
firmer permanent economic base for Scottish industry than

large-scale key industrial developments. However a number of such key industries have also been attracted to Scotland as a result of the government's industrial location policy, most of them requiring considerable government nurturing (by the preferential placing of government contracts for example) in the early years. Heavy dependance on them does of course present potential problems in the event of failure or decline; they could be the shipyards and locomotive workshops of the future. The Ravenscraig steel plant in Motherwell and the Bathgate and Linwood vehicle works are notable developments of manufacturing industry resulting from the location of industry policy, but the rise of the electronics industry is perhaps the most significant achievement. Major world names in this field now have substantial industrial plant in Scotland (Ferranti, Burroughs, Honeywell, IBM, Philips, AEI etc.), especially throughout the central belt.

A great many of the firms in this group of manufacturing industry are foreign owned or based. The attraction of foreign capital investment in manufacturing industry is in fact one of the most obvious results of the location of industry policy as far as Scotland is concerned. Apart from the large English element, non-Scottish investment has been mainly by North American companies, with European companies playing a much less significant role. Although difficult to determine accurately, studies in the early nineteen seventies suggest that American owned firms are now responsible for between ten and twenty per cent of the output of and employment in, manufacturing industry in Scotland.

The present very concentrated distribution of manufacturing industry in Scotland evolved in response to the powerful locational advantages of very small parts of the country at formative stages in its industrial development. In the process, the labour force, capital investment and transport facilities also became regionally concentrated. Very few recent trends suggest a weakening of the established distribution pattern. It is too early yet to assess whether the exploitation of North Sea oil resources will produce great alterations, but it does not seem likely. Very little change has yet occurred either as a result of the deep water port requirements of modern world shipping, except for the development of Invergordon and discussions about the location of new manufacturing enterprises at

192

Plate 13 Construction Industry

A. The Aigas Dam, River Beauly 1961. The building of large structures on site has, in the last two hundred years, temporarily disrupted the local economy in most remote parts of Scotland.

B. North Sea Oil Platform Construction Site, Methil, Fife. The latest in a series of construction booms, affecting especially the East Coast and Clydeside.

Plate 14 Urban Landscapes
A. Glasgow's East End. Mixed industrial, commercial and residential building, mainly nineteenth century. In spite of legislation, atmospheric pollution, especially during winter inversions, is not completely cured.

B. The Centre of Edinburgh. A group of imposing public and commercial buildings.

Hunterston and other coastal sites on the lower Clyde. In
fact the growing interest in the quality of the total
environment of Scotland is exerting increasing pressure to
prevent the spread of manufacturing industry, except on a
very modest scale, into areas where it is not already
developed in some measure.

The location of the construction industry

Although dependant on raw materials, power supplies,
labour and capital, the location of the construction
industry is tied very closely to the market since it is
largely concerned with the construction of fixed installations - buildings, transport routes etc. - on site or
very close to the final site. Since the demand for such
installations is universal, though the level of demand is
related to the size of a region's population, it is not
surprising that there is little variation regionally,
within Scotland, in the proportion of the work force
employed in construction (Fig 27).   Unlike almost all
other industries however, the location of the construction
industry is not fixed for any length of time; the completion of a project also means a move to a new location.
In areas with a largely built environment, such as the major
towns, these movements in location may be relatively short,
and it might be said that such areas in general are
permanently characterised by construction industry sites.
In regions where the elements of the built environment are
much less widespread, locational movements of the construction industry tend to be much greater, and constructional
activities perform a much less permanent role in the local
economy.   During the late eighteenth, nineteenth and early
twentieth centuries, the construction of canals, roads and
railways through the countryside brought large shifting
populations of construction workers to temporary sites in
all parts of Scotland.   The development of the hydro-
electric power resources, mainly ih the Southern Uplands
and the Highlands, continued the pattern into the nineteen
sixties. (Plate 13A).   Since then major industrial
installations and their associated developments in remote
areas, such as the Corpach pulp mill and the Invergordon
smelter have carried on the tradition.   The developments
associated with the exploration for North Sea oil since
1970 have produced a construction industry boom at coastal
sites in many parts of Scotland. (Plate 13B).

Although the actual locations of such construction
industry sites may be temporary, they have been an almost
permanent feature of the scene in remoter parts of Scotland
for some two hundred years.   They have given, and continue
to give, a considerable boost to local raw material exploitation (sand, gravel and aggregate in particular) and
to the local, and indeed the Scottish, economy.   In fact,
at times and in particular places, not entirely necessary
construction work has been undertaken in an effort to
encourage just such local economic growth and to soak up
local unemployment pools.

The location of service industry

Most service industry premises and centres of employment are strongly linked in locational terms to their
markets.   Since these markets are chiefly the public at
large, there is a strong correlation with the distribution
of population.   Strong linkages also operate between
different service industries and between service and other
industries, generating a strong tendency towards concentrations of development.   As a general rule, the number
and range of distributional, insurance, banking, finance,
business, professional, scientific, administrative and
entertainment premises increases with increasing settlement
size.   Edinburgh and Glasgow therefore possess the greatest
concentrations of service industry in Scotland, followed by
other urban centres, down to the small villages with only
a very few retail, office, educational and cultural establishments.   Within the urban areas, many service
industries are strongly pulled towards the accessible
urban centres, creating specialised central business
districts.
The strong central place locational pull for service
industry development breaks down in only a few instances.
Part of the development associated with the gas, electricity
and water supply industries is related to scattered production centres, while in the transport and communications
industries, the manning and operation of the route network
involves a breakdown of the central locational pattern.
In other cases the market for service industries is itself
mobile, and the siting of service establishments is
associated with locational attributes other than centrality.
Thus service industries associated with tourism are widely

194

scattered throughout Scotland because of the widespread distribution of scenic and historic phenomena attractive to tourists. Even so, there is a tendency towards the development of concentrations associated with particular points such as seaside resorts like Ayr, Saltcoats and Troon and mountain resorts like Glencoe, Pitlochry and Aviemore. For some defence and scientific research establishments, remoteness from the main centres of population is a positive advantage. The Uist rocket range, the Dounreay nuclear research establishment and the Rhum nature conservancy research centre are but three examples.

Those elements of service industry relatively free from the locational pull of major central places, especially those associated with tourism, have been encouraged as potential economic growth foci in remoter parts of Scotland where there are few if any locational advantages for other forms of industrial development. The Aviemore tourist and the Dounreay research developments are two good examples. Since the mid-nineteen sixties interest has grown in the possibility of using elements of the service industries which have traditionally been regarded as strongly tied to central places in the same way. As long as reasonable communications, and to a lesser extent transport facilities, are available, there is no reason why all local administrative and business offices should be located in one centre. Nor is there any reason why all national administrative and business head offices should be located in the capital Edinburgh. Large institutions, such as universities, similarly do not have to be located in the largest urban centres. Although these service industries have tended in the past to display strong central ties, they are in fact footloose to some degree. The increasing extension of industrial location policy planning to service industries is beginning to disseminate new developments of service industries more widely amongst the urban settlements of Scotland, including especially the New Towns (the Inland Revenue offices at East Kilbride for example), although not as yet beyond the upper range of the urban hierarchy.

THE INDUSTRIAL LANDSCAPES OF SCOTLAND

Much the greater part of Scotland, somewhere in the region of ninety per cent of the total land area, is dominated by the extensive primary industries of agriculture and forestry. The varying intensities and types of activity and the resulting landscapes of such rural areas of Scotland have already been discussed in chapter 4. The dominant agricultural and forestry landscapes in such areas do, of course, contain small pockets of fishing, mining, manufacturing and service activity, usually on a small scale and associated with the mixed activities of small urban settlements. In just a few instances however concentrations of other industrial activity do give rise to landscapes somewhat distinct from the general rural types.

Manufacturing industry on the cottage scale, even if locally concentrated as in the woollen enterprises of Lewis and the Shetlands, does not produce distinctly different landscapes. But when small-scale specialised factory premises are involved, distinctive landscape elements are produced. The regional concentrations of whisky distilleries in the north-east, especially in Banffshire and Morayshire, and on the Island of Islay are cases in point. Single large-scale industrial developments in the manufacturing and service sectors also introduce atypical landscape features. The aluminium works of Kinlochleven, Invergordon and Fort William, the latter now supplemented by the large-scale pulp mill at Corpach; the nuclear power station at Dounreay; the many hydro-electric power stations in the Highlands and South West; the Aviemore tourist complex - all these impinge sharply on the landscape. Such isolated industrial premises tend to influence the landscape over a much wider area than their actual locations as a result of associated rail, road and transmission line developments. From time to time also large-scale elements of the construction industry disrupt, if only temporarily, the general rural landscape.

On only a very small proportion of the total land area of Scotland do concentrations of mining, manufacturing and service industries dominate the landscape. This is largely because they make very small demands on space compared with extensive activities like forestry and agriculture. In the Central Lowlands, and the neighbouring valleys of the Borders and the east-coast lowlands northward to Aberdeen, where most of such landscapes are found,

196

they are discontinuous. Large areas are still dominated by agriculture, while even in the more urbanised zones considerable areas are dominated in landscape terms by housing developments, or a mixture of land uses, rather than by active or derelict mining, manufacturing and service establishments. This urban element of Scotland is more fully discussed in Chapter 6. In just a few instances however, and over very limited areas, concentrations of particular types of industrial activity do produce landscapes which might be described more accurately as industrial rather than urban in character.

In the strip of country from central Ayrshire through the northern part of Lanarkshire to West Lothian and the eastern part of Stirlingshire, and on both sides of the Forth in southern Fife and the eastern part of Midlothian, discontinuous tracts are dominated by mining landscapes, mainly coal mining but also sand and gravel, clay and oil shale activities. Much of such country is derelict and the landscape characterised by spoil heaps and abandonned small workings rather than large-scale modern mines and quarries. Zones of derelict land also characterise the small areas dominated by concentrations of long-established heavy manufacturing industry, such as the iron and steel landscapes of Lanarkshire east of Glasgow or the shipyard and heavy portside industrial landscapes of the upper Clyde estuary. More varied manufacturing industrial landscapes tend to occur around more active ports and in narrow linear bands along main rail and road arteries leading from the main urban centres. In relation to these transport arteries, the proportion of derelict land and old manufacturing premises declines as the arteries approach the perimeters of the urban centres, giving way to newer, often single-storey factories. Since the late nineteen thirties, this linear pattern of mixed manufacturing industrial expansion has given way increasingly to the planned zoning of factory premises, often on purpose-built factory estates. This has led to the widespread development in all parts of central Scotland, but especially in suburban areas and in the New Towns, of concentrated blocks of mixed, generally small single-storey, manufacturing industrial premises. These small mixed manufacturing industrial zones are an increasingly significant element in the industrial landscapes of Scotland. (Plate 12B).

Small areas within urban Scotland in which the landscape is dominated by concentrations of mixed service

197

industries are also widespread.   They are found to a greater or less extent in the centres of all towns and cities, and at certain suburban nodes in the larger cities.   Such areas are characterised by a mixture, or sometimes distinct zones, of transport, cultural, office and shopping premises.

Single elements of manufacturing or service industry are only rarely on a sufficiently large scale to make a major, rather than a minor local, contribution to the landscape.   Amongst the more space consuming of such premises are air ports and major transport termini, large installations like the Grangemouth oil refinery, the power stations of Kincardine, Cockenzie and Longannet, the assembly plant at Bathgate and Linwood, the larger hospitals and university campuses.   Such large scale developments do stand out from the mixture of industrial and other elements which form the general urbanised landscapes of a small part of Scotland.

6 URBAN SCOTLAND by G. Gordon

Reference has already been made in Chapter 2 to the
scale and nature of the process of urbanisation in Scotland
since the beginning of the nineteenth century, but urbanisation is a complex phenomena involving many components
which vary temporally and spatially.   One fundamental
problem involves the definition of an urban settlement.
Whilst a particular population size is frequently adopted
as a basis for definition at a national or international
scale, any accurate definition needs to include some
element of functional structure, because urban centres are
normally viewed as central places supplying goods and
services to their resident population and to the inhabitants
of a hinterland, the surrounding area or sphere of influence
of that central place.   In Scotland, the Census recognises
cities, large burghs and small burghs, and suggests that
urban centres are burghs with at least 1,000 inhabitants.
Since 1750 various additions have been made to the list of
burghs (as recently as 1951 suburban communities adjoining
Glasgow such as Bearsden and Bishopbriggs attained small
burgh status), but time-lags were inevitable and substantial
urbanised areas did not have burgh status at particular
moments in history.   Amorphous late nineteenth century
mining areas such as Shotts in North Lanarkshire or some of
the oil-shale communities of West Lothian provide examples
stemming from industrial growth in previously agricultural
areas, whilst massive suburban districts such as Newton
Mearns and Clarkston to the south of Glasgow or Currie to
the west of Edinburgh reflect more recent suburban trends.
These time lags in the census definitions stem from an
expanding urban system which increasingly is pervading the
whole way of life of Scottish society and thereby clouding
attempts to establish a simplistic dichotomy between urban
and rural settlements or indeed, ways of life.   This is
shown in Fig 28 where only Sutherland had less than 20 per
cent of its population resident in burghs in 1971.

Significantly many of the upland counties had about half
of their population nucleated in burghs, creating a system
of small market nodes outside the densely populated central
belt.   Fig 28 also emphasises the fact that high levels
of nucleation occur in some Border and Highland counties,
albeit in quite small urban settlements set within counties
which in turn have a small total population.   Thus the
County of Selkirk had 20,868 inhabitants in 1971, some 87
per cent living in the burghs of Galashiels and Selkirk.
The largest counties in terms of resident population,
Lanark (626,790), Renfrew (362,123), Ayr (361,257), Fife
(327,131) and Dunbarton (237,549) all had at least half of
their inhabitants resident in burghs but the proportion
ranged from about 53 per cent in Lanark to 76 per cent in
Dunbarton.   Fig 29 reveals the dominant western focus in
the distribution of Scotland's urban population and the
critical role of Edinburgh, Dundee and Aberdeen which along
with the County of Fife represent the major urban foci in
eastern Scotland, suggesting a contrast between an extensive urbanised western central lowland zone and a more
dispersed nodal pattern on the east coast.

THE EVOLUTION OF THE URBAN HIERARCHY

In its own way the medieval settlement system of
Scotland was structured and did, largely, distinguish
between urban and rural centres.   From the time of David I
the monarch had granted special trading privileges to places
awarded the status of Royal Burgh which effectively established their role as regional service centres commanding
a defined hinterland and acting as the intermediary between
that area and the rest of the national and international
trading system.   Thus Edinburgh for several centuries
controlled the port of Leith, the main port in Scotland
during much of the medieval period.   Trade in the port could
only be conducted by Edinburgh merchants.   Similarly the
burgh charter of Dundee prohibited anyone in the Sheriffdom
of Forfar from buying wool or skins except from the
burgesses of Dundee.   The main focus of medieval Scotland
lay on the east coast reflecting the trading links with
the Baltic and the Low Countries and east coast Royal Burghs
therefore dominated urban life in Scotland until the
eighteenth century.   A second category of burgh, Burghs
of Barony gradually emerged often in the environs of the

200

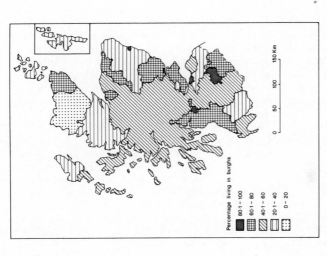

Figure 28.   Degree of urbanisation 1971
(By counties)

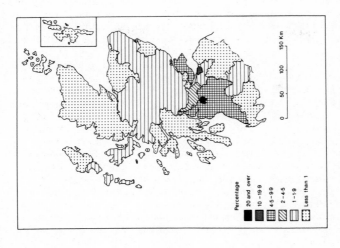

Figure 29.   Distribution of the urban
population 1971 (By counties)

201

larger Royal Burghs.   They frequently attracted trades
and crafts which were unable to find sites in the Royal
Burghs and provided an example of early industrial suburbs.
All of these settlements, even the Royal Burghs, were small:
Glasgow in 1600 had a population of about 5,000 while
Edinburgh in 1707 was estimated to have only 20,000 inhabi-
tants.

The rural settlement pattern was founded upon the
small agricultural hamlet or clachan.   The association
of church and hamlet formed the kirk towns which flourished
after the Reformation and there were also other specialised
hamlets such as milltowns and castletowns.   Marketing,
however, was essentially the privilege of Royal Burghs
which curtailed the development of a network of marketing
villages until the eighteenth century.   Further components
of the rural settlement structure were the small nuclei
of farm labourers' cottages on the large agricultural
estates in parts of the agricultural lowlands of eastern
Scotland while in the eighteenth century planned villages
emerged as a further element in the structure.   These
resulted from various forces including the need to house
surplus rural population, to stimulate the rural economy
and to organise the land use pattern on the large agricultural estates.   Thus a series of new villages were
created throughout Scotland adding new elements to the
market structure and challenging the position of the
smaller Royal Burghs and the baronial markets which had
been established on estates in the sixteenth century.
Some of these planned villages remained small distinct
units but many grew into important nodes as the population
of Scotland increased during the eighteenth and nineteenth
centuries.

By 1801 both Edinburgh and Glasgow housed over 80,000
inhabitants but most urban settlements still had less than
10,000 residents and the distribution was predominantly on
the east side of Scotland.   With population increase and
industrialisation the pattern began to change during the
nineteenth century and gradually the coalfields and Clydeside assumed greater importance in the overall structure.
Figs. 30 to 34 trace the detailed change in the pattern of
distribution of settlements with populations in excess of
5,000 persons.   By 1851, as can be seen from Fig 30,
Glasgow was larger than Edinburgh and Paisley, Greenock
and Kilmarnock were important towns.   In addition, a
girdle of smaller but expanding industrial centres could

be identified around Glasgow including Coatbridge, Airdrie, Rutherglen and Hamilton to the east of the city and Dumbarton, Port Glasgow, Barrhead and Johnstone on the west.   Edinburgh (160,302 inhabitants) was clearly the second largest city and distinctly separated in terms of size from the third and fourth settlements, Dundee (78,931) and Aberdeen (71,973). Within the penumbra of Edinburgh were the port of Leith and the smaller urban nodes of Musselburgh and Dalkeith. The remainder of the urban pattern consisted of a series of distinct and separate market centres and industrial nodes with Perth being noteworthy as a middle-order settlement reflecting the nodal situation of the town.   Outside the Central Lowlands the pattern had a strong coastal tendency with most of the exceptions being route foci.

The pattern for 1881 (Fig 31) reveals an increase in the number of centres with the addition of a further nineteen urban places to the map.   The rank order of the largest settlements is unchanged although all have grown substantially.   The intensification of urban development in west central Scotland is clearly illustrated with the emergence of a series of industrial suburbs adjoining Glasgow, of which Govan was the largest, and extensive industrial urban growth in Lanarkshire, Renfrewshire and Dunbartonshire.   Similarly in Fife, Kirkcaldy and Dysart had grown rapidly and Edinburgh and Dundee had experienced extra-mural expansion at Portobello and Broughty Ferry respectively.   Outwith the Central Lowlands the pattern was more stable with some growth in the Borders and in the North-East.

Many of these trends continued to influence the pattern up to 1911 (Fig 32).   By that time Glasgow housed over three-quarters of a million people and was at the core of a conurbation, a word coined by Geddes at about this period. The other cities were still growing but at a much slower rate.   Edinburgh increased by 91,961 between 1881-1911 and Dundee by only 24,765 over the same period.   One noticeable feature is the increased number of middle-order towns, especially in the 30,000 - 49,999 category which contained nine burghs in 1911 and none in 1881.   Of the nine centres, three were solely products of the industrial expansion, namely Clydebank, Coatbridge and Motherwell whilst of the others Kirkcaldy, Kilmarnock, Falkirk and Hamilton all owed much of their recent growth to industrial development and coal-mining.   Only Ayr and Perth were long established important agricultural centres, although they

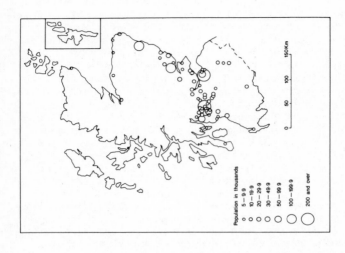

Figure 31.   Burghs with more than 5000
              inhabitants, 1881

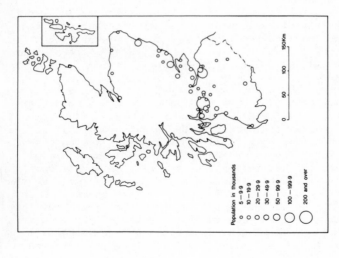

Figure 30.   Burghs with more than 5000
              inhabitants, 1851

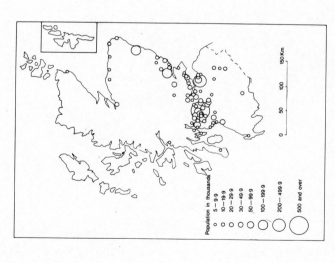

Figure 33.   Burghs with more than 5000
             inhabitants, 1951

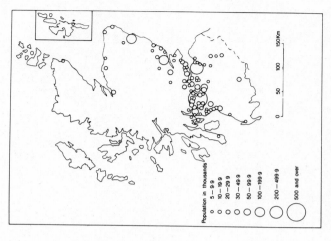

Figure 32.   Burghs with more than 5000
             inhabitants, 1911

205

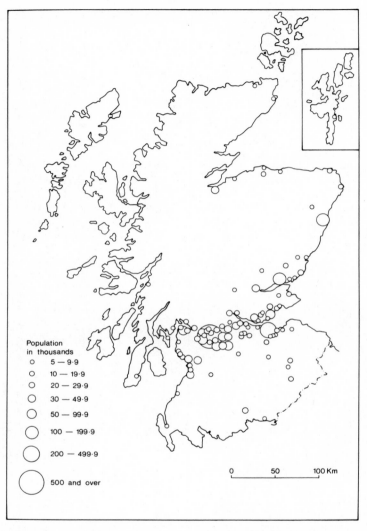

Figure 34. Burghs with more than 5000 inhabitants 1971

too had benefitted to some extent from industrial growth and improved communications which had also added a suburban function to the developing functional structure of these county towns.   Another feature of the map is the appearance of new clusters of urban centres on the Ayrshire coast, in the Falkirk-Stirling area and in Fife.

By 1951 the cities had been extended to incorporate previously independent burghs such as Govan, Pollokshaws, Leith, Portobello, Broughty Ferry and Dysart.   In addition Motherwell and Wishaw had merged to form one burgh as had Bonnyrigg and Lasswade.   Thus the largest centres remained essentially unchanged in rank order (Fig 33) although they had increased in absolute size.   Much of the increase resulted from the urban additions already mentioned. Most centres remained within the same size grade although Dumfries, Dunfermline, Buckhaven and Methil, Saltcoats, Troon, Rothesay, Port Glasgow, Elgin, and Bathgate all moved up one grade in the hierarchy and Prestwick and Bearsden entered as newly-created burghs.   Similarly fourteen burghs entered the 5,000 - 9,999 category for the first time notably around Glasgow, in Ayrshire, West Lothian and Midlothian but also including Blairgowrie, Burntisland, Inverurie and Lerwick.   The urban zone from Ayrshire to Arbroath had become almost continuous by 1951 with the expansion of the Ayrshire coastal settlements, further suburban growth around Glasgow, the emergence of the central node based upon Falkirk and further developments around the Forth and Tay valleys.

The 1971 pattern is shown in Fig 34.   The cities have largely stabilised with Glasgow in fact declining in absolute population size.   Equally the suburban burghs e.g. Bearsden and Bishopbriggs and, even more strikingly, the New Towns have emerged as important urban centres occupying prominent positions in the urban hierarchy.   Of the existing towns, Coatbridge, Kirkcaldy and Inverness all experienced significant growth, as did Kirkintilloch, Johnstone and Grangemouth at a lower order in the hierarchy. The overall pattern reveals the addition of several small urban centres in the environs of Edinburgh and the entry of Stornoway, Thurso, Lossiemouth, Nairn and Annan as centres with at least 5,000 inhabitants.   The rapid emergence of East Kilbride, Cumbernauld, Irvine and, to a lesser extent, Glenrothes has produced a subtle variation in the urban pattern reducing the omnipotence of Glasgow.

Table 24 shows actual and expected rank-size

Rank	1881			1971		
		Actual	Expected		Actual	Expected
1	Glasgow	487,985		Glasgow	897,483	
2	Edinburgh	228,557	243,993	Edinburgh	452,584	448,742
3	Dundee	140,239	162,662	Dundee	182,729	299,161
4	Aberdeen	105,003	121,996	Aberdeen	182,071	224,371
5	Greenock	66,704	97,597	Paisley	95,557	179,497
6	Leith	59,485	81,331	Motherwell and Wishaw	73,658	149,581
7	Paisley	55,638	69,712	Greenock	69,502	128,212
8	Govan	50,506	60,998	East Kilbride	64,118	112,185
9	Perth	28,980	54,221	Coatbridge	52,145	99,720
10	Partick	27,410	48,798	Kirkcaldy	50,360	89,748
11	Kilmarnock	25,844	44,362	Dunfermline	49,897	81,589
12	Kirkcaldy	23,315	40,665	Kilmarnock	48,787	74,790
13	Arbroath	21,873	37,537	Ayr	47,896	69,057
14	Ayr	20,987	34,856	Hamilton	46,349	64,106
15	Dunfermline	19,915	32,532	Clydebank	44,658	59,832
16	Hamilton	18,517	30,499	Perth	43,050	56,093
17	Coatbridge	17,500	28,705	Irvine	42,451	52,793
18	Inverness	17,585	27,110	Airdrie	37,740	49,860
19	Airdrie	16,535	25,683	Falkirk	37,579	47,236
20	Hawick	16,184	24,399	Inverness	34,859	44,874

Table 24.   Urban rank size relationships, 1881 and 1971

Plate 15 Urban Preservation and Change
A. Edinburgh New Town. Stylish buildings, worth preserving in a living city fabric.

B. Glasgow Tenements. Demolition of decayed portions of the urban fabric provides an opportunity for urban improvement.

Plate 16 Two Contrasting Twentieth-Century Urban Projects
A. Kinlochleven. Founded in 1904 with the creation of an aluminium reduction works. A cramped valley site.

B. Cumbernauld New Town. Founded in 1955 as a new self-contained settlement. An open hilltop site.

relationships in 1881 and 1971.   The rank-size rule states
that the population of the second largest settlement should
be half that of the largest and the n th settlement 1/n th
of the premier centre.   In 1881 Edinburgh approximated
quite closely to the expected population figure but the
remainder of the settlements were consistently below the
expected values illustrating the restricted development
of the hierarchy and the dominance of the cities.
Similarly whilst Edinburgh closely approximated to the
expected value in 1971, all of the other centres lay below
the expected values.   Table 25 attempts to summarise the
structural changes in the urban hierarchy between 1851 and
1971 for all burghs with at least 2,500 inhabitants.

Population size group	1851	1881	1911	1951	1971
500,000 +	0	0	1	1	1
200,000 - 499,999	1	2	1	1	1
100,000 - 199,999	1	2	2	2	2
50,000 - 99,999	2	4	5	3	6
30,000 - 49,999	3	0	9	10	11
20,000 - 29,999	2	6	8	7	12
10,000 - 19,999	9	22	23	24	27
5,000 - 9,999	28	29	28	28	40
2,500 - 4,999	42	62	52	48	37
4,000 - 4,999	4	25	22	21	17
2,500 - 3,999	38	37	30	27	20

Table 25.   The urban hierarchy 1851 - 1971

There has been a pronounced upward movement in the
hierarchy reflected by the fact that for all but the
lowest order of settlements 1971 has the maximum number
of members in each settlement category.   (Another minor
exception is caused by Glasgow and Edinburgh falling into
the same category in 1881).   Nevertheless, even in 1971,
Scotland had only ten centres with at least 50,000
inhabitants, a relatively restricted hierarchy compared
with that of Britain as a whole.   With the modal category
falling in the 5,000 to 9,999 group for the first time
in 1971, it previously having fallen in the below 5,000
inhabitants group, another aspect of the nature and development of the hierarchy is revealed.   Since the small

209

urban centres are numerically dominant, in Table 25 the
smallest category has been subdivided to illustrate in more
detail trends between 1851-1971.   Interestingly there
was a notable absence of centres in the 4,000 - 4,999
population range in 1851.   In part at least this may have
been an illustration of the time-lag in according burgh
status to new urban nodes.   Since 1881 both sub-groups
have declined in numbers principally due to the growth of
many individual centres, industrial, suburban and market
centres, and the consequent movement into higher orders of
the hierarchy.

     In 1971 extensive suburban areas were not recorded in
the burgh statistics.   Thus, the First District of Renfrewshire, which included Newton Mearns and Clarkston, had
49,175 inhabitants.   Similarly, the Currie District of
Midlothian had 14,392 residents and the Central No. 1
District of Stirlingshire, (Bannockburn, Cowie, Polmaise
and Sauchie) an old coal-mining district, housed 17,130
people.

     Between 1851 and 1971 the general relationships in the
urban hierarchy have been maintained although several towns
have significantly progressed, notably Coatbridge, Kirkcaldy,
Hamilton, Motherwell and Wishaw, Airdrie, Dunfermline,
Inverness, Falkirk, Buckhaven and Methil, Grangemouth, Bathgate
and the New Towns.   Apart from the cities, which have constantly occupied the first four places in the hierarchy,
several settlements display remarkable consistency at various
levels in the hierarchy.   Paisley and Greenock grew steadily
between 1851 and 1971 but retained a relatively constant
place in the hierarchy.   Montrose and Arbroath have only
experienced minor fluctuations in population size whilst
Brechin, Wick, Lanark, Dalkeith, Stranraer, and Campbeltown
are representatives of one size category continuously from
1851 until 1971.

     The spatial pattern of urban centres in Scotland bears
little obvious resemblance to the neat regularly spaced
pattern postulated by central-place theory, principally
because of the extreme contrasts of population density which
characterise Scotland.   Various specialised settlements
such as industrial, resort and fishing towns, which do not
possess or require the normal service centre-hinterland
relationships for their economic viability, further distort
the pattern.   Although the pattern of urban settlements
in Scotland varies markedly from the theoretical ideal,
much of the broad spatial pattern established by 1881 is

210

retained in 1971, despite infilling, extension and growth.
There is little immediate likelihood of fundamental change,
although the new local government units will appear to alter
the hierarchy as a result of a redefinition of boundaries.

THE MAJOR URBAN CENTRES

The Four Cities

The pattern of population growth in the four cities
(Glasgow, Edinburgh, Dundee and Aberdeen) is outlined in
Chapter 2, although in the case of Glasgow and to a lesser
extent Edinburgh and Dundee striking increases may be
attributable in part to the extension of city boundaries.
In the case of Glasgow major incorporations of surrounding
developed areas occurred in 1846, 1891 and 1912.   Thus,
in 1891, annexation involved the Police Burghs of Crosshill,
Govanhill, Maryhill, Hillhead and Pollokshields with a
combined population of over 50,000.   During the nineteenth
century the area of the city increased from 715 hectares
to 5,134 hectares.   In 1912 another major extension in-
corporated a further 2,512 hectares and 226,335
inhabitants involving the Police Burghs of Partick, Govan
and Pollokshaws and the extensively settled districts of
Shettleston and Tollcross along with the southern suburbs
of Cathcart and Newlands.

Two further extensions in 1926 and 1938 added another
8,095 hectares of largely unsettled lands located mainly
to the north and south of the city which provided many of
the sites of the subsequent local authority housing developments.

Similarly between 1855 and 1914 Edinburgh was engaged
in large-scale physical extension annexing over 2,800
hectares and in the process trebling the area under muni-
cipal control.

In Dundee and Aberdeen much of the boundary extension
has occurred in the twentieth century to facilitate the
need for new housing at lower densities, but in all of the
cities the major phase of boundary extensions ceased after
1946 with the introduction of planning policies favouring
the restriction of city growth.   In the case of Glasgow a
conscious policy of population decline through overspill
agreements and rehousing in the New Towns was reflected
in the 14.9 per cent decrease in the population of the

city between 1961 and 1971 but the other three cities also recorded decreases for that period, ranging from 0.4 per cent in Dundee to 3.2 per cent in Edinburgh. Thus the cities as defined by their now relatively fixed boundaries are all experiencing varying rates of decline or near nil growth.

All of the cities developed on or near rivers although in the case of Edinburgh the strategic qualities of the castle ridge were more influential in guiding the location and emergence of a settlement. There were some functional similarities between the settlements but they differed greatly in detail in terms of site and development.

From the establishment of the settlement until the middle of the eighteenth century, Edinburgh developed within the confines of the crag-and-tail feature dominated by the castle which was set upon an eroded volcanic plug. During this period Edinburgh emerged as the leading urban centre in Scotland, capitalising on its administrative role as seat of the Royal Court and Parliament and commercial centre commanding the leading Scottish seaport, to clearly establish its primacy in almost every walk of Scottish life (Plate 14B). With the founding of the New Town of Edinburgh in the eighteenth century, a phase of urban growth was initiated which continued throughout the nineteenth century by which time the residential boundary extended to the slopes of the Braid Hills in the south and Murrayfield in the west and merged almost imperceptibly in the north with the ports of Granton and Leith. The industrial revolution had a muted impact on Edinburgh although the Forth and Clyde Canal and the major railway termini and sidings did affect the morphology. Major new industrial developments included rubber working, engineering and whisky blending but the traditional activities of brewing, milling and printing retained their industrial primacy. The city also acquired important insurance and banking functions re-inforcing the established administrative and service character.

Glasgow developed beside the Molendinar Burn at the lowest bridging point on the River Clyde. The first stimulus came with the establishment of the Cathedral in the sixth century but until the industrial upsurge of the eighteenth century, the city essentially consisted of a north-south axis (High Street and Saltmarket) and an east-west axis (Gallowgate and Trongate) with a series of wynds and minor streets or alleys leading from those two

thoroughfares.   A phase of spectacular growth was
initiated in the eighteenth century with the commencement
of the Atlantic trade involving sugar, tobacco and cotton.
Between 1780 and 1830 Glasgow's population increased five-
fold.   To accommodate this growth new suburbs were erected
to the west of the medieval core and across the river to
the south, on the lands of Gorbals.   The initial western
growth included the Georgian section of Glasgow equivalent
to the New Town in Edinburgh, but the rate of expansion
was so great that these terraced houses soon became converted to offices and shops.   The spectacular urban and
industrial explosion spawned independent urban nodes such
as Partick and Govan, growth nodes which became physically
joined to the city as a result of continued urban growth
during the nineteenth century (Plate 14A).   Thus by the
end of the nineteenth century Glasgow extended to Maryhill
and Springburn on the north, Bridgeton in the east, Mount
Florida and Langside in the south and Bellahouston in the
west, thereby encompassing, but not as yet incorporating,
Govan and Partick.   Since these burghs were the two
principal areas associated with shipbuilding and marine
engineering, the common assumption that these industries
characterised late nineteenth century Glasgow is, in the
strict sense, inaccurate.   The industrial revolution had,
however, brought a vast array of heavy industries including
engineering and chemicals as well as textiles and numerous
commercial offices to administer the booming commerce of
the emerging Second City of the Empire.

By the sixteenth century, Dundee, a long established
Royal Burgh, was second in wealth only to Edinburgh.   At
that time it performed the characteristic functions of a
Royal Burgh, collecting the goods from the surrounding
agricultural hinterland and handling the exchange of these
goods and the dealings in imported goods.   The medieval
settlement had emerged astride the mouth of the Scouring
Burn on the north bank of the Firth of Tay.   By the
eighteenth century, the simple morphology focused upon
the Marketgait (High Street), served by the Nethergait
and Overgait to the west and the Murraygait and Seagait
to the east.

When a substantial linen industry arose in the
eighteenth century between Arbroath and Perth, the seeds
were sown for the industrial growth of Dundee.   Although
outwith the early natural line of development based on
Strathmore, Dundee could supply the essential labour,

213

capital and business expertise and by the early nineteenth century the offices in Cowgate in Dundee dominated the trade. Shortages of flax encouraged experiments with jute which soon became the predominant industry in the city. The mills and industrial suburbs initially followed the course of the Scouring Burn but urban expansion also occurred to the west and to a lesser extent to the east of the old medieval core, and to the north towards the slopes of the Law.

From early medieval times, Aberdeen has operated as the market and principal port for an extensive hinterland in the north-east. The town grew around two foci, the commercial one at the mouth of the Dee and the other, Old Aberdeen, with ecclesiastical links dating from the sixth century becoming the site of the Cathedral in the twelfth century and the New College of St. Mary (later named King's College) in 1500. The Royal Burgh, on the northern banks of the Dee estuary, was an important craft and trading centre by the sixteenth century. Woollen manufacturing, granite working, shipbuilding and papermaking all became important industries during the post-industrial revolution period and the city also acquired its role as a leading fishing port as rail communications developed in the Victorian era.

A phase of physical extension accompanied this industrial growth and the construction of Union Street, a new street leading west from Castlehill, formed the keystone of these developments. A shallow loch was drained for residential development and the city progressively spread away from the Dee towards Old Aberdeen and also in the direction of the Den Burn.

In all of the Scottish cities the late nineteenth century urban extension was assisted and facilitated by the construction of tramway systems. Both Glasgow and Edinburgh also had suburban railway networks and Glasgow, in addition, had a limited underground pattern whilst commuting by rail affected suburban communities in the case of all four cities.

The principal characteristic of the twentieth century has been the substantial physical extension of the cities largely sponsored by the space demands for housing and new industrial sites. The exact proportions vary from city to city but in every case extensive tracts of local authority houses have been the most notable addition. The cities have also changed in their employment profiles at

both a general and detailed level.   In 1881, for example,
44 per cent of the economically active females were engaged
in domestic service whereas in 1966, using a rather omnibus
category as the nearest equivalent, less than 5 per cent
were engaged in this activity.   Between 1911 and 1961 the
percentage of the occupied population in Dundee engaged in
manufacturing industry fell from the very high figure of
67 per cent to 44 per cent although this was still a larger
percentage than the other Scottish cities, notably Aberdeen
(24 per cent).   In general there has been a switch to the
tertiary sector which accounted for 73 per cent of the
employment in Edinburgh and Aberdeen in 1961 and 63 per
cent in Glasgow.

Within manufacturing industry considerable shifts
have occurred.   In Dundee, for example, employment in
textiles, largely jute, had declined from about 48,000 in
1911 to just 10,200 by 1966.   Some 38,000 jobs in shipbuilding, marine engineering, textiles and metal manufacturing were lost between 1954 and 1967 on Greater
Clydeside.   Since over 90 per cent of post-war shipbuilding
and marine engineering employment on the Upper Clyde was
concentrated in Clydebank, Partick and Govan these areas
had suffered most from the continued declining fortunes
of these industries in the 1950's and 1960's.   Similarly
Paisley and the Bridgeton district of Glasgow have borne
the brunt of the reductions in employment in the textile
industry.   In 1967 these areas accounted for almost half
of the regional employment in this industry and they
shared almost 60 per cent of the redundancies which occurred
between 1954 and 1967.   During this period almost 9,000
jobs were lost in the traditional metal manufacturing
industries, notably at Parkhead, Springburn (with the
collapse of the locomotive industry) and Govan.   To some
extent these declines have been offset by the emergence
of light industries based on industrial estates, with
Hillington, the largest, providing some 20,000 jobs.   The
provision of sufficient employment opportunities to com-
pensate for decline in traditional industries has proved
a persistent problem in Glasgow in recent years.   Between
1951 and 1966 whilst the total city population fell by
113,200 inhabitants, the working population was reduced
by some 42,000.

In Dundee similar changes have occurred but from a
narrower initial industrial base.   Here the manufacturing
growth sectors have been electrical engineering and office

machinery, principally associated with two large post-war immigrant companies, National Cash Registers and United States Time Corporation and the general emergence of several industrial estates notably beside Kingsway, as a major component of the industrial pattern.

Aberdeen and Edinburgh had respectively 24 and 25 per cent of their occupied population engaged in manufacturing industry in 1961, compared with about 36 per cent in Glasgow and 44 per cent in Dundee. Both Aberdeen and Edinburgh have experienced decline in traditional industries such as granite working in Aberdeen, with the closure of Rubislaw Quarry in 1970, and rubber working in Edinburgh, with the removal of the Uniroyal plant to a new site at Newbridge near the M.8. However neither city had ever been as deeply committed to large-scale manufacturing employment as Dundee and Glasgow and, therefore, they have at least avoided the most acute problems of the massive upheaval and change of employment structure which has troubled Glasgow and, to a lesser extent, Dundee. The absence of a major heavy industrial sector has ultimately proved at least a partial advantage for Aberdeen and Edinburgh. Nevertheless with about one person in twelve estimated to be engaged directly or indirectly in the fishing and associated industries Aberdeen has not entirely avoided economic vicissitudes in recent years. Equally increasing disquiet has been voiced in Edinburgh as many industries have departed in search of more spacious and accessible sites in the Lothians and few new industries were attracted to the city in the 1960's after the completion of the principal industrial estate at Sighthill.

Table 26 shows the socio-economic structure of the cities in 1966 based upon the occupations of economically active males. Significantly Glasgow and Edinburgh generally display opposite patterns, with Edinburgh having the highest proportions in managerial and professional and intermediate and junior non-manual occupations and the lowest proportions in skilled manual, semi-skilled and non-manual occupations, whilst Glasgow has the highest proportion in skilled manual and unskilled manual occupations and the lowest in managerial and professional employment. This does not, however, mean that there is an acute shortage of professional and managerial occupations in Glasgow but rather that the respresentatives of these groups largely resided outwith the city in suburban communities such as Bearsden and Newton Mearns.

216

In 1966 for example the principal male occupations in Glasgow (as opposed to the occupation of resident males) were: engineering and allied trades (44,710), transport and communications (30,300); professional, technical and artists (27,050); sales (26,380); labourers (24,200); clerical (23,360); service, sport and recreation (18,760); administrators and managers (11,790). Together these groups account for almost 73 per cent of all male employment in Glasgow and illustrate the increasingly vital role of the service sector and the continuing importance of traditional industries.

	1 – 4[1]	5 & 6[1]	8 & 9[1]	10[1]	11[1]	7 & 12[1]	13–17[1]
Glasgow	8.9	17.7	40.7	15.2	13.6	2.9	1.2
Dundee	11.2	15.3	39.1	18.9	11.1	3.3	1.2
Aberdeen	14.0	18.9	36.5	15.5	10.3	3.8	0.9
Edinburgh	17.3	22.1	33.5	11.8	9.4	3.7	2.2
Scotland	11.9	15.8	36.5	15.0	10.4	3.1	7.5

[1]Groups 1 – 4 employers, managers and self employed professional workers
5 & 6 intermediate and junior non-manual
8 & 9 foremen, supervisors and skilled manual
10 semi-skilled manual
11 unskilled manual
7 &12 personal service workers and self employed non-professional
13 –17 farmers, agricultural, armed forces and indefinite

Table 26. Socio–Economic Groups in the Scottish Cities 1966

In Edinburgh in 1966, the principal male occupations were: professional, technical, artists (16,810); transport and communications (14,690); clerical (14,100); engineering and allied trades (13,600); sales (12,650); labourers (9,900); service, sport and recreational (9,710); administrators and managers (6,160). Collectively these groups represented 70 per cent of total male employment in Edinburgh and demonstrate some of the detailed differences and similarities between Edinburgh and Glasgow: the same eight groups are represented but in different rank order. In Dundee the main occupation groups in 1966 were: engineering and allied trades (8,900); labourers

(4,860); transport and communications (4,530); textiles (4,370); professional, technical, artists (4,340); sales (4,060); service, sport, recreational (3,320); clerical (3,310). These groups accounted for 70 per cent of male employment and apart from the presence of textiles reflecting the traditional specialism of the city, the small number in the administrators and managers class (1,760) and the relatively low ranking of clerical occupations, reveals a distinction between the major cities and Dundee. The principal male occupation groups in Aberdeen in 1966 were: transport and communications (6,040); sales (5,400); engineering and allied trades (5,230); professional, technical, artists (4,970); labourers (3,820); service, sports, recreational (3,460); clerical (3,160); food, drink, tobacco (2,460). Together these groups accounted for 68 per cent of male employment and again local specialisms featured, e.g. food processing industries. As in Dundee, administrators and managers (1,860) were not a major group, involving fewer men than the farmers, foresters and fishermen group (1,920).

Between 77 per cent and 83 per cent of female employment in Glasgow, Aberdeen and Edinburgh in 1966 was accounted for by four groups (clerical; sales; service, sport, recreational; and professional, technical and artists) but in Dundee, the proportion fell to 63 per cent due to large numbers in textiles (5,940) and engineering and allied trades (2,880). In Glasgow, over 15,000 women were employed in textiles and clothing industries in 1966.

Despite some measure of similarity in employment profiles the four cities retain many distinctive qualities. Locational changes have also occurred, especially with the progressive abandonment of old central factory sites dating from the canal and railway eras in favour of newer suburban locations conveniently situated in relation to road networks.

New Towns

The total population of the New Towns in 1971 was 179,028, just slightly less than Dundee or Aberdeen. The population of Cumbernauld had risen from 4,924 in 1961 to 31,557 in 1971, that of East Kilbride from 31,970 to 64,118, Glenrothes from 12,750 to 27,335, Irvine from 32,716 to 42,451 and Livingston from 2,063 to 13,567. The New Towns Act, 1946 provided the legislative mechanism for new town development in Scotland but the concept dates back to

218

Victorian visionaries such as Ebenezeer Howard, the initiator
of the famous garden cities of Letchworth and Welwyn Garden
City near London.   The need for new towns in Scotland was
identified in the Clyde Valley Plan, principally to provide
proper housing facilities in a pleasant modern environment
for the overcrowded and inadequately accommodated population
of Glasgow.   The first Scottish New Town, East Kilbride,
was designated in 1947 on an undulating and elevated site
only twelve kilometres south-east of Glasgow.   From the
outset the town was given a large area (4,148 hectares)
mainly to permit the maintenance of a pronounced green
zone on the northern boundary, thereby clearly separating
the town from the nearby urban and suburban centres of
Eaglesham, Busby, Rutherglen and Cambuslang.   The average
altitude of around 160 metres, heavy rainfall, boulder clay
subsoil and undulating site crossed by several winding,
narrow valleys provided a challenge to the planners.   The
initial plan was based upon a series of neighbourhoods,
each with a local service centre, schools and churches
but dependent upon the town centre for specialised
shopping and services.   The industrial areas were distinctly segregated and placed in peripheral locations
reflecting the planning philosophy of separation of
industrial and residential land uses.   Originally the
planned target population of East Kilbride was set at
45,000 but, in 1960, this was raised to 70,000 and this
has since been increased to 82,500, which with subsequent
natural increase would produce a settlement of about 100,000
people.
      East Kilbride encompassed an existing small dormitory
settlement which provided valuable services during the early
stages of the construction and evolution of the new town
centre.   From a population of only about 3,000 in 1950
East Kilbride mushroomed to 31,557 residents by 1961.   A
formal overspill agreement was signed with Glasgow in 1959
but from the outset East Kilbride was intended to provide
an essential housing and industrial growth point to ease
the problems of Glasgow.   By 1973 the population was
69,000 and there were 275 industries employing 17,290 people.
In addition 192 shops employed 1,660 people and 81 offices
accounted for a further 2,750 jobs.   The factory area
totalled 532,000 square metres which was more than double
the figure of any other Scottish New Town, as was the office
area of 255 square metres.   In the latter case, the presence
of an Inland Revenue Computer Centre accounts for much of

the office employment and office space and has provided
an invaluable source of white-collar jobs, and added variety
to local employment opportunities.   Sufficient jobs have
now been created to equal the working population of East
Kilbride but the town experiences substantial daily journey-
to-work flows.   About one third of those who work in the
town commute from other areas, notably Glasgow, Rutherglen
and adjacent parts of North Lanarkshire, whilst an approximately equal number leave the town for work, with Glasgow
as the principal destination.   In 1968 almost half of
the 16,000 tenants of Development Corporation houses did
not work in East Kilbride.   To some extent these patterns
are changing as the town matures and diversifies, but
complex journey-to-work flows are a typical feature of
modern large urban regions reflecting high levels of
personal mobility and the increasing dispersal of the location of employment opportunities.

The new shopping plaza in the town centre and the
opening of a branch of Marks, and Spencer Ltd. will firmly
establish East Kilbride as a regional shopping centre with
a catchment population of nearly 250,000.   For several
years the town has attracted weekend shoppers from Hamilton,
Motherwell and Wishaw, Paisley and the southern suburban
fringe of the Clydeside conurbation.   In general, East
Kilbride has been remarkably successful and in less than
thirty years a dynamic and vital community has been created.

The original master plan for the second Scottish New
Town, Glenrothes, in central Fife, was for a town of 32,000
people with only modest provision of industrial sites
because it was assumed that about one in eight of the
population would be employed in the Rothes coal-mine.   The
failure of this project and the ultimate abandonment of the
mine in 1961 caused a major re-assessment of the function
and future of Glenrothes.   With an area of 2,333 hectares,
situated between Leslie and Markinch on a gentle northward-
sloping site above the Leven Valley, Glenrothes, which was
started in 1948, was intended to become a growth node in an
established but scattered mining area which also had high
levels of unemployment.   It was also designed on a neighbourhood basis, each neighbourhood consisting of precincts based
upon a small shopping cluster.   In the 1950's the rate of
development and population growth was slow to some extent
related to inevitable problems involved in the construction
of a New Town but exacerbated by the economic problems of
the Rothes pit.

220

In the late 1950's the strategy for Glenrothes was
revised with the emphasis being firmly placed on attracting
industry.   The plan for the town was redrawn to accommodate
a new target population of 70,000 inhabitants.   Between
1957 and 1967, twenty eight new factories were established,
increasing to 115 by 1973 employing over 8,000 people.
These are located in five industrial estates, with a
pronounced cluster on the southern periphery of the town,
although the oldest estate, Queensway, lies to the north
of the town centre, beside an earlier paper mill.   A wide
variety of light industries have located in Glenrothes
including a number of companies engaged in the field of
electronics.   The opening of the Forth Road Bridge undoubtedly aided Glenrothes in its search for industry.
        About 9,000 houses have been built in Glenrothes in
nine housing precincts, each based upon a local primary
school, and with a distinct architectural style.   There
is only one tall block of flats, Raeburn Heights, which,
as in similar developments in East Kilbride and Cumbernauld,
has proved most popular with single professional people.
Glenrothes has been less successful in attracting offices,
only 75 square metres by 1973, but a nine-storey office
block is currently being built in the town centre.   The
slow population growth also impeded the development of the
town centre although an extension is under construction
and the existing area is being converted into an enclosed
shopping mall.   Many of the residents use Kirkcaldy as
a regional shopping centre because of the wider choice and
range of shops.   Most of the residents of Glenrothes have
moved from other parts of Fife, especially from the old
mining communities such as Cowdenbeath and Lochgelly,
attracted by the prospects of employment and modern housing.
        Apart from the details of its developmental history,
Glenrothes differs from other New Towns such as East
Kilbride and Cumbernauld in a locational context, being
50 and 93 kilometres respectively from Edinburgh and
Glasgow.
        Cumbernauld designated in 1955, lies some twenty two
kilometres to the north east of Glasgow.   The site had
been mentioned as a possibility in the Clyde Valley Plan
of 1946 but, at that time, it seemed unlikely that Glasgow
citizens would be willing to move to such a location.   By
the mid 1950's the continuing need to overspill population
and the fact that many of the potential sites had either
been developed or were no longer suitable had altered this

view.   The Development Corporation were instructed to
provide a balanced community of 50,000 persons, about four
in every five being attracted from Glasgow.   The initial
site, of 1,680 hectares, largely astride a long narrow hill
with a maximum elevation of about 150 metres provided a
challenge to the planners and architects. (Plate 16B). The
difficult and exposed site was constricted by areas of
coal-mining to the north-west and fireclay workings to the
south-east.   At the time of designation about 3,000 people
lived on the site, mainly in the villages of Cumbernauld
and Condorrat.   The planners elected to adopt an unusual
design with the town centre on the top of the hill and the
whole residential area grouped around this focus and linked
to it by walkways and a northern and southern loop road
system which fed on to the central road passing underneath
the elevated town centre.   Initially no neighbourhoods
were planned although the residential pattern was not
structureless, the distinction referring to shop and
service provision rather than housing design and physically
distinguishable residential units.   Subsequently the
target population was increased to 70,000 which would then
rise by natural increase to about 100,000.   This has
necessitated a boundary extension incorporating a further
1,327 hectares and has involved some modification of the
original plans to incorporate a number of relatively self-
contained outlying neighbourhoods, and the integration of
a new area to the north of the A80.   The planners have
consistently aimed at the separation of pedestrians and
vehicles by incorporating elements from various design
forms including cul-de-sacs and the Radburn approach.
     The principal industrial areas are Wardpark on the
north-eastern periphery (the site of the largest single
employer in the town, Burroughs Office Machines Ltd.) and
Blairlinn on the south-western perimeter beside the railway.
By 1973 143 companies employed about 6,000 people and 58
offices provided a further 1,100 jobs.   Compared with
other Scottish New Towns, Cumbernauld has been relatively
more successful in attracting office than industrial
employment.   A substantial number of people commute daily
to Glasgow by bus, train and car especially for jobs in
the white-collar sector although planned office developments in the town will help to alleviate this problem.
     The town centre is now being extended and a Woolco
department store opened in 1974.   With extensive

222

car-parking facilities this store has provided a valuable addition to the town centre and is attracting increasing numbers of weekend shoppers from nearby Airdrie and Kirkintilloch.

Livingston, the fourth Scottish New Town, designated in 1962, was planned to provide a major growth point in West Lothian whilst simultaneously aiding the overspill requirements of Glasgow. Situated 25 kilometres from Edinburgh and 50 kilometres from Glasgow the M8 traverses the northern periphery of the town and the River Almond flows through the heart of the settlement. On the valley slopes a grid iron urban design will ultimately house 100,000 people and act as a regional centre between Falkirk and Edinburgh. The linear town centre will sit astride the River Almond and about half of the planned population will live close to this centre. The remainder will occupy the higher valley slopes served by three district centres. By 1973 55 industries at the Houston and Deans industrial estates employed 4,250 people with Cameron Iron Works as the largest employer. Before the New Town development the main employment opportunities in the area were in the oil-shale industry and in coal-mining. The designated area of 2,708 hectares included about 2,000 people in the small communities of Livingston, Livingston Station and Bell's Quarry. By 1973 Livingston had 20,000 residents, but this figure was rather low if the target population were to be achieved by 1985. (Projected 1973 population was 28,600). Offices and an enclosed shopping centre are currently being built and Livingston anticipates rapid growth during the remainder of the 1970's.

Irvine, the fifth New Town, is rather different from the others in that it used an established settlement base, the burghs of Irvine and Kilwinning. The coastal location is also unique in the Scottish context. Within the designated area of 5,022 hectares the plan is to integrate established settlements into a coherent structure with a target population of about 100,000 people which will act as a growth node in Northern Ayrshire. Situated 40 kilometres from Glasgow, 12 kilometres from Kilmarnock and 17 kilometres from Ayr, the New Town incorporates an old coal-mining area and adjoins an important chemical complex. It represents the progressively more sophisticated use of New Towns to attempt to simultaneously embrace industrial, employment, environmental and housing problems in the designated area and also elsewhere, e.g. Glasgow overspill

223

needs. By 1973 the town had 48,000 residents and a total employment of 20,250. Since designation the number of industries and employees have doubled. Part of the merit of using pre-existing established settlements is the attainment of quite high shopping and service levels from the outset but this also involves the later transformation of the old cores through redevelopment and this process is now actively progressing in Irvine with the construction of a new shopping complex astride the river.

Collectively the Scottish New Towns possess a number of distinct demographic characteristics. The proportion of persons over pensionable age was extremely low, in 1971, when compared with the Scottish average. Of the population of Livingston, only 2.7 per cent of males were aged 65 and over and 5.8 per cent of females were aged 60 and over, compared with 9.7 per cent of males and 20.6 per cent of females for Scotland as a whole. Cumbernauld, East Kilbride and Glenrothes all reflected this pattern although in Irvine the figures were closer to the Scottish average. Thus migration to New Towns would appear to be age-selective. Equally the proportions of males and females under 15 years were significantly higher than the Scottish rates, again with the exception of Irvine. Of the population of the New Towns in general, between 86 and 94 per cent were born in Scotland. This resembles the figures for the four cities although the New Towns as major growth nodes might have been expected to attract a higher proportion of immigrants from elsewhere. Instead they seem to be fulfilling their planned role as overspill reception centres and foci for regional population redistribution, experiencing only limited long distance migration.

In part the explanation may be in the housing allocation policy of the New Towns for most houses are rented from the local authority, Development Corporation or Scottish Special Housing Association, the figures ranging from 80.8 per cent in Irvine to 96.6 per cent in Livingston. Most of the New Towns are attempting to extend the private housing sector by the construction of blocks of executive flats and estates of private houses but this sector plays a minor role at present.

Terraced and semi-detached houses played an important part in the early developments at East Kilbride and Glenrothes but the New Towns now contain quite a wide variety of house types and designs including maisonettes, multi-storey blocks and more traditional four-storey blocks.

224

In general, the New Towns have a high standard of
household amenities: the proportion of households with
exclusive use of a hot water supply, fixed bath, and an
inside water-closet is 95 per cent in Irvine and over 99
per cent in the other New Towns. These figures reflect
the standard facilities of modern houses and are comparable
to the figures for suburban districts in the cities such
as Camperdown in Dundee, and Provan and Knightswood in
Glasgow. The degree of improvement can be measured by the
fact that even in 1971 only 14 per cent of the houses in
the Kingston Ward (an old central area) of Glasgow had exclusive use of these three facilities. In addition to the
provision of facilities the houses are all built to modern
space and design standards with the nineteenth century stone
tenements now superseded by brick buildings and other modern
structures faced by harling or rough-casting. These
materials are used universally now, of course, but the impact
is perhaps most apparent in the New Towns because most of
the settlement is of comparatively recent origin.

Despite differences in site and developmental history,
the New Towns constitute an important and distinct economic,
physical and social group in the modern settlement pattern
of Scotland.

Other urban centres

Apart from cities and New Towns, almost all of the
large and small burghs are characterised by functional
specialisation, normally in the field of manufacturing
industry. Sometimes this dates from the pre-industrial
revolution period but it is predominantly of palaetechnic
origin. In most cases such specialisation is diminishing
as traditional industries decline and all settlements
develop a substantial service sector. Few settlements
have remained unifunctional for long but often a few
activities have dominated the urban economic base. For
example, as recently as 1951 almost 30 per cent of the
labour force in Paisley were engaged in the textile
industry. Engineering and metal industries still feature
prominently in the economy of Motherwell and Wishaw,
Airdrie, Coatbridge and Rutherglen. Shipbuilding and marine
engineering maintain an important role in Greenock and Port
Glasgow but the previously heavy dependence of Clydebank
on this specialism is gradually reducing as a result of the

eclipse of many local shipyards and the emergence of modern light engineering industries. Hamilton is now an administrative focus and service centre rather than the heart of a coal-mining district and the unique concentration of linoleum production in Kirkcaldy has been reduced to one representative producing a wide range of floor-covering products. The Border textile towns retain much of their specialisation although their employment predominance has also been reduced.

During the nineteenth century the railways enabled a number of settlements to acquire a tourist function, notably coastal resorts near the cities, such as Largs, Troon, Dunoon, North Berwick and Carnoustie. They were often also able to act as commuter settlements. Increased mobility and affluence and changing tastes have largely transformed many of these settlements into short stay rather than major holiday resorts but this has generally been more than compensated by the enlarged dormitory function which has followed from the twentieth century trend toward increased commuting over progressively greater distances. Other specialised nineteenth century urban creations include the spas e.g. Bridge of Allan, which enjoyed a short-lived popularity. St. Andrews could legitimately, if a little simplistically, be classed as a University town and the dominant role of the naval dockyard at Rosyth is reflected in the impression that almost everyone there is employed by the Admiralty. The aluminium works dominate Kinlochleven (Plate 16A) as do the whisky distilleries in many small Speyside communities. Numerous coal-mining settlements remain in the Central Lowlands, distinct communities despite the sharply reduced role of mining employment. The fishing communities of the north-east remain functionally specialised and often socially segregated from the surrounding areas.

In most parts of Scotland urban settlements of varying age and function are juxtaposed although broad regional trends do emerge as in the textile towns of the Border valleys or the fishing, agricultural and market communities of the north-east. The vagaries of urbanisation have left medieval market centres in the midst of coalfield-based industrial settlements. Chance industrial implantations sparked off some unusual nineteenth century manufacturing specialisms and subsequent variations in fortunes have allowed some settlements to diversify to a greater degree

226

than others.   Among the major current trends are
industrialisation in parts of the north-east and Highlands,
new and expanded tourist functions largely in the
Highlands and further extension and expansion of dormitory
functions within the commuting fields of the cities, the
New Towns and some of the large burghs.

SPHERES OF INFLUENCE

Urban centres are assumed to perform a series of
specialised functions to satisfy the needs of their
residents and the inhabitants of the hinterland or sphere
of influence of the settlement.   These functions include
provision of retail services, distribution, administration,
professional services and entertainment and recreational
facilities.   Variation occurs in the level of specialisation of each function reflecting the nature and
organisation of the function and expressed in the concepts
of threshold and range.   Threshold defines the minimum
population required for economic viability, and range the
distance-decay characteristics of the function from the
minimum distance measured by threshold to the farthest
distance a dispersed population is willing to go to obtain
a good or service at a place.   In central place theory
different orders of settlements are hypothesised involving
higher levels of specialisation, larger thresholds,
increased range and hence progressively fewer centres.
Hinterlands of small centres combine to form the spheres
of influence of larger settlements.   The structure
implicitly assumes less frequent contact with increased
levels of specialisation so that cities, for example, are
expected to have extensive hinterlands.   With few exceptions
the more specialised the function, the more probable a city
location.   Recent trends have strengthened this tendency
by favouring fewer major administrative bodies.   So each
of the Scottish cities has an extensive sphere of influence
based upon administration, professional services and
specialised shopping such as clothing, jewellery and furniture.   Within each hinterland intensity of contact is
greatest near the city or regional centre and declines with
distance although a simple distance-decay relationship is
distorted by transport networks and the distribution of
middle-order centres which can offer a measure of competition.
Indeed outside the intensive hinterlands of the major

regional centres, the spheres of influence of middle-order centres represent the normal activity systems of most people in terms of their usage of urban functions.   The distribution of Marks and Spencer stores provides a potential guide (Fig 35) to the pattern of middle-order centres.   The stores are entirely contained within the densely populated zone between Ayr and Aberdeen reflecting the high turnover and threshold population requirements of this type of shop. The next level in the hierarchy includes centres which have a branch of F. W. Woolworth, banks, a range of shops and other services.

There is not a perfect correlation between the distribution of the Woolworth stores shown in Fig 36 and middle-order centres and some substantial settlements, e.g. Coatbridge, Bearsden, Bishopbriggs and Grangemouth, are not sites of these stores, whilst they occur in much smaller places, e.g. Castle Douglas and North Berwick.   Equally although several branches occur in the cities, these are scaled in relation to larger threshold population levels than some of the stores in less urbanised situations. These variations are a natural outcome of calculations concerning factors such as competition, demand, accessibility and the availability of suitable sites.   These factors help to explain why there is a store in the resort of Leven rather than in the nearby larger settlement of Buckhaven and Methil.

The majority of middle-order centres, however, do include a branch of Woolworth, a branch of at least two of the major Scottish banks, a selection of non-convenience shops (i.e. clothing, footwear, furniture, hardware and electrical goods), a convenience sector dominated normally by representatives of regional or national supermarket groups and an array of specialised services including solicitors, surveyors, opticians, dentists and doctors.   Each centre will serve a surrounding area of limited spatial extent in the densely populated Central Lowlands but often involving considerable areas in the more sparsely peopled Highlands and Southern Uplands.   At this level the service and shopping centrality is frequently reinforced by the presence of a secondary school or a local newspaper.   Below this level in Scotland clear differences in the structure of service centres are difficult to identify but progressively specialisation declines.   Many cottage hospitals remain in urban foci in sparsely-populated areas, remnants of the days of slower transport and restricted communications and

228

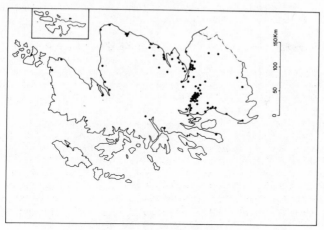

Figure 36. Distribution of Woolworths stores

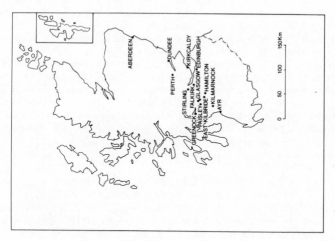

Figure 35. Distribution of Marks and Spencer stores

229

distort attempts to measure specialisation or centrality.
The Census has suggested that burghs with 1,000 inhabitants
could be termed urban and many settlements of that size do
possess distinct service components such as shops, a bank,
a post-office and often a doctor although in sparsely
populated areas, the latter might serve more than one
community.

The number and range of services varies substantially
between settlements of a similar size at this point in the
hierarchy reflecting differences in hinterland population
size and the availability of alternative shopping and
service opportunities.   Thus isolated urban nodes such
as Lochgilphead or Duns attain relatively high levels of
specialisation because of the distance to alternative
central places.   In contrast, many of the small mining
communities, in Lanarkshire, Stirlingshire, West Lothian
and Midlothian, often have a relatively poorly developed
service provision with the local Co-operative Society
acting as the principal retail outlet.   Some settlements
have apparently greater significance as service centres
than their population size might suggest.   The county
towns of Ayr, Stirling, Perth and Inverness are examples
partly because of historical administrative functions
but also because they possess high levels of nodality in
their respective regions.   Similarly many resorts have
more service facilities than would be expected for their
resident population because of the seasonal variation in
the service population.

Changes in transport routes can alter spheres of
influence e.g. the opening of the Forth Road Bridge, the
Tay Road Bridge and the Erskine Bridge.   The major reorganisation of local government in Scotland in 1975 will alter
many administrative hinterlands but will not necessarily
alter journey-to-service patterns correspondingly.   The
emergence of new centres such as the New Towns also
necessitates adjustment of the pattern as people react to
new opportunities.

Within cities and conurbations it is also possible to
identify a structure of service centres.   The Central
Business District, the commercial core of the city, dominates
the structure.   Maximum land values occur in the principal
shopping thoroughfares within the central business district
such as Argyle Street and Sauchiehall Street in Glasgow,
Princes Street in Edinburgh, Overgate and Murraygate in
Dundee and Union Street in Aberdeen.   The structure then

consists of nodal and linear components.　Leading from the
city centre linear shopping streets line the main roads, e.g.
Duke Street and Dumbarton Road in Glasgow or Gorgie Road
and Leith Walk in Edinburgh.　Many of the shops sell foodstuffs but there are also some specialised outlets retailing
standard items of clothing and hardware and service
establishments such as hairdressers.　The most important
secondary nodes are the outlying business centres such as
Shawlands in south Glasgow or Broughty Ferry in Dundee.
With a considerable degree of regional accessibility due to
a convergence of roads, a sufficiently large threshold
population is generated to warrant small department and
variety stores, insurance and building society offices,
estate agents and a wide range of quite specialised shops
and services.　Major linear components can also occur
such as the arterial ribbons largely composed of convenience
shops which stretch out to the 1914 city boundaries, e.g.
Maryhill Road and Springburn Road in Glasgow and Gorgie
Road and Nicolson Street-Clerk Street in Edinburgh.　More
discreet spatial clusters characterise post 1918 development, initially stimulated by the appreciably lower
population densities of the inter-war local authority and
private housing areas, and subsequently by planning
direction favouring land-use segregation and discouraging
ribbon tendencies.　In the cities new service nodes have
developed at the heart of the large post-1945 local
authority housing schemes.　Thus, in Glasgow, Drumchapel
and Castlemilk, both housing more people than Perth, have
important service centres including branches of Woolworths,
large supermarkets and a wide array of other shops.
Similarly, in Edinburgh, a new centre has been constructed
at the recently developed Wester Hailes estate which includes
a hotel in addition to a variety of shops.　However these
centres normally concentrate upon frequent demand goods
and tend to lack the specialised infrequent demand goods
or services which would occur in towns of equivalent
population size.
　　Changes have also affected the intra-urban hinterlands.　Increased personal mobility has allowed car-
owners to use ring roads to frequent service centres with
car-parking facilities which are often located in relatively
peripheral locations.　The impact of East Kilbride drawing
shoppers from the southern fringe of the intensive Glasgow
hinterland has already been mentioned.　The development

231

of supermarkets and the increased use, firstly, of refriger-
ators and more recently, of freezers has facilitated the
beginnings of the American pattern of weekly shopping trips
to out-of-town shopping centres. Various plans are under
discussion and planning evaluations well advanced for the
construction of hypermarkets around the fringe of Glasgow.
Already a number of enlarged supermarket-department stores
have been built. Cumbernauld has one of the nine Woolco
stores in Britain and the first in Scotland and another is
planned at Livingston. At Wester Hailes, a large new
local authority estate on the western periphery of Edinburgh
near the Sighthill industrial estate, the shopping centre
includes a branch of AILSA, another embryonic hypermarket,
whilst the eastern flank of the city is similarly served
by a branch of ASDA. In central Glasgow an AILSA branch
has recently opened at Anderston near the ring road and
the Kingston Bridge, stressing the role of the car in
modern accessibility calculations.

Between 1960 and 1975 the extending commuting fields
of the major cities and urban agglomerations stimulated
residential growth in numerous small towns and villages
which, in turn, sponsored improvements in service provision
in these centres. Normally the shopping sector reacted
quickly by extending the type of goods carried and by the
opening of some new outlets, although on occasions,
especially after 1968, complete freedom of commercial
response was tempered by the conservation policies of the
local planning authority.

In certain respects the sphere of influence of
Edinburgh or Glasgow extends over the whole of Scotland.
Edinburgh is the home of the National Library of Scotland,
the Royal Scottish Museum, the Scottish Office, the official
residence of the Secretary of State for Scotland, the
General Assembly of Scotland and the International Festival.
Glasgow plays a dominant role in trade and industry and
has the headquarters of various boards and administrative
bodies. Tradition accords to Edinburgh the status of
capital and administrative centre and to Glasgow primacy
in trade and commerce. However the activities of modern
economic and social life and the behavioural decision-
making of most people are scarcely affected by such lofty
considerations of prestige and rank. People may commute
daily from the suburban fringes to the major cities and
during the course of the day use the facilities of the city
centre but much of the remainder of their activity patterns

232

occur in the suburban areas. These are the residential
foci for the bulk of the urban population of present day
Scotland.

TOWNSCAPES

Considerable alterations have occurred since 1900 in
the townscapes of urban settlements in Scotland. In the
cities the characteristic nineteenth century working class
housing unit was the four-storey tenement entered by a
common stair and composed of one, two or three room units
often with shared washing or toilet facilities. In most
of the large burghs and some of the cities, two storey rows
of flatted units often reached by pends leading to rear
access stairs and outside balconies on the upper storey,
were typical of working class nineteenth-century housing
districts. In the first half of the nineteenth century
large terraced houses were favoured by the middle class
and the wealthy but during the Victorian era the detached
or semi-detached stone built villa set in low-density
green suburbs became very fashionable although some elected
to remain fairly central and favoured the large flats in
select tenement districts such as Marchmont in Edinburgh.
During the inter-war period the bungalow emerged as the
typical new middle-class dwelling at least in part due to
the fact that it attracted a government subsidy for much
of the 1920's. The trend towards social segregation
which had clearly emerged in the nineteenth century was
at least maintained if not extended by the construction
of large estates of bungalows such as those at Corstorphine
in Edinburgh. The supply of working-class housing for
rent became an unattractive proposition early in the twentieth century and in 1920 the government placed the
responsibility for the provision of houses for the working
classes in the hands of local authorities. They were
initially encouraged to build at a maximum of thirty houses
per hectare and many of the early schemes consisted of
semi-detached and flatted villas (sometimes called Scottish
quadruple blocks) set in attractive green surroundings e.g.
Mosspark scheme in Glasgow. However, by 1930 in the
cities and many of the large industrial burghs between one-
fifth and one-quarter of the existing housing stock was
either unfit for human habitation or overcrowded. Attention
was therefore turned after 1930 to dealing with this problem

and numerous local authority estates, large and small, sprang up on peripheral sites in towns and cities.   In Edinburgh and Glasgow a modern version of a four-storey tenement block was increasingly adopted e.g. at Blackhill in Glasgow and Craigmillar in Edinburgh.   By 1935 these cities had also generated a large number of people who did not wish to purchase a villa or bungalow but did seek non local authority rented accommodation with a suburban location.   With the aid of local authority loans a series of estates of flatted villas for private renting were constructed in Edinburgh and Glasgow between 1935 and 1939, adding a further component to the townscape.

The virtual cessation of house-building between 1939 and 1945, apart from a few estates of hastily constructed prefabricated houses which remained in use for over twenty years, and the inherited housing shortage combined with the upsurge in new families, produced acute housing problems in the post-war period.   The introduction of various items of planning legislation tended to circumscribe simple extensionist growth after 1946 and by the mid 1950's many authorities, notably Glasgow, faced a serious housing problem with little new land available for further peripheral construction and the growing need for central redevelopment. Redevelopment schemes have a pedigree dating from the mid-nineteenth century in Scotland but this was on a completely new scale.   Glasgow defined twenty-nine Comprehensive Development Areas involving most of the nineteenth century working class tenement districts. (Plate 15B).   Similarly in Edinburgh most of the old core of Edinburgh and Leith and the nineteenth century industrial suburbs were zoned for redevelopment.   In all of the Scottish cities re-development coincided with the entry of the multi-storey block of flats into the urban fabric of modern Scottish settlements.   The era of multi-storey blocks has been relatively brief because most authorities have now abandoned this house type and reverted to the more tra-ditional four storey block.   Between 1953 and 1975 Glasgow will have constructed 303 multi-storey blocks accommodating some 90,000 people.   Multi-storey flats were adopted because they seemed to combine the attributes of reasonably high densities with quite large areas of open space.   They have principally been abandoned because of enormous building costs although they have also been the subject of extensive social and sociological criticism.

234

The gradual abandonment of some of the older central industrial areas, such as the railway locomotive industrial sites at Springburn in Glasgow, combined with extensive redevelopment of the zone of transition and the innermost residential district has substantially altered the urban environment and fabric in recent years. In Glasgow the currently incomplete pattern tends to accentuate dereliction and detract from the sections which are finished but in central Edinburgh, where the scale was more restricted, the environmental improvements have been striking.

In the four cities between 1961 and 1971 there was a population shift from the central wards to the more out-lying wards reflecting slum clearance activity heralding, at least, the beginning of redevelopment. There was a decrease in the number of persons per private household and an increasing provision of household amenities, especially outside the central area. In each case the proportion of owner-occupation had increased but the 1971 levels ranged from 20 per cent in Dundee to almost 47 per cent in Edinburgh. The proportion of houses rented from the local authority or the Scottish Special Housing Association had also increased but again the 1971 proportions ranged from 32 per cent in Edinburgh to almost 60 per cent in Dundee. The role of the private rented sector was inevitably being curtailed with the progressive demolition of the old tenement districts.

In general, the cities display a broadly sectoral land use structure. The tendency towards both western and southern high rent zones in Glasgow and Edinburgh emerged in Victorian times and has been broadly maintained. In the case of Glasgow for example twentieth century extensions have occurred in the suburban communities of Bearsden and Newton Mearns. The two-storey villa, detached or semi-detached, has re-emerged as the dominant post-1945 house type although materials and building methods have changed and recent estates incorporate currently fashionable design features such as the abandonment of the fencing of front gardens and attempts at pedestrian and traffic segregation by using linked walkways. Small blocks of luxury flats have provided a minor component since the 1920's often attracting retired couples or professional people in the pre-child bearing stage of the life-cycle. Some of these flats have been built upon sites produced by demolishing Victorian villas but others have successfully sought more peripheral locations.

235

Escalating maintenance costs and changing housing tastes have stimulated change in the Victorian villa districts. Where they lie in the path of the advancing office zone as it extends from the town centre, many villas have been readily converted to offices as terraced houses were at an earlier period. They also make excellent small hotels and all of the cities illustrate this trend, e.g. at Murrayfield and Newington in Edinburgh. In some cases the site is cleared and a more modern hotel or office block constructed but often only minor conversion and extension is undertaken retaining much of the original physical fabric. The Victorian villas have also been subdivided into flatted units as a means of producing smaller and more manageable houses and limiting maintenance costs.

In the town or city centre old buildings have been replaced by modern units. This process often results in the elimination of residential land use from the shopping centre and a general tidying and restructing of the land use pattern in the central area. Within the last decade at least partial redevelopment has occurred in the main street of most Scottish towns. This is often accompanied by pedestrianisation of part of the shopping area or at least traffic regulation schemes restricting parking and introducing one-way traffic flows. In many towns substantial new shopping sections have been constructed such as the shopping plaza at Paisley situated astride the River Cart, the new town centre at Grangemouth, the Callander Riggs development at Stirling and the St. James centre at the eastern end of Princes Street in Edinburgh. Frequently such schemes involve the extension of the central business district, in some cases even away from the preceding dominant growth direction, by invading and replacing part of the mixed land-use transition zone which characteristically adjoin parts of the central area of the town or city.

Many offices operate successfully from converted residential buildings but there has been a marked upsurge in new office construction since 1960. In the cities this has introduced a new vertical component into the skyline through the medium of multi-storey office blocks. Some of these blocks have been an integral part of new town or city centre projects as in the St. James Centre in Edinburgh but many isolated speculative ventures have also occurred.

For some land uses accessibility no longer dictates a

position in the central area of the city. Thus the fruit markets, in both Glasgow and Edinburgh, have recently moved to more spacious modern premises at some distance from the city centre, for example in Glasgow from Candleriggs to Blochairn. In Edinburgh, a number of merchant schools have abandoned traditional central sites in favour of more spacious suburban locations. This process of land use re-adjustment is natural and inevitable reflecting changing locational considerations, land values and demand factors. The upsurge in University education since 1955 has stimulated spatial expansion of the University precincts through the process of invasion and replacement of existing land uses.

Equally in many of the towns and cities the local government sector has experienced a pronounced spatial expansionist phase over a similar time period, often involving invasion of existing structures and the construction of new buildings. Other land uses seek to modernise on their existing site partly because they require centrality and also due to the lack of suitable alternative locations, e.g. large hospitals.

Special factors, such as the conservation of the New Town area of Edinburgh, distort and influence townscape adjustment and alteration, and create variations in the rate and scale of urban change in different settlements. (Plate 15A).

The cities have been constrained in the extent of their suburban growth since 1945 by formal or informal green belt policies. Edinburgh, for example, has operated a fairly strict policy refusing urban growth in a defined zone engirdling the city and effectively pushing growth further out beyond that zone. The more extensively urbanised situation of the Greater Glasgow area prevented the adoption of a simple green girdle but the overall intention has been to try and maintain buffer zones of green space between communities and discourage urban sprawl. These policies have tended to affect the direction of suburban development. In Edinburgh, for example, growth was allowed at Currie because of existing nuclei and linear components, while beyond the green belt new dormitory suburbs have been built in small towns such as Penicuik, Kirkliston and Haddington. A few major incursions have occurred into the rural-urban fringe of Edinburgh, notably the Heriot-Watt University at Riccarton, but these have been limited.

237

In the West of Scotland pressure from a multiplicity of nodes has placed great strain on the operation of even an informal green belt policy. The overspill housing needs of Glasgow alone have necessitated not only the growth of new towns but substantial urban extensions elsewhere. Many of the burghs in the conurbation have also implemented redevelopment schemes and constructed new peripheral housing estates. Industrial growth and relocation has largely occurred on new land outwith the pre 1945 urban area. New road developments have consumed substantial tracts of land and further eroded the spatial separation of communities. In many ways the fringe is an active zone of land-use competition with planning limiting completely free interplay and structuring developments.

The basic blueprint of the settlement geography until 1990 has already been drawn by the planners although the detail is largely undecided. The achievement of the broad design, however, depends on the accuracy of the projections and the operation of variables such as technology, social attitudes, economic climate and government policy. These factors will determine the rate and scale of future changes in the pattern and fabric of urban settlements.

BIBLIOGRAPHY

The Bibliography contains both sources of information used in the compilation of the text and suggestions for further reading. It excludes for the most part very specific regional, or limited topical, articles, university research publications and planning reports of which there are almost unlimited numbers. For convenience, the more general works are listed first, with more specific works listed under chapter headings and subheadings. In each list, statistical sources are placed first.

General Sources on the British Isles

The Atlas of Britain and Northern Ireland 1963. Oxford.
The Reader's Digest Complete Atlas of the British Isles 1968.
Central Statistical Office. Annual Abstract of Statistics.
Central Statistical Office. Abstract of Regional Statistics.
Ashton, J. and Long, W.H. The Remoter Rural Areas of Britain (1972).
Best, R.H. and Coppock, J.T. The Changing use of Land in Britain (1962).
Chisholm, M. Resources for Britain's Future (1970).
Chisholm, M. and Manners, G. Spatial Policy Problems of the British Economy (1971). Cambridge.
Clout, H.D. Rural Geography, 1972.
Coates, B.E. and Rawstron, E.M. Regional Variations in Britain (1971).
Dury, G. The British Isles: a Systematic and Regional Geography (1968).
House, J.W.(Ed). The UK Space: Resources, Environment and the Future (1973).
Institute of British Geographers. Land Use and Resources: Studies in Applied Geography. Special Publication No. 1 (1968).
Manners, G., Warren, K., Rodgers, H.B. and Keeble, D.E. Regional Development in Britain (1972).

Mitchell, J.B. and Morgan, M.A. (Eds.). Great Britain:
  Geographical Essays (1967). Cambridge.
Smith, W. An Historical Introduction to the Economic
  Geography of Great Britain (1968).
Stamp, L.D. and Beaver, S.H. The British Isles:
  A Geographic and Economic Survey (1971)
Watson, J.W. and Sissons, J.B. The British Isles:
  A Systematic Geography (1964)

General Sources on Scotland

Scottish Statistical Office. Digest of Scottish Statistics
  (to 1970). Edinburgh.
Scottish Office. Scottish Abstract of Statistics (1971-   ).
  Edinburgh.
Scottish Office. Scottish Economic Bulletin (1971-   ).
  Edinburgh.
Credland, G. and Murray, G.T. Scotland: A New Look (1969).
  Glasgow.
Glen, A. and Williams, M. Scotland from the Air (1971).
McIntosh, I.G. and Marshall, C.B. The Face of Scotland
  (1966).
Miller, R. and Watson, J.W. Geographical Essays in Memory
  of Alan G. Ogilvie.
Millman, R.N. The Making of the Scottish Landscape (1974)
Munro, R.W. Johnston's Gazetteer of Scotland (1973).
Murray, G.T. Scotland: The New Future (1973). Glasgow.
Rae, G. and Brown, C.E. Geography of Scotland (1966).
Rait, Sir R.S. and Pryde, G.S. Scotland (1954)
Scottish Council (Development and Industry). Natural
  Resources In Scotland (1961). Edinburgh.
Scottish Office and Central Office of Information.
  Scotland Today (1974). Edinburgh.
Select Committee on Scottish Affairs. Land Resource Use
  in Scotland. Vols. I - V (1972).
Statistical Account of Scotland (Old) (1791-99). Edinburgh.
Statistical Account of Scotland (New) (1845). Edinburgh.
Statistical Account of Scotland (Third) (1950-). Edinburgh.
Tivy, J. (Ed.). The Organic Resources of Scotland (1973).

Regional Sources on Scotland

British Association Handbooks. The Glasgow Region (1958).
  Glasgow.

British Association Handbooks. The North East of Scotland
(1963). Dundee and District (1968). The Stirling
Region (1974). Stirling.
Bailey, P. Orkney (1971). Newton Abbot.
Carmichael, A. Kintyre (1974). Newton Abbot.
Clapperton, C.M. (Ed.). North East Scotland Geographical
Essays (1972). University of Aberdeen.
Cruickshank, A.B. and Jowett, A.J. The Loch Linnhe District.
British Landscape Through Maps 15. (1972). Sheffield.
Darling, F.F. (Ed.). West Highland Survey: An Essay in
Human Ecology. (1955).
Darling, F.F. and Boyd, J.M. The Highlands and Islands
(1964). Oxford.
Department of Agriculture and Fisheries for Scotland.
Land-use in the Highlands and Islands (1964). Edinburgh.
Howe, G.M. (Ed.). Atlas of Glasgow and the West Region
of Scotland (1972). Edinburgh.
Lindsay, M. The Lowlands of Scotland. County Books Series
(1973).
Macnab, P.A. The Isle of Mull (1971). Newton Abbot.
Munro, I.S. The Island of Bute (1973). Newton Abbot.
Murray, W.H. The Islands of Western Scotland (1973).
Nicolson, J.R. Shetland (1972). Newton Abbot.
O'Dell, A.C. and Walton, K. The Highlands and Islands of
Scotland (1962). Edinburgh.
Small, A. and Smith, J.S. The Strathpeffer and Inverness
Area. British Landscape through Maps. 13. (1971) Sheffield.
Thompson, F. Harris and Lewis, Outer Hebrides (1968)
Newton Abbot.
Thompson, F. St. Kilda and other Hebridean Outliers
(1970). Newton Abbot.
Thompson, F. The Uists and Barra (1974) Newton Abbot.
Turnock, D. Patterns of Highland Development (1970).
Turnock, D. Scotland's Highlands and Islands (1974).
Oxford.

Sources on the Introduction

Dunnett, A.M. (Ed.). Alistair Maclean introduces Scotland
(1972).
Glen, D. (Ed.). Whither Scotland? (1971).
Kellas, J.G. Modern Scotland (1968).
Marwick, W.H. Scotland in Modern Times (1964).
Meikle, H.W. Scotland. A Description of Scotland and
Scottish Life. (1947).

Murray, C. de B. How Scotland is Governed (1947).

Sources on Chapter 1

The Land

Bremner, A. 'The Origin of the Scottish River System'.
Scottish Geographical Magazine. 58. (1942)
15, 54 and 99.
Craig, G.Y. (Ed.). The Geology of Scotland (1965).
Edinburgh.
Godard, A. Recherches de Geomorphologie en Ecosse du
Nord-Ouest 1965. Paris.
Fitzpatrick, E. 'An Introduction to the Periglacial
Geomorphology of Scotland'. Scottish Geographical
Magazine 74. (1958) 28.
Hollingsworth, S.E. 'The Recognition and Correlation of
High-level Erosion Surfaces in Britain: a Statistical
Study. Quarterly Journal of the Geological Society. 94
(1938). 55.
Linton, D.L. 'Problems of Scottish Scenery'. Scottish
Geographical Magazine. 67. (1951). 65.
MacGregor, M. and MacGregor, A.G. Midland Valley of
Scotland British Regional Geology (1948). Edinburgh.
Memoirs of the Geological Society.
Murray, J. and Pullar, L. Bathymetric Survey of the
Freshwater Lochs of Scotland (1910). Edinburgh.
Phemister, J. Northern Highlands. British Regional Geology
(1948). Edinburgh.
Pringle, J. South of Scotland. British Regional Geology
(1948). Edinburgh.
Read, H.H. and MacGregor, A.G. Grampian Highlands. British
Regional Geology (1948). Edinburgh.
Richey, J.E. Tertiary Volcanic Districts. British Regional
Geology (1948). Edinburgh.
Sissons, J.B. The Evolution of Scotland's Scenery (1967).
Sissons, J.B. 'Some Aspects of Glacial Drainage Channels
in Britain'. Scottish Geographical Magazine. 76.
(1960). 131 and 77 (1961). 15.
Steers, J.A. 'The Coastline of Scotland'. Geographical
Journal 118 (1952). 180.
Steers, J.A. The Coastline of Scotland (1973).
Weir, T. The Scottish Lochs (1972).

Climate

Meteorological Office. _British Rainfall_.
Green, F.H.W. 'The Climate of Scotland' in Burnett, J.H.
  (Ed.). _The Vegetation of Scotland_ (1964). 15.
Gresswell, R.K. _The Weather and Climate of the British
  Isles_ (1961).
Manley, G. _Climate and the British Scene_ (1952).
Manley, G. 'The Range and Variation of the British
  Climate'. _Geographical Journal_. 117. (1951). 43.
Taylor, J.A. and Yates, R.A. _British Weather in Maps_
  (1967).

Vegetation and Soils

Burnett, J.H. (Ed.). _The Vegetation of Scotland_ (1964).
Department of Agriculture and Fisheries for Scotland.
  Scottish Peat Surveys. (1965). Edinburgh.
Ferreira, R.E.C. 'Scottish Mountain Vegetation in Relation
  to Geology'. _Transactions of the Botanical Society
  of Edinburgh_. 37. (1959). 229.
Fitzpatrick, E.A. 'The Soils of Scotland' in Burnett, J.H.
  (Ed.). _The Vegetation of Scotland_ (1964). 36.
McVean, D.N. and Lockie, J.D. _Ecology and Land Use in
  Upland Scotland_ (1969). Edinburgh University.
McVean, D.N. and Ratcliffe, D.A. _Plant Communities in
  the Scottish Highlands_ (1962).
Memoirs of the Soil Survey of Great Britain: Scotland.
Ogg, W.G. 'The Soils of Scotland'. _Empire Journal of
  Experimental Agriculture_ (1935). 174 and 241.
Pears, N.W. _The Present Tree-line in the Cairngorm
  Mountains of Scotland and its Relation to Former
  Tree-lines_. Ph.D. Thesis (1965). London.
Pears, N.V. 'Wind as a Factor in Mountain Ecology'.
  Scottish Geographical Magazine. 83. (1967). 118.
Pearsall, W.H. _Mountains and Moorlands_ (1950)
Steven, H.M. and Carlisle, A. _The Native Pinewoods of
  Scotland_ (1959). Edinburgh.
Tansley, A.G. _Britain's Green Mantle_ (1949).

Sources on Chapter 2

Population

General Register Office. _Census Reports_. Edinburgh.

Registrar General for Scotland. Annual Reports. Edinburgh.
Hutchinson, B. Depopulation and Rural Life in Scotland
(1963).
Johnston, R.J. 'Population Change in an Urban System - the
examples of the Republic of Ireland and Scotland'.
Scottish Geographical Magazine. 85. (1969). 132.
Jones, H.R. 'Migration within Scotland'. Scottish
Geographical Magazine. 83. (1967). 151.
Jones, H.R. 'Migration to and from Scotland since 1960'.
Transactions of the Institute of British Geographers.
49. (1970). 145.
Kyd, J.G. Scottish Population Statistics. 1952. Edinburgh.
Moisley, H.A. 'Population Changes and the Highland Problem'.
Scottish Studies. 6. (1962). 94.
Robertson, I.M.L. 'Scottish Population Distribution:
Implications for Locational Decisions'. Transactions
of the Institute of British Geographers. 63. (1974). 111.
Scottish Development Department Central Planning Research
Unit. The Size and Distribution of Scotland's Population
(1972).

Social and Economic Planning

Committee on Public Participation in Planning
(Skeffington Committee). People and Planning (1969).
Committee on Land Utilisation in Rural Areas
(Scott Committee). Report (1942).
Cullingworth, J.B. Town and Country Planning in Britain
(1972)
Expert Committee on Compensation and Betterment
(Uthwatt Committee). Report (1942).
Highlands and Islands Development Board. Annual Reports
(1967-   ).
McCrone, G. Regional Policy in Britain (1969).
Robinson, E.A.G. Economic Planning in the United Kingdom
(1967).
Royal Commission on the Distribution of the Industrial
Population (Barlow Commission). Report (1940).
Scottish Development Department. Development Plans: A
Scottish Manual on Form and Content. (1971). Edinburgh.
Turnock, D. 'Regional Development in the Crofting Counties'.
Transactions of the Institute of British Geographers.
48. (1969). 189.

Notable Regional Plans include:

Scottish Council (Development and Industry). Oceanspan. A Maritime Based Strategy for a European Scotland. 1970.
Scottish Council (Development and Industry). A Future for Scotland. 1973.
Scottish Development Department. Lothians Regional Survey and Plan (1966). Edinburgh.
Scottish Development Department. North-east Scotland: A Survey of its Development Potential (1969). Edinburgh.
Scottish Development Department. A Strategy for South West Scotland. (1970). Edinburgh.
Scottish Development Department and University of Dundee. Tayside: Potential for Development (1970). Edinburgh.
Scottish Office. The Scottish Economy 1965-70: A Plan for Expansion (1966). Edinburgh.
Scottish Office. The Central Borders: A Plan for Expansion (1968). Edinburgh.
Scottish Office. The Grangemouth/Falkirk Regional Survey and Plan (1968). Edinburgh.

Sources on Chapter 3

Administration

Royal Commission on Local Government in Scotland. 1966-9 (Wheatley Commission). Report (1969). Edinburgh.
Scottish Office. Scottish Administration (1967). Edinburgh.

Transport

National Ports Council. Digest of Port Statistics.
Appleton, J.H. The Geography of Communications in Great Britain (1962).
Bird, J. The Major Seaports of the United Kingdom (1969).
British Railways Board. The Reshaping of British Railways (Beeching Report). (1963).
British Railways Board. The Development of the Major Railway Trunk Routes (1965).
Coull, J.R. and Willis, P.D. 'The Air Services in the Northern Isles'. Geography. 247. (1970). 204.
Desbarats, J.M. 'A Geographical Analysis of the Clyde's Forelands'. Tijdschrift voor Economische en Sociale Geografie. 62. (1971). 249.

Highland Transport Board. <u>Highland Transport Services</u> (1967).
Edinburgh.
Jones, H.R. and Pocock, D.C.D. 'Some Economic and Social
Implications of the Tay Road Bridge'. <u>Scottish
Geographical Magazine</u>. 82. (1966). 93.
Kinniburgh, I.A.G. 'New Developments in Clydeport'.
<u>Scottish Geographical Magazine</u>. 82. (1966). 144.
Lindsay, J. <u>The Canals of Scotland</u> (1968). Newton Abbot.
MacGregor, D.R. 'Social and Economic Effects of the Forth
Road Bridge'. <u>Scottish Geographical Magazine</u>. 82 (1966) 78.
Moir, D.G. 'The Roads of Scotland'. <u>Scottish Geographical
Magazine</u>. 73 (1957). 101 and 167.
Skewis, W.I. <u>Transport in the Highlands and Islands</u>.
Ph.D. Thesis (1962). University of Glasgow.
Turnock, D. 'Hebridean Car Ferries'. <u>Geography</u>.
229. (1965). 375.

Energy

National Coal Board. <u>Annual Reports</u>.
North of Scotland Hydro-electric Board. <u>Annual Reports</u>.
Edinburgh.
Scottish Gas Board. <u>Annual Reports</u>. Edinburgh.
South of Scotland Electricity Board. <u>Annual Reports</u>.
Edinburgh.
United Kingdom Atomic Energy Authority. <u>Annual Reports</u>.
Ball, N.R. 'The East Coast of Scotland and North Sea Oil'.
<u>Geography</u>. 258. (1973). 51.
Jones, J.H. and Marshall, C.B. 'The Longannet Power Project'.
<u>Geography</u>. 241. (1968). 410.
Lea, K.J. 'Hydro-electric power generation in the Highlands
of Scotland'. <u>Transactions of the Institute of British
Geographers</u>. 46. (1969). 155.
McNeil, J. 'The Fife Coal Industry 1947-67'. <u>Scottish
Geographical Magazine</u>. 89. (1973). 81 and 163.
North of Scotland Hydro-electric Board and South of
Scotland Electricity Board. <u>Scottish Electricity: Plans
for the Future 1963-70</u>. (1963). Edinburgh.
Royal Scottish Geographical Society. <u>Scotland and Oil</u>.
Teachers Bulletin No. 5 (1973). Edinburgh.
Simpson, E.S. <u>Coal and the Power Industries in Postwar
Britain</u> (1966).

Water

Water Resources Board and Scottish Development Department.
  Surface Water Year Book of Great Britain.
Scottish Development Department. The Water Service in
  Central Scotland. (1963). Edinburgh.
Scottish Development Department. A Measure of Plenty:
  Water Resources in Scotland. A General Survey (1973).
  Edinburgh.
Smith, K. Water in Britain (1972).

Sources on Chapter 4

Rural Landscape Evolution

Adams, I.H. 'The Land Surveyor and his Influence on the
  Scottish Rural Landscape'. Scottish Geographical Magazine.
  84 (1968). 248.
Caird, J.B. 'Changes in the Highlands and Islands of
  Scotland'. Geoforum 12. (1972). 5.
Caird, J.B. 'The Making of the Scottish Rural Landscape'.
  Scottish Geographical Magazine. 80. (1964). 72.
Dodgshorn, R.A. 'The Nature and Development of Infield-
  Outfield in Scotland'. Transactions of the Institute
  of British Geographers. 59. (1973). 1.
Gailey, R. 'The Evolution of Highland Rural Settlement'.
  Scottish Studies. 6. (1962). 153.
Handley, J.E. The Agricultural Revolution in Scotland
  (1963). Glasgow.
Millman, R. 'The Marches of Highland Estates'. Scottish
  Geographical Magazine. 85. (1969). 172.
Millman, R. 'The Landed Properties of Northern Scotland'.
  Scottish Geographical Magazine. 86. (1970). 186.
Millman, R. 'The Landed Estates of Southern Scotland'.
  Scottish Geographical Magazine. 88. (1972). 126.
Prebble, J. The Highland Clearances (1963)
Storrie, M. 'Landholding and Settlement Evolution in the
  West Highlands of Scotland'. Geografiska Annaler.
  47. (1965). 138.

Agriculture

Department of Agriculture and Fisheries for Scotland.
  Agricultural Statistics: Scotland. Edinburgh.

Beilby, O.J. 'The Changing Face of Scottish Agriculture'.
Scottish Agriculture. 50. (1970). 131.

Bowler, I.R. 'Co-operation: A Note on Government
Promotion of Change in Agriculture'. Area. 4. (1972) 169.

Carlyle, W.J. 'The Marketing and Movement of Scottish Hill
Lambs'. Geography. 57. (1972). 10.

Carlyle, W.J. 'The Away-wintering of Ewe Hoggs from Scottish
Hill Farms'. Scottish Geographical Magazine. 88. (1972).
100.

Collier, A. The Crofting Problem (1953).

Coppock, J.T. An Agricultural Geography of Great Britain
(1971).

Crofters Commission. Annual Reports.

Darling, F.F. Crofting Agriculture (1945). Edinburgh.

Dickson, D.R. 'Changes in Land Use on Farms which grew
Sugar Beet'. Scottish Agricultural Economics. 23 (1973)
217.

Edwards, A.M. and Wibberley, G.P. An Agricultural Land
Budget for Britain 1965-2000 (1971).

McQueen, J.D.W. 'Milk Surpluses in Scotland'. Scottish
Geographical Magazine 77. (1961). 93.

Moisley, H.A. 'The Highlands and Islands: A Crofting
Region?' Transactions of the Institute of British
Geographers 31. (1962) 83.

Russell, T.P. 'The Size and Structure of Scottish
Agriculture'. Scottish Agricultural Economics. 20 (1970).

Shirlaw, G. An Agricultural Geography of Great Britain
(1971).

Symon, J.A. Scottish Farming Past and Present (1959).

Tarrant, J.R. Agricultural Geography (1974) Newton Abbot.

Warrings, A.R. 'Scottish Agriculture'. Scottish
Geographical Magazine. 80. (1964). 96.

Whitby, H. 'Some Developments in Scottish Farming since
the War'. Journal of Agricultural Economics. 21 (1970) 1.

Forestry

Edlin, H.C. 'The Forestry Commission in Scotland 1919-69'.
Scottish Geographical Magazine. 85. (1969). 84.

Forestry Commission. Forest Park Guides.

Forestry Commission. Forest Policy (1972).

Forestry Commission. Pamphlets.

Forestry Commission. Postwar Forest Policy (1943).

H.M.S.O. Forestry in Great Britain: an Interdepartmental
Cost/Benefit Study (1972).

248

Holtham, B. 'Forestry and its Related Industries in Scotland'. Scottish Forestry 23. (1970). 173.

McLay, J.D. 'The Work of the Forestry Commission in South-west Scotland'. Scottish Geographical Magazine. 85. (1969). 96.

Mather, A.S. 'Problems of Afforestation in North Scotland'. Transactions of the Institute of British Geographers 54. (1971). 19.

Taylor, C.J. (Ed.). A History of Scottish Forestry (1967). Edinburgh.

Outdoor Recreation

British Travel Association. The British on Holiday (1969).

Carter, M.R. 'A Method of Analysing Patterns of Tourist Activity in a large Rural Area: The Highlands of Scotland'. Regional Studies. 5. (1971). 29.

Coppock, J.T. 'The Recreational Use of Land and Water in Rural Britain'. Tijdschrift voor Economische en Sociale Geographie. 57. (1966). 81.

Coppock, J.T. Recreation in the Countryside.

Coppock, J.T. (Ed.). Leisure and the Countryside (1971).

Coppock, J.T. (Ed.). The Touring Caravan in Scotland (1971).

Cosgrove, I. and Jackson, R. The Geography of Recreation and Leisure (1972).

Countryside Commission for Scotland. A Planning Classification of Scottish Landscape Resources (1971) Perth.

Linton, D.L. 'The Assessment of Scenery as a Natural Resource'. Scottish Geographical Magazine. 84. (1968).

Millman, R. Outdoor Recreation in the Highland Countryside (1971).

Patmore, J.A. Land and Leisure (1970). Newton Abbot.

Pears, N.V. 'Man in the Cairngorms. A Population/Resource Balance Problem'. Scottish Geographical Magazine 84. (1968).

Perry, A.H. 'Climatic Influences on the Scottish Skiing Industry'. Scottish Geographical Magazine 87. (1971). 197.

Scottish Tourist Board. Annual Reports. Edinburgh.

Scottish Tourist Board. Caravanning and Camping in Scotland. (1969). Edinburgh.

Scottish Tourist Board. Tourism in Scotland (1972). Edinburgh.

Seeley, I.H. Outdoor Recreation and the Urban Environment
(1973).
Stamp, L.D. Nature Conservation in Britain (1969).

Rural Land Competition and Planning

Carter, I. 'Economic Models and the Recent History of the
Highlands'. Scottish Studies. 15. (1971). 99.
Countryside Commission for Scotland. Annual Reports.
Department of Education and Science. Forestry, Agriculture
and the Multiple Use of Rural Land (1966).
James, P.G. 'An Economic Appraisal of the Use of Hills
and Uplands for Forestry and Agriculture Respectively'.
Farm Economist 10. (1965). 12.
Lovejoy, D. (Ed.). Land Use and Landscape Planning. (1974).
Martin, P.C. 'The Hills – Farming or Forestry?' Occasional
Paper 1 (1970). Economics Department, East of Scotland
College of Agriculture.
Mather, A.S. 'Red Deer Land Use in the Northern Highlands'.
Scottish Geographical Magazine 80. (1972). 36.
Natural Resources (Technical) Committee (Zuckerman Committee).
Forestry, Agriculture and Marginal Land (1957).
Whitby, M.C. et al. Rural Resource Development (1974).
Wibberley, G.P. The Future of Britain's Rural Land (1970).
Newton Abbot.

Sources on Chapter 5

Board of Trade. Reports on the Census of Production
(1958, 1968 and 1970).
Board of Trade and Department of Trade and Industry. Report
on the Census of Distribution and other Services (1966).
Department of Agriculture and Fisheries for Scotland.
Scottish Sea Fisheries: Statistical Tables. Edinburgh.
Department of Trade and Industry. Report on the Census of
Production (1971).
Department of Industry. Report on the Census of Production
(1972).
British Steel Corporation. Iron and Steel. Annual
Statistics for the United Kingdom.
Beckles, N.I. 'Textiles and Port Growth in Dundee'.
Scottish Geographical Magazine. 84. (1968). 90.
Carter, C. 'Some Changes in the Post War Industrial
Geography of the Clydeside Conurbation'. Scottish
Geographical Magazine. 90 (1974). 14.

Chapman, K. 'The Structure and Development of the Oil-based complex at Grangemouth'. Scottish Geographical Magazine. 90 (1974). 98.

Clyde Estuary Development Corporation. Report on Possible Industrial Developments in the Clyde Estuary (1969).

Coull, J.R. 'Modern Trends in Scottish Fisheries'. Scottish Geographical Magazine. 84 (1968). 15.

Dunning, J.H. and Thomas C.J. British Industry (1963).

Gale, W.K.U. The British Iron and Steel Industry (1967). Newton Abbot.

Heal, D.W. The Steel Industry in Post-war Britain (1974). Newton Abbot.

Hood, N. 'A Geography of Competition: The Scottish Woollen Textile Industry'. Scottish Geographical Magazine. 89 (1973). 74.

Johnston, T.L., Buxton, N.K. and Moir, D. Structure and Growth of the Scottish Economy (1971).

McLellan, A.G. 'Geomorphology and the Sand and Gravel Industry of West Central Scotland'. Scottish Geographical Magazine. 85 (1969). 162.

Oakley, C.A. Scottish Industry. An Account of What Scotland makes and Where she makes it (1953).

Pacione, M. 'Traditional and New Industries in Dundee'. Scottish Geographical Magazine. 88. (1972). 53.

Scottish Council Development and Industry. Annual Reports.

Storrie, M.C. 'The Scotch Whisky Industry'. Transactions of the Institute of British Geographers. 31 (1962). 97.

Turner, W.H.K. 'The Concentration of the Jute and Heavy Linen Manufacturing Industry in East Central Scotland'. Scottish Geographical Magazine. 82 (1966). 29.

Warren, K. 'Locational Problems of the Scottish Iron and Steel Industry since 1760'. Scottish Geographical Magazine. 81 (1965). 18 and 87.

Watts, H.D. 'The Location of Aluminium Reduction Plant in the United Kingdom . Tijdschrift voor Economische en Sociale Geografie. 61 (1970). 148.

Welch, R.V. 'Immigrant Manufacturing Industry Established in Scotland Between 1945 and 1968: Some Structural and Locational Characteristics'. Scottish Geographical Magazine. 86. (1970). 134.

Welch, R.V. 'Manufacturing Change in Greater Clydeside in the 1950's and 1960's'. Scottish Geographical Magazine 90 (1974). 168.

Sources on Chapter 6

General Register Office. Census Reports. Edinburgh.
Coull, J.R. 'The Historical Geography of Aberdeen'. Scottish Geographical Magazine. 79 (1963). 80.
Diamond, D.R. 'The Central Business District of Glasgow' in Norborg, K. (Ed.). Lund IGU Symposium in Urban Geography (1960).
Evans, H. 'Britain's New Towns: Facts and Figures'. Town and Country Planning (January 1974).
Freeman, I. 'Some Aspects of Edinburgh's Capital Status and its Regional Implications for Office Development'. Regional Studies Group Bulletin 10 (1970).
Gordon, G. The Status Areas of Edinburgh: A Historical Analysis. Ph.D. Thesis (1971). University of Edinburgh.
Green, P. 'Some Planning Problems of a Large Burgh: Hamilton - Clydeside'. Scottish Geographical Magazine. 83 (1967). 174.
Jones, H.R. 'Recent Migration to and from Dundee'. Scottish Geographical Magazine. 84 (1968). 99.
Kearsley, G.W. and Srivastava, S.R. 'The Spatial Evolution of Glasgow's Asian Community'. Scottish Geographical Magazine. 90 (1974). 110.
McGovern, P.D. 'The New Towns of Scotland'. Scottish Geographical Magazine. 84 (1968). 29.
Mellor, R.E.H. 'Building Use in Aberdeen'. Scottish Geographical Magazine. 79 (1963). 95.
Miller, R. 'The New Face of Glasgow'. Scottish Geographical Magazine. 86 (1970). 5.
Pocock, D.C.D. 'Shopping Patterns in Dundee: Some Observations'. Scottish Geographical Magazine. 84 (1968). 108.
Pocock, D.C.D. 'The Fair City of Perth'. Scottish Geographical Magazine. 85 (1969). 3.
Reports of the Cumbernauld, East Kilbride, Glenrothes, Irvine and Livingston New Town Development Corporations.
Scottish Development Department. Summary Report of an Investigation to Identify Areas of Multiple Deprivation in Glasgow City. Central Planning Research Unit Working Paper No. 7 (1973). Edinburgh.
Scottish Development Department. Aspects of Population Change in Glasgow. Central Planning Research Unit Working Paper No. 1 (1972).
Smith, P.J. 'Changing Objectives in Scottish New Towns Policy'.

<u>Annals of the Association of American Geographers</u>
56. (1966). 492.

Smith, P.J. 'Glenrothes: Some Geographical Aspects of New Town Development'. <u>Scottish Geographical Magazine</u> 83 (1967). 17.

Turner, W.H.K. 'The Growth of Dundee'. <u>Scottish Geographical Magazine</u>. 84 (1968). 76.

Whitehand, J.W.R. and Alauddin, K. 'The Town Plans of Scotland'. <u>Scottish Geographical Magazine</u>. 85 (1969). 109.

Whitehand, J.W.R. 'Building Cycles and the Spatial Pattern of Urban Growth'. <u>Transactions of the Institute of British Geographers</u>. 56 (1972). 39.

ACKNOWLEDGEMENTS

The authors are indebted to individuals far too numerous to name, without whose help this book could not have been written.   It has been distilled from information gained from, and ideas stimulated by, the written and spoken words of people in all walks of life, Scottish and non-Scottish, over a period of many years.   We thank them all.

On a more practical level, we are extremely grateful for the help of the secretarial and technical staff of the Department of Geography, University of Strathclyde: Miss Anne Laing, Mrs. Jane Simpson and Mrs. M. MacLeod for typing the manuscript;   Mrs. Diane Holme and Mrs. Linda MacIver for preparing the cartographic material;   and Mr. Brian Reeves for help with the photography.

Photographs are by K. J. Lea, except for Plates 11A (B. Reeves), 14B and 15A (G. Gordon).

All maps are based on the Ordnance Survey Map with the sanction of the Controller of H.M. Stationery Office, Crown Copyright reserved.   Figures 2, 3 and 4 are adapted from pages 8, 7 and 18 respectively in the Atlas of Great Britain and Northern Ireland, Clarendon Press (1963); and are also based on Crown Copyright Geological Maps, by permission of the Controller of H.M. Stationery Office. Figure 25 is based on maps produced in the Edinburgh and Lanark volumes of Leisure and the Countryside (1971), edited by J. T. Coppock.   Figure 26 is derived from a series of maps published in The Geographical Magazine, London in 1973.

INDEX

Aberdeen, 214, 215-8
Accessibility, 90, 92, 190,
    fig 17;   to the country-
    side, 157, 160-2, 164
Act of Union (1707), 7ff
Administrative infra-
    structure, 79-89
Afforestation, 149ff, 163
Agricultural revolution, 61
Agriculture, 60, 61, 121,
    126-48; coefficient of
    localization, 143-4;
    spatial concentration and
    dispersion, 143-4; trends,
    142-8, table 17; workforce,
    65: see also Farm and under
    individual farm types
Air: flows, 33ff; masses,
    34; transport, 90,101-3,
    table 6
Alpine orogeny, 21
Altitudinal range, 13,plate
    1, figs 1, 14
Amenity (visual), 157, 167
Architecture, 8

Barley, 138, 142, 148
Basalt, 17
Beef cattle, 132, 136, 138,
    141, 142, 148
Birth rate, 48, 64, fig 9,
    table 1
Blizzards, 35
Braken, 45, 136
Bridges rail, 96; road, 93,
    94

Broadcasting services, 90
Burghs, 56, 58, 79ff, 199,
    figs 30-34; of Barony,
    200; Royal, 200, 202

Caledonian orogeny, 20, 21
Cambrian age, 18, 19
Canals, 89, 99, 118
Carboniferous age, 16
Castle towns, 202
Central business district,
    230
Central place theory, 210
Centres, middle order, 228
Chemical industry, 171ff
Cities, 56, 58, 199, 207,
    210, 211-8: see also under
    individual cities
City: boundary extensions,
    211, 214; population trends,
    211-2; regions, 85
Clachan, 202
Clay, 20; boulder, 27-9
Clearances, 61, 127
Climate, 13, 32-8, figs 5,
    6
Coal, 19, 104, 105-8, 111,
    114, table 8; fields, 105;
    mining, 105
Coastal landforms, 17, 19,
    30-2
Coke ovens, 112
Colliery closures, 107
Commercial enterprise, 61
Communities: locality, 84,

255

Fluvio-glacial processes,
28–30
Fog, 35
Folding, 20–21
Food industries, 60, 171ff
Forest: distribution, 151–2;
ownership, 149–51; parks,
68, table 19; utilisation,
152–4
Forestry, 148–56, 168,
fig 24, table 18; and
agriculture, 155–6;
Commission, 125, 150ff;
financing, 150; income and
employment, 156; villages,
156
Fragmentation of estates,
122
Frost, 35
Fruit farming, 140

Gaelic, 8
Gas, 104, 111–3, table 10;
consumption, 113; works,
111, 113
Glaciation, 25, 26–30
Glasgow, 212–3, 215–8
Glasshouses, 140
Glenrothes, 220–1
Gleys, 39, 40, 45
Gneiss, 18, 19
Granite, 15–16
Grassland, 40ff
Grazing, 41ff: see also
Rough grazing
Green belts, 68, 237
Greywackes, 19
Grouse moors, 42, 163, 164

Hamlets, 202
Hardwoods, 149
Heath, 40
Hedgerows, 44
Hercynian orogeny, 21
High forest, 152, 153

Highlands and Islands:
Development Board, 69,
165; problem, 69
Horticulture, 139
Housing, 225; council estates,
67; multistorey, 234; New
Town, 224–5; types, 233–4
Hydro-electric power, 104,
116–8

Ice: age, 25ff, 31, 35;
sheets, 25
Igneous rocks, 15–17, 41
Immigration, 50
Imports, 101
Improvement Movement, 126,
127, 149
Industrial: centres, 202,
203, 210, 225–7; develop-
ment, 73, 75; estates,
72, 197; imbalance, 177,
178; landscapes, 196–8;
linkage, 186, 189, 194;
location, 182–95; produc-
tion, 173, 178; production
trends, 175, 178; region,
66; Revolution, 59; structure,
168–79; trends, table 22,
23
Industrialisation, 48, 60,
202
Industry, 168–198, plates
11–13; distribution of,
179–182; employment in,
169, 171, 177ff, 190–191,
193; employment trends in,
171ff; Government inter-
vention in, 184ff; regional
concentration of, 181, 186,
188, 192ff
Insolation, 34
Intensive farming, 139–140
Intermediate Areas, 75
Iron and steel industry, 60,
171ff

257

258

DAVID & CHARLES BOOKS ON SCOTLAND

HISTORY

Ancient Scotland
A Guide to the Remains
Lloyd Laing
216 x 138mm   illustrated

Here is a book which develops Scotland's history as interpreted through the many archaeological finds and sites of all periods. The remains of Scotland's past are detailed and listed in an easy-to-follow reference section which will inform the reader of what is available in his own locality as well as encourage him to visit these sites and to consider for himself the markers which time has left all around him.

The Military Roads in Scotland
William Taylor
216 x 138mm   illustrated

In Part I the military roads are placed in their historical context with details of origins, development, method of construction and subsequent use or abandonment, while Part II describes in detail and pinpoints with six figure references and sketch maps the precise lines of the road and their present condition.

Orkney and Shetland: An Archaeological Guide
Lloyd Laing
210 x 145mm   illustrated

Orkney and Shetland possess more ancient monuments per square mile than any other county in the British Isles, and also boast several of the most important and impressive. This book is intended as a general guide to the archaeology of the islands from the earliest settlements in Neolithic times until the seventeenth century and later, and sets the archaeology of the Northern Isles in a wider perspective of British archaeology as a whole.

Reminiscences of My Life in the Highlands
Volume 1 (1883)
Volume 2 (1884)
Joseph Mitchell
216 x 138mm

Joseph Mitchell is remembered chiefly as the projector of the Highland Railway, although he also constructed harbours along the West coast of Scotland. The first volume describes the far-reaching social and economic changes resulting from the vastly improved lines of communication he engineered, the second covers his career as a railway engineer. Controversial and suppressed in their day, these books give an unusually interesting picture of engineering in the Victorian period.

Scotland: The Shaping of a Nation
Gordon Donaldson
216 x 138mm   illustrated

One of Scotland's leading historians takes a broad view of the country
— its history, its culture and current status, with separate chapters on
the Church, politics, the Union, Scottish society and so on. The Highlands have their own telling chapter and the book ends with an appraisal
of Scottish society from early medieval times to the present day.
Chronological tables, thematic maps and a discursive bibliography are
among this important book's outstanding features.

Scottish Military Uniforms
Robert Wilkinson-Latham
235 x 185mm   illustrated

This authoritative history of Scottish and Highland regimental uniforms
is fully illustrated with drawings and photographs. It traces their evolution, how they were modified by battle distinctions, the preferences of
succeeding monarchs, the changing demands of warfare or simply fashion,
and the text relates the various colourful legends, traditions and incidents
surrounding the uniforms, to make an attractive and informative book
for all interested in this aspect of military history.

The Scottish Revolution 1637-1644
The Triumph of the Covenanters
David Stevenson
216 x 138mm   illustrated

The Scottish revolution has until now been the most neglected of the
three which confronted Charles I within five years of his coronation. It
came before its English and Irish counterparts and, at least until 1646,
determined their course. Dr Stevenson redresses the earlier imbalance
created by historians who have concentrated too much on the part
played by the Church in Scottish seventeenth century affairs ignoring
the role of the laymen.

INDUSTRIAL HISTORY

Great Pit Disasters
Helen and Baron Duckham
216 x 138mm   illustrated

Violent death on a large scale in the mines of Britain was an all too
regular occurrence until the comparatively recent past. Accidents of
appalling suddenness might put an end to hundreds of lives, leaving
whole communities virtually bereft of their menfolk. This book recounts
from first-hand sources many of the blackest underground catastrophes
of folding, explosion and entombment. It is a record of anguish and of
heroism.

The Industrial Archaeology of Galloway
South West Scotland including Wigtown, Kirkcudbright and adjoining
parts of Dumfries
Ian Donnachie
210 x 145mm   illustrated

This province has a rich heritage of rural and industrial archaeology,
some of it quite recent. Few areas of Britain preserve in such diversity
the evidence of past economic activity — from country mills to long-
deserted harbours. The main text is followed by a gazetteer which
details a wide range of interesting sites, with an extended bibliography
of books, documents and maps.

New Ways Through the Glens
Highland Road, Bridge and Canal Makers of the Early Nineteenth Century
A R B Haldane
216 x 138mm   illustrated

A detailed account of the work of the great engineer Thomas Telford
and his colleagues in the Highlands. The author discusses the background
of social and economic distress in the Highlands which forced the
government into action, then describes the difficult and exciting work
involved in opening up the area and finally the benefits brought by the
new communications.

North Sea Oil and Gas
A Geographical Perspective
Keith Chapman
216 x 138mm   illustrated

Only ten years after the first rig moved into position, 90 per cent of
the United Kingdom's gas supply comes from the North Sea. But how
does North Sea oil fit into the world oil network? How can conflicting
national and commercial interests be reconciled? Dr Keith Chapman
assesses the problems and potential of North Sea energy in these first
exciting years of its discovery.

Robert Owen
Prince of Cotton Spinners
Edited by John Butt
216 x 138mm   illustrated

Robert Owen of New Lanark, born in 1771, was associated with every
important social agitation of his day — factory reform, education, poor
law and housing — and became the inspiration of the working classes in
the 1830s. The contributions to this study cover his social and economic
thought, his attitude towards education, his career as a factory reformer
and his place in the history of British business. Based on a wide range of
primary and secondary sources, they challenge many traditional views
and cast new light on neglected aspects of his career.

DAVID & CHARLES BRUNEL HOUSE NEWTON ABBOT